VARIETIES OF ENVIRONMENTALISM: ESSAYS NORTH AND SOUTH

RAMACHANDRA GUHA

AND

J. MARTINEZ-ALIER

EARTHSCAN PUBLICATIONS LTD, LONDON

First published in the UK in 1997 by Earthscan Publications Ltd

Reprinted 2000

A catalogue record for this book is available from the British Library

ISBN: 1 85383 324 X (hardback), 1 85383 329 0 (paperback)

Typesetting and page design by Carl Inwood Studios

Printed and bound by Biddles Ltd, Guildford and King's Lynn

Cover design by Andrew Corbett

For a full list of publications, please contact
Earthscan Publications Limited
120 Pentonville Road
London N1 9JN
Tel: 020 7278 0433
Fax: 020 7278 1142
email: earthinfo@earthscan.co.uk
http://www.earthscan.co.uk

Earthscan is an editorially independent subsidiary of Kogan Page Ltd
and publishes in association with WWF-UK and the International
Institute for Environment and Development.

In memory of Paul Kurian
and E. P. Thompson

CONTENTS

PREFACE

Although the essays it contains were written in the last few years, this book draws upon interests and activities that go back almost two decades. *Varieties of Environmentalism* elaborates in detail ideas first tentatively put forward in Martinez-Alier's history of ecological economics, published in 1987, and in Guha's history of the Chipko movement, published two years later. Those books each ended by noting the differences between environmentalism in First and Third World contexts. That contrast became one focus of our subsequent research, the results of which are presented here.*

Over the years we have discussed varieties of environmentalism with many colleagues, among them Bina Agarwal, Tariq Banuri, Frank Beckenbach, Mike Bell, Peter Brimblecombe, Bill Burch, Fred Buttel, Madhav Gadgil, Enrique Leff, James O'Connor, Martin O'Connor, Paul Richards, Joel Seton, LoriAnn Thrupp, Victor Toledo, Stefano Varese and Donald Worster. These colleagues have pursued for a long time – 20 years in some cases – lines of research parallel to our own. The notion of an 'environmentalism of the poor' developed in this book will not be a novelty to them.

An especial word of thanks is owed to the Social Science Research Council (SSRC), whose Joint Committee on Latin American Studies convened a series of meetings on the environmentalism of the poor. Several of the ideas put forward here were first discussed at those meetings in Oxford, New York and New Delhi. At the SSRC, Enrique Mayer and Lawrence Whitehead, both members of the Joint Committee, and Eric Hershberg, Programme Officer, gave strong support to our work.

The authors of this book met in August 1988, when Martinez-Alier came to India at the invitation of Paul Kurian, an economist and social activist then with the Institute for Cultural Research and Action in Bangalore. Paul Kurian, who died tragically in 1993, not yet 40, had a wide range of intellectual and political interests. A student of New Delhi's Jawaharlal Nehru University in its halcyon years (the early 1970s), he later worked with a pioneering trade union, the Chattisgarh Mines Shramik Samiti; wrote scholarly essays on Solidarity in Poland; and lived for a time in Sandinista-ruled Nicaragua. He then developed a keen interest in ecological economics, and was at work on a doctorate in the field at the

---

* Chapters 1,4,5,8 and 10 have been authored by RG; chapters 2,3,6,7 and 9 are by JMA.

time of his death.

We dedicate this book to India's Paul Kurian and to England's Edward Palmer Thompson, another friend who is no longer with us. E. P. Thompson is, of course, one of the most influential historians of our time, but it is not so well known that he had an abiding interest in the environment. Signs of this interest appear, indirectly, in his biography of that great early 'red-green' thinker, William Morris, and in his involvement in the peace movement. It was also expressed more directly in personal conversation and in some of his later writings; as for instance his book *Customs in Common* (1991), which refers to 18th century peasant protesters as 'premature Greens', and to John Clare as one who 'may be described, without hindsight, as a poet of ecological protest'. Two years later, in what was very likely the last review he wrote, of a book on Indian environmental history, Thompson wondered why 'so much ecological writing should be so deeply depressing'. He noted that 'despite all exploitation and abuse, that vast area of fissured land, from the Himalaya to the tip of the peninsula, is so rich still in so many resources and species that one wonders if one might be permitted a glimmer of utopian encouragement.' Full of optimism until the end, and with not just the Indian sub-continent in mind, he asked, 'Might the downward drift not yet be turned around?'

In remembering Paul Kurian and E. P. Thompson we invoke not so much personal friendships as a wider socialist tradition of thought and hope, a tradition that needs to be renewed and revitalised for the future. In 1991, shortly after the collapse of the Soviet Union, a group of distinguished Marxist scholars published, under the auspices of a distinguished Marxist press, a volume of essays with the gloomy title *After the Fall*. The authors of the present book, however, felt no sense of failure at the happenings in eastern Europe; on the contrary, we felt a sense of relief, at being able to go back, in a spirit of fraternity and open-ness, to alternative traditions of left-wing thought crushed by some 70 years of Marxist and (especially) Leninist arrogance. Before Bolshevism became the Big Brother on the Left, traditions of anarchism, syndicalism, and peasant populism – to name only three – existed on more or less equal terms with it. An ecological politics for the next century must, we believe, build on the insights of these 'other' varieties of socialism in their pristine 19th century forms and as they have been elaborated by an array of 20th century thinkers, some of whom are duly honoured in these pages.

This book is in the first instance a work of comparative history, an account and analysis, over time and across societies, of the varieties of environmentalism that we understand to be characteristic of the modern world. But we must also own up to another and not always hidden agenda: the bringing into dialogue of socialism and environmentalism, two radical traditions that have tended to talk past rather than talk to each other.

Ramachandra Guha and Juan Martinez-Alier
Bangalore and Barcelona
November 1996

INTRODUCTION

In the winter of 1925–6, the English writer Aldous Huxley embarked with his wife on a six month tour of Asia, his first sojourn outside Europe. Landing in Bombay, they cut a wide swathe through the sub-continent: the northern Himalaya, the Rajasthan desert, the towns of Benares and Lucknow in the Indo-Gangetic Plain and the colonial city of Calcutta. From India the couple proceeded to Burma, then on to Malaya, Java and the Philippines. Leaving the tropics behind them, the Huxleys spent a few days in Japan before returning home in June 1926.

Like other English writers of his generation, Huxley went abroad only to write about it. He published a diary of his Indian travels, *Jesting Pilate*, that enraged his hosts for its negative portrayal of Indian music, Indian architecture and Indian religion. The book aroused intense feelings at the time, not least for its dismissal of the Taj Mahal ('Marble', Huxley said, 'conceals a multitude of sins'). But *Jesting Pilate* was not the only literary work that resulted from his travels. Huxley also wrote an essay with the intriguing title 'Wordsworth in the Tropics', an essay that attracted little attention when it was published, and appears to be wholly forgotten now.[1] But so far as we can tell, it was the first published contribution to the comparative study of environmentalism, which is why we resurrect it here.

'Wordsworth in the Tropics' exhibits the easy confidence of one who has just enlarged his own range of experience. Huxley deems it a pity that Wordsworth himself 'never travelled beyond the boundaries of Europe'. For a 'voyage through the tropics would have cured him of his too easy and comfortable pantheism. A few months in the jungle would have convinced him that the diversity and utter strangeness of nature are at least as real and significant as its intellectually discovered unity. The 'Wordsworthian who exports his pantheistic worship of Nature to the tropics', claims Huxley, 'is liable to have his religious convictions somewhat rudely disturbed.'

In Huxley's view, the appreciation and love of nature could only flourish in benign temperate ecologies: it could scarcely be exported to the dark, forbidding and (to Europeans, at any rate) dangerous tropics. The worship of Nature came easily, almost naturally, to those who lived 'beneath a temperate sky and in the age of Henry Ford'. But this adoration was possible only 'in a country where Nature has been nearly or quite enslaved to man'. For 'Nature, under a vertical sun, and nourished by the equatorial rains, is not at all like the chaste, mild deity who presides over the... prettiness, the cosy sublimities of the Lake District'. It 'is easy to love a feeble and already conquered enemy', remarks Huxley, but 'an enemy with whom one is still at war, an unconquered, unconquerable, ceaselessly active enemy – no; one does not, one should not, love him'. For despite its beauty, the tropical forest was terrifying and sinister, its 'vast masses of swarming vegetation alien to the human spirit and hostile to it'.[2]

Two years after Huxley's essay appeared, another British intellectual–aristocrat offered a somewhat different interpretation of why, and how, the love of Nature came to be a cultural force in the modern West. This was the Cambridge scholar G. M. Trevelyan, whose contribution to the environmental debate[3] is as little remembered today as is 'Wordsworth in the Tropics'.

By training a social historian, Trevelyan located the wellsprings of Nature-love not in a distinctive and benign ecology but within secular changes in economic and social life. What is for the writer an incidental and throwaway comment ('the age of Henry Ford') becomes for the scholar the central explanatory variable. The 'love of nature in its most natural and unadulterated form', notes Trevelyan, 'has grown *pari passu* with the Industrial Revolution. James Watt and George Stephenson were contemporaries of Rousseau and Wordsworth, and the two movements have gone on side by side ever since, each progressing with equal rapidity'. One movement furthered the appreciation and understanding of natural beauty; the other movement intensified the rate at which Nature was destroyed. As Trevelyan perceptively remarks: 'No doubt it is partly because the destruction is so rapid that the appreciation is so loud'. This sense of nostalgia was heightened by the conditions of city life, the condition now of the vast majority of English people. Their separation from the natural world, enforced by urban living, fostered a yearning to return periodically and for short spurts to Nature – 'and for that reason, if for no other, the real country must be preserved in sufficient quantity to satisfy the soul's thirst of the town dweller'.

Illustrative here was the change in English perceptions of the Alps and the Scottish Highlands; once regarded as hostile they were, by the time Trevelyan wrote, the epitome of what was wild and, therefore, beautiful. This change in attitude towards mountain scenery, observes the historian, 'is almost identical in time and progress with the march of the industrial revolution, and has, I think, a certain causal connection with it'. In his explanation, the

Modern aesthetic taste for mountain form, is connected with a moral and intellectual change, that differentiates modern civilized man from civilized man in all previous ages. I think that he now feels the desire and need for the wildness and greatness of untamed, aboriginal nature, which his predecessors did not feel. One cause of this change is the victory that civilized man has now attained over nature through science, machinery and organization, a victory so complete that he is denaturalizing the lowland landscape. He is therefore constrained to seek nature in her still unconquered citadels, the mountains.[4]

Huxley and Trevelyan were both spokesmen for the progressive and privileged intelligentsia of England. At this time, nature appreciation was restricted by and large to writers and professionals of the upper classes, and was not the mass phenomenon it subsequently became. With hindsight, the historian's interpretation seems to have worn better than the novelist's. The diversity and 'utter strangeness' of nature in the tropics, which Huxley felt would put off Western nature lovers, is indeed what is increasingly attracting them to it. Western man, having denaturalised his lowlands *and* his mountains, can find aboriginal nature only in the rainforests of the Amazon or of Borneo, with their astonishing diversity of animal, insect and plant life, all of which seem now so appealing to him. Saving the rainforest, those 'vast masses of swarming vegetation', is, with the possible exception only of saving the whale, the great environmental cause of our times. Even if most nature lovers come no closer to the rainforest than watching a television programme set there, the readiness with which they part with cash to save it testifies to a spirit of kinship with – not, as Huxley supposed, hostility to – the tropical forest.

In contrast, Trevelyan anticipates, in several crucial respects, the core arguments of historians of modern environmentalism. From the 1960s, as the movement for environmental protection acquired deep roots in one industrialised country after another, a series of writers offered interpretations which, albeit unknowingly, took as their point of departure the Trevelyan thesis that rapid industrialisation and urbanization lead both to a separation from nature and to a greater and self-conscious move to protect and identify with it. In 1963, the year after Rachel Carson published her landmark book, *Silent Spring*, one historian commented upon the 'paradoxical ability' of the American people 'to devastate the natural world and at the same time to mourn its passing.'[5]

This has been, in fact, an ability widely shared across the North. Consider Sweden, a wealthy industrial nation of some 8.5 million people, 600,000 of whom have country cottages and even more own leisure boats. In their working life these people are caught up in 'the landscape of industrial production', ruled by 'rationality, calculation, profit and effectiveness', escaping only on holidays and weekends to 'another landscape of recreation, contemplation, and romance'. Two Swedish anthropologists present – should one say (re)present? – in their formal language the conclusions that the Cambridge historian arrived at half a century earlier. 'It is the alienation from the natural world', they write, 'that is a prerequisite for the new sentimental attachment to it. Nature must first become exotic in order to become natural.'[6]

The Trevelyan thesis might also be viewed as a precursor of the theory of 'post-materialism' which, by the late 1970s, was to acquire hegemonic status in the literature on the environmental movement. The political scientist Ronald Inglehart, who coined the term, argued that rapid economic growth since World War II had, through the creation of a mass consumer society, led to the satisfaction of material needs and expectations for the vast majority of the population.[7] Opinion polls now showed an increasing desire for 'post-materialist' pursuits, such as the enjoyment of a beautiful and clean environment. The growing popular interest in nature was not so much a rejection of the modern world as a proper fulfilment of it. As a British journalist crisply put it, 'when everyone turns environmental, prosperity has truly arrived. Greenness is the ultimate luxury of the consumer society'.[8]

The theory of post-materialism, or Trevelyan updated, provides a clear and in many respects persuasive explanation for the development and popularity of the environmental movement in the North. What resonance does it have outside? Although Inglehart and Trevelyan were both silent on this question, it appears that the postmaterialist framework does not allow for the expression of environmental concern in the less developed world. For example, the influential Anglo–American journal *World Development* invites papers which study 'the implications for the development efforts of the Third World of Western concerns for the environment', meaning, of course, that the Third World itself has none.[9] Likewise, in February 1986 a left-wing columnist wrote in the *New Statesman* that ecology movements 'are or seem luxuries affordable only in societies which have a high degree of control over the natural environment; equally, they are only necessary in those societies'.[10] Later the same year, an editorial in the *New York Times* deplored the hostility to technology displayed by the sentimental cult of nature among some American environmentalists, cautioning against its export overseas. 'To African villagers or Asian peasants', it remarked, 'nature is not a friend but a hostile force to be propitiated. Salvation [for them] lies not in organic gardening but in fertilisers, pesticides and fungicides, indeed the very stuff produced at [the Union Carbide plant in] Bhopal', the accident in which had given renewed strength to the opponents of modern technology.[11]

The implication is that the poor are not green either because they lack awareness (with no taste for environmental amenities when faced with more immediate necessities), or because they have not enough money (yet) to invest in the environment, or both reasons together. One also notices a beguiling linearity in these formulations. Indeed, some commentators argue that on the environmental as much as the economic front, the more developed country shows the less developed one the image of its future. 'The Third World', claims the Executive Director of the Sierra Club, 'looks upon having a system of national parks and protected areas as an indication of the country's level of development'.[12] The expression of environmentalism here becomes a mark of acceptance into the club of rich nations, a shedding of the embarrassing euphemism 'less developed' for a label ('developed') which can be worn with honour. When, in the early 1990s, a wave of environmental protests rocked South Korea, Western commentators viewed this as the 'inevitable' consequence of growing affluence, the sign that Korea was now 'waking up to the environment'.[13]

Wisdom may be deemed conventional when it unites ideologues of the left and right, scholars as well as journalists. The views quoted above, excerpted from the British and American press, find strong confirmation in more academic appraisals of the origins of environmental concern. Writing with the magisterial air that seems to come naturally to economists, Lester Thurow claims that 'If you look at the countries that are interested in environmentalism, or at the individuals who support environmentalism within each country, one is struck by the extent to which environmentalism is an interest of the upper middle class. *Poor countries and poor individuals simply aren't interested'*.[14] Even Eric Hobsbawm, that most learned of modern historians, himself a pioneer in the study of social protest, suggests in his recent history of the 20th century that

It is no accident that the main support for ecological policies comes from the rich countries and from the comfortable rich and middle classes (except for businessmen who hope to make money by polluting activity). The poor, multiplying and under-employed, wanted more 'development', not less.[15]

EXAMPLES OF ENVIRONMENTAL CONFLICT

Project Tiger

The Chenchus are a community of hunters and gatherers living in the hills and forests of the Krishna basin in the southern Indian state of Andhra Pradesh. In the early decades of this century their forests were taken over by the state (the princely state of Hyderabad); the new rulers of the forest, the Nizam's Forest Department, sharply restricted Chenchu access to fruit, food and game.[16] More recently, parts of the Chenchu habitat have been constituted as a tiger reserve under Project Tiger, India's most ambitious conservation programme. This has meant more restriction on the movement of Chenchus and on their access to forest produce. The problem, as the Chenchus see it, is that 'they have to pay for the protection of tigers while no one pays for the conservation of their communities'. As one tribal told a visitor from the state capital, 'If you love tigers so much, why don't you shift all of them to Hyderabad and declare that city a tiger reserve?'[17]

The Siberian Programme

Several thousand miles to the north, on the Siberian coast, a joint Russian–American programme was lauched three years ago to save the endangered Siberian tiger, a species even more vulnerable, at an estimated 200 to 250 animals, than its Indian cousin, which numbers in excess of 2000. Ecologists from around the world now descend upon a region suddenly made accessible after decades of isolation, much 'to the bemusement of the 5,000 locals who believe their own suffering is more important than that of the tiger'. The project is under threat from local hunters and fisherfolk who wonder why no one makes a fuss about *their* predicament. For the condition of the Russian economy is appalling, and there are few sources of employment or income – one of which is the poaching of the said tiger. This can yield upwards of U.S. $5,000 in tiger skin and bones (used in Chinese medicine).[18]

The Galapagos Islands

These islands off the coast of Ecuador have a unique place in the natural history of the globe because of Charles Darwin and the giant tortoises he studied there. The conservation programmes on the islands are funded in large part by an international foundation, named after Darwin. As much as 97percent of the Galapagos archipelago enjoys the status of a national park. There is too a Charles Darwin Research Station, manned by Northern scientists. A 'corps of dedicated conservationists is fighting for the long-term preservation of the islands', but they face increasing hostility from local residents. Fisherfolk are bitter about the ban on catching lobsters and on shark fishing: moreover, the meat of the protected tortoise forms part of the islanders' diet. In October 1993 the fishermen burnt in procession an effigy of a leader of the Darwin Foundation; the following April some islanders organised a raid on a colony of tortoises, killing 31 of them and leaving another seriously injured. The scientists at the Darwin station first wanted to fly out a veterinarian from the University of Florida to treat the injured animal, but then decided to fly it to the United States 'apparently because they feared that Galapagos residents would rise up in anger if the tortoise were treated at a local clinic built for humans'. Fifteen months later the conflict had shifted to another protected species. On January 1995, a group of *pepineros* (sea-cucumber fishermen) marched on and seized control both of the Darwin research station and the headquarters of the Galapagos National Park in Puerto Ayora, on the island of Santa Cruz. Masked and armed with clubs and machettes, the *pepineros* demanded that the ban on fishing sea-cucumbers, imposed in December 1994, be lifted forthwith.[19]

These three cases are widely separated in space, yet a common thread runs through them. They seem to collectively exemplify the post-materialist thesis that the countries of the South (among whom Russia must now be reckoned) are too poor, too narrow-minded, or too relentlessly focused on the short-term to be Green. Sometimes, indeed, this interpretation takes on the nature of a self-fulfilling prophecy, so that it is advanced not only by Northern sociologists or ecologists but by people in the South. 'It's beautiful to speak of ecology when you have your pockets full of bills', remarks Alberto Granja, a native of the Galapagos, 'but what's it worth when you are dying of hunger?'[20]

The converse of this thesis, that the South is 'too poor to be Green', is the belief that programmes of environmental protection in the Third World are nothing but a form of conservation imperialism, a Northern conspiracy to keep the Third World forever underdeveloped. This argument was eloquently put forward by the Indian Prime Minister, at the United Nations Conference on the Human Environment, held in Stockholm in June 1972. Mrs Gandhi appears later to have gone back on this position, but it is still widely held by Third World intellectuals and by some politicians too. The Indian cartoonist and columnist Abu Abraham has talked of an 'international vested interest in blocking the progress of the poorer nations, especially if they want to develop their own resources and become economically independent'. And so he deeply suspects 'advice that comes from foreign sources. I mistrust the Gandhism and the environmentalism that is often imparted to us from London, Bonn or Washington'.[21]

This distrust has been expressed rather more forcefully and influentially by the Malaysian Prime Minister, Dr Mahathir bin Mohamad. Some years ago, a British schoolboy wrote to Dr Mahathir conveying his anguish at the destruction of the rainforest in that country. 'I am ten years old', wrote Darrell Abercrombie, and

When I am older I hope to study animals in the tropical rain forests. But if you let the lumber companies carry on there will not be any left. And millions of animals will die. Do you think that it is right just so one rich man gets another million pounds or more. I think it is disgraceful.

And this, in part, is Dr Mahathir's reply:

I hope you will tell the adults who made use of you to learn all the facts. They should not be too arrogant and think they know how best to run a country. They should expel all the people living in the British countryside and allow secondary forests to grow and fill these new forests with wolves and bears etc. so you can study them before studying tropical animals.[22]

Here we find an uncanny congruence between the Chenchu of the Andhra forest and the Malaysian Head of State. 'Take your tigers to the city', says one, speaking for his tribe. 'Grow back your forests and bring back the animals you have destroyed', says the other, speaking for his nation. We can't *afford* to be green, say both.

Or do they?

OTHER EXAMPLES OF CONFLICT

Introduction of Eucalyptus Trees

Throughout the world, forestry departments have accorded the eucalyptus tree 'most favoured species' status. It grows quickly, has a variety of economic uses as fuel and pulpwood, and requires little or no supervision as it is not browsed by goats or cows. In consequence it has spread far and wide outside its native habitat, becoming unquestionably the best-known Australian export, but not the best-loved. Take the tree's introduction to the Pakham district of Thailand, which is close to the border with Kampuchea. In its pursuit of an export-oriented development strategy, the Thai government has encouraged the production of wood chips and paper pulp. Quite often, existing deciduous forests are cleared to make way for monocultures of the Australian tree. In the forests of Pakham these schemes have threatened peasants who settled these areas towards the end of the last century. When the Thai Royal Forestry Department gave a contract to a private company to plant eucalyptus trees, it was immediately opposed by the villagers, who said their rice did not grow well near this water-guzzling and soil-depleting tree. Led by a Buddhist monk, Phra Prajak Khuttajitto, peasants protested by burning a eucalyptus nursery in 1988, an act repeated the following year. But theirs was a programme of destruction *and* of renewal, for they also collaborated with the monk in a replanting programme using local species.[23]

The Ogoni People

In November 1995, nine years after insisting that ecological concern was an exclusively Northern phenomenon, the *New York Times* was forced to front-page the activities of an African environmentalist. The circumstances were tragic, for the man in question, Ken Saro-Wiwa, had just been executed by the military rulers of his country, Nigeria. Saro-Wiwa, a playwright of international renown, had been mobilising his Ogoni people against the destruction of their homeland by oil drilling. The Ogoni live in the delta of the Niger river, where the Anglo–Dutch company Royal Shell operates deep and vastly profitable oil wells. Starting operations in 1958, Shell had taken out an estimated 900 million barrels of crude from the region. The Nigerian Federal Government also benefited handsomely from these operations, earning revenues in excess of US$15 billion. As only 1. 5 percent of this money was ploughed back into the oil-bearing areas, the Ogoni remained without jobs, schools or hospitals. Thirty-five years of drilling had instead led to death and devastation – 'a blighted countryside, an atmosphere full of ... carbon monoxide and hydrocarbon; a land in which wildlife is unknown; a land of polluted streams and creeks, a land which is, in every sense of the term, an ecological disaster'. It fell to Saro-Wiwa and his associates to organise the Movement for the Survival of the Ogoni People (MOSOP). MOSOP's efforts culminated in a mass meeting on 4 January 1993, when an estimated 300,000 men and women marched in solidarity and protest, holding twigs, their chosen environmental symbol. Saro-Wiwa then underwent prolonged periods of incarceration before being judicially murdered on never-proven charges of abetting the killing of four pro-government Ogoni chiefs.[24]

The Dutch Environment

Aldous Huxley notwithstanding, there have by now been thousands of European travellers in search of unspoiled tropical forests to explore, praise and protect. In a notable and possibly unique reversal of this traffic, the Dutch Alliance for Sustainable Development invited, in late 1991, four Southern scholars to write a report on the Dutch environment. A Brazilian anthropologist, an Indian sociologist, a Tanzanian agronomist and an Indonesian activist, two men, two women, spent six weeks in the Netherlands, travelling the country and talking to a cross-section of its citizens and public officials. Their investigations culminated in a critical but not always cold look at how the Dutch were managing their environment. In their 'addiction to affluence' – as exemplified in an overreliance on the motor car, dependence on the lands and resources of other countries, and the high levels of pollution this consumption engendered – the Dutch were seen to be a microcosm of the North as a whole. Posing the sharp question, 'Can Dutch society put limits to itself', the four critics thought the developed political culture offered possibilities of self correction – but only if political action was accompanied by technical change, individual restraint, and a wider resolve to share their wealth with the less-advantaged societies of the South.[25]

If our previous illustrations 'proved' that environmentalism was of no concern to the poor, this second set of three cases seems to show the opposite, to wit, the existence of a clearly articulated environmentalism in the countries of the South. There are, of course, many varieties of environmentalism, and it is one of the objects of this book to show, with reference to different individuals, communities and nations, which variety attracts and which repels. One might broadly say (while reserving the refinements and qualifications for later chapters) that poor countries and poor individuals are not interested in the mere protection of wild species or natural habitats, but do respond to environmental destruction which directly affects their way of life and prospects for survival. For as the Pakham monk Phra Prajak Khuttajitto points out, 'even the Buddha and his disciples knew the importance of the harmony and interdependence between man and nature'. This activist monk saw the eucalyptus project as symptomatic of a wider process of development in Thailand, one insensitive to local needs and the environment. The Forestry Department, he remarks, is but a 'tool' of outside profiteers – it has 'let the forest become destroyed because it was intended as a reserve for the use of capitalists'. Prajak thus calls 'for a decentralisation of power structures, local and more equitable resource management, and the use of sustainable cultural practices leading towards a new self-reliance'.[26]

Likewise, while European supporters of Ken Saro-Wiwa, such as the British novelist William Boyd, saw his predicament in terms of the violation of human rights by a brutal and authoritarian regime, the Ogoni leader himself understood his struggle to be as much environmental as it was political. The underlying philosophy of MOSOP, he wrote, is 'ERECTISM, an acronym for Ethnic Autonomy, Resource and Environmental Control'. Like the Buddhist monk, Saro-Wiwa the playwright outlined an alternative to the dominant development path which has, as its building blocks, self-reliance, decentralisation, social justice and hence, environmental integrity. Finally, the authors of *A Vision from the South* offer a global perspective consistent with these local ones. By urging the people of the North to 'de-consumerise', to 'cut down on their life-style of overproduction and overconsumption', they show how 'sustainability will only come with equity among nations and a shift in the West's cherished assumptions about nature, science and other peoples' cultural ways'.[27] Following these four Southerners, one might respond to the question posed by the editors of *World Development* by asking, in turn: 'What are the implications for the *de*-development effort of the West of Third World concerns for the environment'?

CONCLUSION

This book offers to the conventional wisdom of Northern social science an alternative and sometimes oppositional framework for more fully understanding both the 'full-stomach' environmentalism of the North as well as the 'empty-belly' environmentalism of the South. *Varieties of Environmentalism* deals, for the most part, with the perceptions and valuations of nature among subordinated social groups, such as peasants and fisherfolk. The environmentalisms of the poor, we argue, originate in social conflicts over access to and control over natural resources: conflicts between peasants and industry over forest produce, for example, or between rural and urban populations over water and energy. Many social conflicts often have an ecological content, with the poor trying to retain under their control the natural resources threatened by state takeover or by the advance of the generalised market system. This ecological content is then made visible by writers and intellectuals associated with such movements. We explore, in different societies and historical periods, the origins, articulations and ideologies of conflicts over nature. In interpreting social conflict against a backdrop of physical deterioration and natural resource crises, we depart from the prevailing tendency to view environmentalism in largely mental terms as a question of values affirmed or denied, 'post-materialist' or 'anti-materialist'.[28]

The main focus of this book is on environmental conflicts in South Asia and Latin America. We introduce historical and comparative perspectives into the study of environmentalism, including gender issues, and also analyse the international ecological conflicts that have sharpened since the Earth Summit of June 1992. Essays on the 'ecology of affluence', which draw on our research in Europe and the United States, are included as well. Thus we place in context some peculiarly North American types of environmentalism, as for instance the cult of the wilderness, but we also note and comment on the recent upsurge of a quite different type of environmentalism in the United States, the 'Environmental Justice' movement.

The book begins with a case study of environmental conflict in the Indian state of Karnataka. Chapter 2, moving upwards from the local to the national and the global, presents a framework for understanding what we call 'ecological distribution conflicts'. It presents a detailed classification of the varieties of environmentalism in the modern world, outlining a research agenda towards the fulfilment of which this book takes but a few, tentative steps. Anticipating the economist's objection – 'It may work in practice, but does it work in theory?' – Chapter 3 then takes apart the argument (advanced most influentially in the Brundtland Report of 1987) that poverty is a prime cause of environmental degradation. We thus establish, in theory as well as in practice, that to be poor is very often a very good reason to be green. From these 'materialist' analyses we move in Chapter 4, to a comparative study of environmental ideas, understood generically and with reference to India and the United States. We next turn to North–South conflicts, potential and actual, with a polemic against 'deep ecology' followed by a study of the competing claims over biodiversity of indigenous and peasant communities, multinationals, and nation-states. Finally, Chapter 7 studies ecological ideas in an urban context (a context neglected by environmentalists and by environmental historians); thus Part I, which began with an essay of one author's home state, ends with a study of the other's home city.

In Part II we rehabilitate three forgotten (or at any rate insufficiently honoured), exemplars whose thought has a surprisingly contemporary ring. To the All-American holy trinity of John Muir, Aldo Leopold and Rachel Carson we offer three other names for inclusion in the environmentalist's pantheon: the Indian spiritualist and politician Mahatma Gandhi; the (emigré) Romanian economist Nicholas Georgescu-Roegen; and the American polymath Lewis Mumford. Our choices are dictated not so much by a policy of geographical correctness as by our own familiarity with these thinkers, and by our utter conviction that their ideas provide both a deeper understanding and a plausible way out of the global environmental crisis.

Varieties of Environmentalism ranges over a number of disciplines and regions. One of us is an economist and anthropologist of Latin America and Europe; the other a sociologist and historian of South Asia and North America. Only Africa, of the major continents of the world, is not covered here. The essays move geographically from Karnataka in southern India to the Pacific Rim (mainly California, Ecuador and Peru), via Europe, with visits to the German Greens and the Olympic city of Barcelona. Historically, these essays look back sometimes over 100 years, to the exploitation of guano in Peru, or the establishment of huge, state-managed programmes of forest management in British India. Sometimes they look back even further, to the demographic collapse in the Americas after 1492. But most of the essays are contemporary, reaching out to the ongoing struggle against the Narmada dam in central India and the court case brought by some of the indigenous people of Ecuador against Texaco in New York.

Diverse in their location and in their illustrative examples, these essays none the less have, we believe, a strong thematic unity. They are united by a shared analytical aproach, deriving from ecological history and political economy, and consolidated by several years of close interaction and collaboration. They are united, too, by a shared research strategy: the combination of archival and field materials, the focus on conflict, the exploration of the ideologies that underpin or justify environmental movements of the poor and of the rich. Above all, they are united by the urge to see each case comparatively, to set the North by, and sometimes against, the South. We are interested, certainly, in what neo-Wordsworths might say or do in the Tropics, but also in what old Gandhians might say and do in the Temperate Zone.

PART ONE

Chapter 1

The Environmentalism of the Poor[1]

The environmentalists in any area seemed very easy to identify. They were, quite simply, members of the local aristocracy... The environmental vision is an aristocratic one... It can only be sustained by people who have never had to worry about security.

(US journalist William Tucker, 1977)

The first lesson is that the main source of environmental destruction in the world is the demand for natural resources generated by the consumption of the rich (whether they are rich nations or rich individuals and groups within nations)... The second lesson is that it is the poor who are affected the most by environmental destruction.

(Indian journalist Anil Agarwal, 1986)

THE ORIGINS OF CONFLICT

When India played South Africa in a cricket international in Calcutta, the great Indian cricketer, Sunil Gavaskar, was asked by a fellow television commentator to predict the likely winner. 'I tried to look into my crystal ball,', answered Gavaskar 'but it is clouded up by the Calcutta smog.' He might well have added: 'To clear it I then dipped my crystal ball in the river Hooghly [which flows alongside the city's cricket stadium], but it came up even dirtier than before.'

The quality of air and water in Calcutta is representative of conditions in all Indian cities; small wonder that foreign visitors come equipped with masks and bottles of Perrier. Less visible to the tourist, and to urban Indians themselves, is the continuing environmental degradation in the countryside. Over 100 million hectares, or one-third of India's land area, has been classed as unproductive wasteland. Much of this was once forest and land ground; the rest, farmland destroyed by erosion and salinisation. The uncontrolled exploitation of groundwater has led to an alarming drop in the water table, in some areas by more than five metres. There is an acute shortage of safe water for drinking and domestic use. As the ecologist Jayanta Bandyopadhyay has remarked, water rather than oil will be the liquid whose availability (or lack of it) will have a determining influence on India's economic future.[2]

The bare physical facts of the deterioration of India's environment are by now well established.[3] But more serious still are its human consequences, the chronic shortages of natural resources in the daily life of most Indians. Peasant women have to trudge further and further for fuelwood for their hearth. Their menfolk, meanwhile, are digging deeeper and deeper for a trickle of water to irrigate their fields. Forms of livelihood crucially dependent on the bounty of nature, such as fishing, sheep-rearing or basket-weaving, are being abandoned all over India. Those who once subsisted on these occupations are joining the band of 'ecological refugees', flocking to the cities in search of employment. The urban population itself complains of shortages of water, power, construction material and (for industrial units) of raw material.

Such shortages flow directly from the abuse of the environment in contemporary India, the too rapid exhaustion of the resource base without a thought to its replenishment. Shortages lead, in turn, to sharp conflicts between competing groups of resource users. These conflicts often pit poor against poor, as when neighbouring villages fight over a single patch of forest and its produce, or when slum dwellers come to blows over the trickle of water that reaches them, one hour each day from a solitary municipal tap. Occasionally they pit rich against rich, as when the wealthy farmers of the adjoining states of Karnataka and Tamil Nadu quarrel over the water of the river Kaveri. However, the most dramatic environmental conflicts set rich against poor. This, for instance, is the case with the Sardar Sarovar dam on the Narmada river in central India. The benefits from this project will flow primarily to already pampered and prosperous areas of the state of Gujarat, while the costs will be disproportionately borne by poorer peasants and tribal communities in the upstream states of Madhya Pradesh and Maharashtra. These latter groups, who are to be displaced by the dam, are being organised by the Narmada Bachao Andolan (Save the Narmada Movement), which is indisputably the most significant environmental initiative in India today.

The 'Indian environmental movement' is an umbrella term that covers a multitude of these local conflicts, initiatives and struggles. The movement's origins can be dated to the Chipko movement, which started in the Garhwal Himalaya in April 1973. Between 1973 and 1980, over a dozen instances were recorded where, through an innovative technique of protest, illiterate peasants – men, women and children – threatened to hug forest trees rather than allow them to be logged for export. Notably, the peasants were not interested in saving the trees *per se*, but in using their produce for agricultural and household requirements. In later years, however, the movement turned its attention to broader ecological concerns, such as the collective protection and management of forests, and the diffusion of renewable energy technologies.[4]

The Chipko movement was the forerunner of and in some cases the direct inspiration for a series of popular movements in defence of community rights to natural resources. Sometimes these struggles revolved around forests; in other instances, around the control and use of pasture, and mineral or fish resources. Most of these conflicts have pitted rich against poor: logging companies against hill villagers, dam builders against forest tribal communities, multinational corporations deploying trawlers against traditional fisherfolk in small boats. Here one party (e.g. loggers or trawlers) seeks to step up the pace of resource exploitation to service an expanding commercial–industrial economy, a process which often involves the partial or total dispossession of those communities who earlier had control over the resource in question, and whose own patterns of utilisation were (and are) less destructive of the environment.

More often than not, the agents of resource-intensification are given preferential treatment by the state, through the grant of generous long leases over mineral or fish stocks, for example, or the provision of raw material at an enormously subsidised price. With the injustice so compounded, local communities at the receiving end of this process have no recourse except direct action, resisting both the state and outside exploiters through a variety of protest techniques. These struggles might perhaps be seen as the manifestation of a new kind of class conflict. Where 'traditional' class conflicts were fought in the cultivated field or in the factory, these new struggles are waged over gifts of nature such as forests and water, gifts that are coveted by all but increasingly monopolised by a few.

There is, then, an unmistakable material context to the upsurge of environmental conflict in India; the shortages of, threats to and struggles over natural resources. No one could even suggest, with regard to India, what two distinguished scholars claimed some years ago with regard to American environmentalism, namely that it had exaggerated or imagined the risk posed by ecological degradation.[5] All the same, the environmentalism of the poor is neither universal nor pre-given – there are many parts of India (and the South more generally) where the destruction of the environment has generated little or no popular response. To understand where, how and in what manner environmental conflict articulates itself requires the kind of location-specific work, bounded in time and space, that social scientists have thus far reserved for studies of worker and peasant struggles.

This chapter focuses on an environmental conflict that was played out between 1984 and 1991 in the southern Indian state of Karnataka. This conflict is perhaps not as well known outside India as the Chipko or Narmada movements. But its unfolding powerfully illustrates the same, countrywide processes of resource deprivation and local resistance.

CLAIMING THE COMMONS IN KARNATAKA

On 14 November 1984, the government of Karnataka entered into an agreement with Harihar Polyfibres, a rayon-producing unit located in the north of the state; the company forms part of the great Indian industrial conglomerate owned by the Birla family. By this agreement a new company was formed, called the Karnataka Pulpwoods Limited (KPL), in which the government had a holding of 51 per cent and Harihar Polyfibres held 49 per cent. KPL was charged with growing eucalyptus and other fast-growing species of trees for the use by Harihar Polyfibres. For this purpose, the state had identified 30,000 hectares of common land, spread over four districts in the northern part of Karnataka. This land was nominally owned by the state (following precedents set under British colonial rule, when the state had arbitrarily asserted its rights of ownership over non-cultivated land all over India), but the grass, trees and shrubs standing on it were extensively used in surrounding villages for fuel, fodder and other materials.[6]

The land was granted by the state to KPL on a long lease of 40 years, and for a ridiculously low annual rent of one rupee per acre. As much as 87. 5 per cent of the produce was to go directly to Harihar Polyfibres; the private sector company also had the option of buying the remaining 12.5 per cent. All in all, this was an extraordinarily advantageous arrangement for the Birla-owned firm. The government of Karnataka was even willing to stand guarantee for the loans that were to finance KPL's operations: loans to be obtained from several nationalised banks, one of which was, ironically, the National Bank of Agriculture and Rural Development.

For years before the formation of KPL the wood-based industry, faced with chronic shortages of raw material, had been clamouring for captive plantations. Forests were being depleted all over India; in fact, this deforestation had itself been caused primarily by over-exploitation of trees to meet industrial demand. Although the state had granted them handsome subsidies in the provision of timber from government forests, paper, rayon and plywood companies were keen to acquire firmer control over their sources of supply. Indian law prohibited large-scale ownership of land by private companies: in the circumstances, joint-sector companies (i.e., units jointly owned by the state and private capital) provided the most feasible option. Indeed, no sooner had KPL been formed then industrialists in other parts of India began pressing state governments to start similar units with their participation and for their benefit.

But, of course, paper and rayon factories were not alone in complaining about shortages of woody biomass. A decade earlier, the Chipko movement had highlighted the difficulties faced by villagers in gaining access to the produce of the forests. In the wake of Chipko had arisen a wide-ranging debate on forest policy, with scholars and activists arguing that state forest policies had consistently discriminated against the rights of peasants, tribals and pastoralists, while unduly favouring the urban–industrial sector.[7]

There was little question that, as a result of these policies, shortages of fuel and fodder had become pervasive throughout rural India. In Karnataka itself, one study estimated that while the annual demand for fuelwood in the state was 12. 4 million tonnes (mt), the annual production was 10. 4 mt – a shortfall of 16 per cent. In the case of fodder, the corresponding figures were 35. 7 and 23 mt, respectively – a deficit of as much as 33 per cent.[8]

The fodder crisis in turn illustrated the crucial importance of species choice in programmes of reforestation. From the early 1960s, the government's Forest Department had enthusiastically promoted the plantation of eucalyptus on state-owned land. In many parts of India, rich, diverse natural forests were felled to make way for single-species plantations of this tree of Australian origin. As in the Thai district of Pakham (discussed in the Introduction), this choice was clearly dictated by industry, for eucalyptus is a quick growing species sought after by both paper and rayon mills. But it is totally unsuitable as fodder – indeed, one reason eucalyptus was planted by the Forest Department was that it is not browsed by cattle and goats, thus making regeneration that much easier to achieve. Environmentalists deplored this preference for eucalyptus, which was known to have negative effects on soil fertility, water retention and on biological diversity generally. Eucalyptus was, moreover, a 'plant which socially speaking has all the characteristics of a weed', in that it benefited industry at the expense of the rural poor, themselves hard hit by biomass shortages. These critics advocated the plantation and protection instead of multi-purpose, indigenous tree species more suited for meeting village requirements of fuel, fodder, fruit and fibre.[9]

In the context of this wider, all-India debate, the formation of KPL seemed a clearly partisan move in favour of industry, as the lands it took over constituted a vital, and often irreplaceable, source of biomass for small peasants, herdsmen and wood-working artisans. Within months of its establishment, the new company became the object of severe criticism. In December 1984, the state's pre-eminent writer and man of letters, Dr Kota Shivram Karanth, wrote an essay in the most popular Kannada daily, calling on the people of Karnataka to totally oppose 'this friendship between Birlas and the government and the resulting joint-sector company'.

The opposition to KPL grew after 15 July 1986, the date on which the state actually transferred the first instalment of land (3,590 hectares) to KPL. Even as the company was preparing the ground for planting eucalyptus, petitions and representations were flying thick and fast between the villages of north Karnataka (where the land was located) and the state capital of Bangalore, 250 miles to the south. The Chief Minister of Karnataka, Ramkrishna Hegde, was deluged with letters from individuals and organisations protesting against the formation of KPL; one letter, given wide prominence, was signed by a former Chief Minister, a former Chief Justice and a former Minister, respectively. Meanwhile, protest meetings were organised at several villages in the region. The matter was also raised in the state legislature.[10]

In the forefront of the movement against KPL was the Samaj Parivartan Samudaya (Association for Social Change, SPS), a voluntary organisation working in the Dharwad district of Karnataka. The SPS had in fact cut its teeth in a previous campaign against Harihar Polyfibres. It had organised a movement against the pollution of the Tungabhadra river by the rayon factory, whose untreated effluents were killing fish and undermining the health and livelihood of villagers living downstream. On 2 October 1984 (Mahatma Gandhi's birth anniversary), SPS held a large demonstration outside the production unit of Harihar Polyfibres; then in December 1985, it filed a public interest litigation in the High Court of Karnataka against the State Pollution Control Board for its failure to check the pollution of the Tungabhadra by the Birla factory.[11]

Before that petition could come up for hearing, SPS filed a public interest writ against Karnataka Pulpwoods Limited, this time in the Supreme Court of India in New Delhi. SPS was motivated to do so by a similar writ in the state High Court, filed by a youth organisation working among the farmers in the Sagar *taluka* (county) of the adjoining Shimoga district. Here, in a significant judgement, Justice Bopanna issued a stay order instructing the Deputy Commissioner of Shimoga to ensure that common land was not arbitrarily transferred to KPL, and that villagers be allowed access to fodder, fuel and other usufruct from the disputed land.[12]

Submitted in early 1987, the Supreme Court petition was primarily the handiwork of SPS. The petitioners spoke on behalf of the 500,000 villagers living in the region of KPL's operations, the people most directly affected by the action of the state in handing over common land to one company. The transferred land, said the petition, 'is the only available land vested in the village community since time immemorial and is entirely meant for meeting their basic needs like fodder, fuel, small timber, etc. Neither agriculture could be carried out, nor the minimum needs of life, such as leaves, firewood and cattle fodder could be sustained without the use of the said lands.'

In this context, the petition continued, the arbitrary and unilateral action of the state amounted to the passing of 'control of material resources from the hands of common people to capitalists'. This was a 'stark abuse of power', violating not just the general canons of social justice but also two provisions of the Indian Constitution itself: the right to fair procedure guaranteed by Article 14, and the right to life and liberty (in this case, of the village community) vested under Article 21 of the Constitution. Finally, the petitioners contended that the planting of monocultures of Eucalyptus, as envisaged by KPL, would have a 'disastrous effect on the ecological balance of the region'.[13]

The arguments of equity and ecological stability aside, this petition is notable for its insistence that the lands in contention were common rather than state property, 'vested in the village community since time immemorial'. Here the claims of time and tradition were counterposed to the legal status quo, through which the state both claimed and enforced rights of ownership. In this respect the petition was perfectly in line with popular protests in defence of forest rights, which since colonial times have held the Forest Department to be an agent of usurpation, taking over by superior physical force land which by right belonged to the community.[14]

On 24 March 1987, the Supreme Court responded to the petition by issuing a stay order, thus preventing the government of Karnataka from transferring any more land to KPL. Encouraged by this preliminary victory, SPS now turned to popular mobilisation in the villages. In May, it held a training camp in non-violence at Kusnur, a village in Dharwad district, where 400 hectares of land had already been transferred to KPL. A parallel organisation of villagers, the Guddanadu Abhivruddi Samiti (Hill Areas Development Committee) was initiated to work alongside SPS. The two groups held a series of preparatory meetings in Kusnur and other villages nearby for a protest scheduled for 14 November 1987, to coincide with the third anniversary of the formation of KPL.

On 14 November, about 2,000 people converged at Kusnur. Men, women and children took an oath of non-violence in a school yard, and then proceeded for a novel protest, termed the Kithiko-Hachiko (Pluck-and-Plant) *satyagraha*. Led by drummers, waving banners and shouting slogans, the protesters moved on to the disputed area. Here they first uprooted 100 saplings of Eucalyptus before planting in their place tree species useful locally for fruit and for fodder. Before dispersing, the villagers took a pledge to water and tend the saplings they had planted.[15]

The next major development in the KPL case was the partial vacation, on 26 April 1988, by the Supreme Court of the stay it had granted a year previously. Now it allowed the transfer of a further 3,000 hectares to KPL (such interim and ad hoc grants of land were also allowed in 1989 and

9

1990).[16] The court seeming to have let them down, SPS prepared once more for direct action. They commenced training camps in the villages, planned to culminate in a fresh Pluck-and-Plant *satyagraha*. Meanwhile, journalists sympathetic to their movement intensified the press campaign against KPL.[17]

The mounting adverse publicity, and the prospect of renewed popular protest, forced the government of Karnataka to seek a compromise. On 3 June 1988, the Chief Secretary of the state government (its highest ranking official) convened a meeting attended by representatives of SPS, KPL and the Forest Department. He suggested the setting up of a one-man commission, comprising the distinguished ecologist Madhav Gadgil, to enquire into the conflicting claims (and demands) of the villagers and KPL. Until the commission submitted its report, KPL was asked to suspend its operations in Dharwad district, and SPS to withdraw its proposed monsoon *satyagraha*.

The setting up of committees and commissions is of course a classic delaying tactic, in India resorted to by colonial and democratic governments alike, to defuse and contain popular protest. In this case, the government had no intention of formally appointing the Madhav Gadgil Commission, for the ecologist was known to be a critic of the industrial bias of state forest policy,[18] and likely to report adversely on KPL. Thus the commission was never set up; in response, SPS started organising another Pluck-and-Plant *satyagraha* for 8 August 1988. This time, however, the protesters were arrested and removed before they could reach KPL's eucalyptus plot.

In later years, non-violent direct action continued to be a vital plank of SPS's strategy. In an attempt to link more closely the issues of industrial pollution and the alienation of common land, it organised in August 1989, in the towns of Hangal and Ranibennur, public bonfires of rayon cloth made by Harihar Polyfibres. The burning of mill-made cloth recalled the bonfires of Manchester textiles during India's freedom movement. Whereas that campaign stood for national self-reliance or *swadeshi*, this one affirmed *village* self-reliance by rejecting cloth made of artificial fibre. The following year, 1990, SPS reverted to its own patented method of protest. On Indian independence day (15th August), it invited the respected Chipko leader Chandi Prasad Bhatt to lead a Pluck-and-Plant *satyagraha* in the Nagvand village of the Hirekerrur taluka of Dharwad.[19]

While these protests kept the issue alive at the grassroots, SPS continued to make use of the wider political and legal system to its advantage. Through friendly contacts in the state administration, it obtained copies of four orders issued in 1987 by the Chief Conservator of Forests (General), an official known to be particularly close to the Birlas. By these orders he had transferred a further 14,000 hectares of forest land to

KPL, an area far in excess of what the Supreme Court had allowed. On the basis of these 'leaked' documents, SPS filed a further Contempt and Perjury petition in October 1988.

Meanwhile, the SPS persuaded public sector banks to delay the release of funds to KPL, pending the final hearing and settlement of the case in the Supreme Court. It had also effectively lobbied the government of India in New Delhi to clarify its own position on KPL-style schemes. In February 1988, an official of the Union Ministry of Environment and Forests, making a deposition in the Supreme Court, stated unambiguously that the raising of industrial plantations by joint-sector companies required the prior permission of the government of India. Later the same year, a new National Forest Policy was announced, which explicitly prohibited monocultural plantations on grounds of ecological stability. In June 1989 the Secretary of the Ministry of Environment and Forests wrote to the government of Karnataka expressing his disquiet about the KPL project.

Within Karnataka, resolutions asking the government to cancel the KPL agreement were passed by local representative bodies, including several *Mandal Panchayats*, local councils each representing a group of villages, as well as the *Zilla Parishad* (district council) of Dharwad. This was followed by a letter to the Chief Minister, signed by 54 members of the state legislature and sent on 11 July 1990, asking him to close down KPL so as 'to reserve village common land for the common use of villagers'. With public opinion and the central government arrayed against it, and possibly anticipating an adverse final judgement in the Supreme Court, the government of Karnataka decided to wind up KPL. The company's closure was formally announced at a board meeting on 27 September 1990, but by then KPL had already ceased operations. In its report for the previous financial year (April 1989 to March 1990) the company complained that 'during the year the plantation activity has practically come to a standstill, excepting raising 449 hectares of plantations'– a tiny fraction of the 30,000 hectares of common land it had once hoped to capture for its exclusive use.

A VOCABULARY OF PROTEST

The struggle against KPL had as its mass base, so to speak, the peasants, pastoralists, and fisherfolk directly affected by environmental abuse. Yet key leadership roles were assumed by activists who, although they came from the region, were not themselves directly engaged in production. Of the SPS activists involved more or less full-time in the movement, one had been a labour organiser, a second a social worker and progressive farmer, a third a biology PhD and former college lecturer, and a fourth an engineer who had returned to India after working for years in the United States. Crucial support was also provided by intellectuals more distant from the action. These included the greatest living Kannada writer, Dr Shivram Karanth, a figure of high moral authority and for this reason the first petitioner in the Supreme Court case against KPL. A co-petitioner was the Centre for Science and Environment, a respected Delhi-based research and advocacy group whose influence in the media and in the government was shrewdly drawn on by the activists from Karnataka.

This unity, of communities at the receiving end of ecological degradation and of social activists with the experience and education to negotiate the politics of protest, has been characteristic of environmental struggles in India. In other respects, too, the SPS-led struggle was quite typical. For underlying the KPL controversy were a series of oppositions that frame most such conflicts in India: rich versus poor, urban versus rural, nature for profit versus nature for subsistence, the state versus the people. However the KPL case was atypical in one telling respect, for environmental movements of the poor only rarely end in emphatic victory.

To put it in more explicitly ecological terms, these conflicts pit 'ecosystem people' – that is, those communities which depend very heavily on the natural resources of their own locality – against 'omnivores', individuals and groups with the social power to capture, transform and use natural resources from a much wider catchment area; sometimes, indeed, the whole world. The first category of ecosystem people includes the bulk of India's rural population: small peasants, landless labourers, tribals, pastoralists, and artisans. The category of omnivores comprises industrialists, professionals, politicians, and government officials – all of whom are based in the towns and cities – as well as a small but significant fraction of the rural élite, the prosperous farmers in tracts of heavily irrigated, chemically fertilised Green Revolution agriculture. The history of development in independent India can then be interpreted as being, in essence, a process of resource capture by the omnivores at the expense of ecosystem people. This has in turn created a third major ecological class: that of 'ecological refugees', peasants-turned-slum dwellers, who eke out a living in the cities on the leavings of omnivore prosperity.[20]

In this framework, the 'environmentalism of the poor' might be understood as the resistance offered by ecosystem people to the process of resource capture by omnivores: as embodied in movements against large dams by tribal communities to be displaced by them, or struggles by peasants against the diversion of forest and grazing land to industry. In recent years, the most important such struggle has been the Narmada Bachao Andolan (NBA), the movement representing the ecosystem people who face imminent displacement by a huge dam on the Narmada river in central India. The movement has been led by the forty-year-old Medha

Patkar, a woman of courage and character once described by a journalist as an 'ecological Joan of Arc'.

A detailed analysis of the origins and development of the Narmada conflict cannot be provided here,[21] but there is one aspect of the movement that is of particular relevance to this book; namely, its flexible and wide-ranging vocabulary of protest.

The term 'vocabulary of protest' is offered as an alternative to Charles Tilly's well-known concept of the 'repertoire of contention'. Tilly and his associates have done pioneering work on the study of dissent and direct action. Their work has focused on the techniques most characteristic of different societies, social groups or historical periods. Tilly's own understanding of direct action tends to be a narrowly instrumental one, with participants drawing on, from a broader repertoire of contention, those techniques which most effectively defend or advance their economic and political interests.[22] But in fact techniques of direct action have at the same time an utilitarian and an expressive dimension. In adopting a particular strategy, social protesters are both trying to defend their interests *and* passing judgement on the prevailing social arrangements. The latter, so to say, ideological dimension of social protest needs to be inferred even when it is not formally articulated – the fact that protesting peasants do not distribute a printed manifesto does not mean that they do not have developed notions of right and wrong. In field or factory, ghetto or grazing ground, struggles over resources, even when they have tangible material origins, have always also been struggles over meaning. Thus my preference for the term 'vocabulary of protest' – for 'vocabulary' more than 'repertoire', and 'protest' more than 'contention' – helps to clarify the notion that most forms of direct action, even if unaccompanied by a written manifesto, are both statements of purpose and of belief. In the act of doing, protesters are saying something too. Thus the Kithiko-Hachiko *satyagraha* was not simply an affirmation of peasant claims over disputed property: as a strategy of protest, its aim was not merely to insist, 'This land is ours', but also, and equally significantly, to ask, 'What are trees for?'

To return to the Narmada Bachao Andolan. Like the anti-KPL struggle, the Narmada movement has operated simultaneously on several flanks: a strong media campaign, court petitions, and the lobbying of key players such as the World Bank, which was to fund a part of the dam project. Most effectively, though, it has deployed a dazzlingly varied vocabulary of protest, in defence of the rights of the peasants and tribal communities which were to be displaced by the dam.

These strategies of direct action might be classified under four broad headings. First, there is the collective *show of strength*, as embodied in demonstrations (Hindi: *pradarshan*) organised in towns and cities. Mobilising as many people as they can, protesters march through the town, shouting slogans, singing songs, winding their way to a public meeting that marks the procession's culmination. The aim here is to assert a presence in the city, which is the locus of local, provincial or national power. The demonstrators carry a message that is at once threatening and imploring: in effect, telling the rulers (and city people in general), 'do not forget us, the dispossessed in the countryside. We can make trouble, but not if you hand out justice'.

Second, there is the *disruption of economic life* through more militant acts of protest. One such tactic is the *hartal* or *bandh* (shut-down strike), wherein shops are forced to down shutters and buses to pull off the roads, bringing normal life to a standstill. A variation of this is the *rasta roko* (road blockade), through which traffic on an important highway is blocked by squatting protesters, sometimes for days on end. These techniques are rather more coercive than persuasive, spotlighting the economic costs to the state (or to other sections of the public) if they do not yield to the dissenters.

Whereas the *hartal* or *rasta roko* aim at disrupting economic activity across a wide area, a third type of action is more sharply focused on an individual target. For instance, the *dharna* or sit-down strike is used to stop work at a specific dam site or mine. Sometimes the target is a figure of authority rather than a site of production; thus protesting peasants might *gherao* (surround) a high public official, allowing him to move only after he has heard their grievances and promised to act upon them.

The fourth generic strategy of direct action aims at putting moral pressure on the state as a whole, not merely on one of its functionaries. Pre-eminent here is the *bhook hartal*, the indefinite hunger strike undertaken by the charismatic leader of a popular movement. This technique was once used successfully by Sunderlal Bahuguna of the Chipko movement; in recent years, it has been resorted to on several occasions by Medha Patkar, the remarkable leader of the Narmada Bachao Andolan. In the *bhook hartal*, the courage and self-sacrifice of the individual leader is directly counterposed to the claims to legitimacy of the state. The fast is usually carried out in a public place, and closely reported in the media. As the days drag on, and the leader's health perilously declines, the state is forced into a gesture of submission – if only the constitution of a fresh committee to review the case in contention.

The *bhook hartal* is most often the preserve of a single, heroic, exemplary figure. A sister technique, also aimed at *shaming the state*, is more of a collective undertaking. This is the *jail bharo andolan* (literally, 'movement to fill the jails'), in which protesters peacefully and deliberately court arrest by violating the law, hoping the government would lose face by putting behind bars large numbers of its own citizens. The law most often breached is Section 144 of the Criminal Procedure Code, invoked, in anticipation of social tension, to prohibit gatherings of more than five people.

The *pradarshan, hartal, rasta roko, dharna, gherao, bhook hartal* and *jail bharo andolan* are some of the techniques which make up the environmental movement's vocabulary of protest. This is a vocabulary shared across the spectrum of protesting groups, but new situations constantly call for new innovations. In the 1970s, peasants in Garhwal developed the idiosyncratic but truly effective Chipko technique; in the 1980s, the SPS in Dharwad, opposing eucalyptus plantations, thought up the Kithiko-Hachiko *satyagraha*; and now, in the 1990s, the Narmada Bachao Andolan has threatened a *jal samadhi* (water burial), saying its cadres would refuse to move from the villages scheduled for submergence even after the dam's sluice gates are closed and the waters start rising.

The techniques of direct action itemised above have, of course, deep and honourable origins. They were first forged, in India's long struggle for freedom from British rule, by Mohandas Karamchand 'Mahatma' Gandhi. In developing and refining this vocabulary of protest, Gandhi drew on Western theories of civil disobedience as well as traditions of peasant resistance within India itself.[23]

In fact, Mahatma Gandhi provides the environmental movement with both a vocabulary of protest and an ideological critique of development in independent India. (The 'environmental' ideas of Mahatma Gandhi are discussed more fully in Chapter 8.) The invocation of Gandhi is thus conducted through what might be called a rhetoric of betrayal. For the sharpening of environmental conflict has vividly brought to light the failed hopes of India's freedom struggle. That movement commanded a mass base among the peasantry, assiduously developed by Gandhi himself, and freedom promised a new deal for rural India. And yet, after 1947 the political élite has worked to ensure that the benefits of planned economic development have flown primarily to the urban–industrial complex.

The KPL case illustrates this paradox as well as any other. On one side were the peasants and pastoralists of north Karnataka; on the other, an insensitive state government in league with the second largest business conglomerate in the country. As one protester expressed it in Kusnur: 'Our forefathers who fought to get rid of the foreign yoke thought that our country would become a land of milk and honey once the British were driven out. But now we see our rulers joining hands with the monopolists to take away basic resources like land, water and forests from the (village) people who have traditionally used them for their livelihood.' In much the same vein, a Chipko activist once told the present writer: 'After independence, we thought our forests would be used to build local industries and generate local employment, and our water resources to light our lamps and run our flour mills.' But to his dismay, the Himalayan forests continued to service the paper and turpentine factories of the plains, and the rivers were dammed to supply drinking water to Delhi and electricity to the national grid which feeds into industries and urban agglomerations all over India. While private industry has thus gained privileged access to natural resources, the burden of environmental degradation has fallen heavily on the rural poor. To invoke a slogan made famous by the Narmada Bachao Andolan, this has been a process of 'destructive development' – destructive both of rural society and of the natural fabric within which it rests. In a bitter commentary on this process, the common people of Dharwad district have come to refer to the noxious air outside Harihar Polyfibres as 'Birla Perfume', to the water of the Tungabhadra river as 'Birla Teertha' (holy water of the Birlas), and to the eucalyptus as 'Birla Kalpataru' (the Birla wonder tree).[24]

The environmental movement's return to Gandhi is then also a return to his vision for free India: a vision of a 'village-centred economic order' that has been so completely disregarded in practice. Perhaps it is more accurate to see this as a rhetoric of betrayal *and* of affirmation, as symbolised in the dates most often chosen to launch (or end) programmes of direct action. These dates are 2 October, Gandhi's birth anniversary; 15 August, Indian Independence Day; and most poignantly, 8 August, on which day in 1942 Gandhi's last great anti-colonial campaign was launched, the Quit India movement – in invoking this environmentalists are asking the state and the capitalists, the rulers of today, to 'quit' their control over forests and water.

TWO KINDS OF ENVIRONMENTALISM

In the preceding sections of this chapter, the KPL controversy has been used to outline the origins, trajectory and rhetoric of the environmental movement in India. In conclusion, let us broaden the discussion by briefly contrasting the 'environmentalism of the poor' with the more closely studied phenomenon of First World environmentalism. This analysis derives, for the most part, from my own research on the United States and India, two countries, ecologically and culturally diverse, but at very different 'stages' of economic development. These are the countries and environmental movements I know best, and yet, because of their size and importance, they might be taken as representative, more generally, of the North and the South.[25]

I begin with the origins of the environmental impulse in the two contexts. Environmental movements in the North have, I think, been convincingly related to the emergence of a post-materialist or post-industrial society. The creation of a mass consumer society has not only enlarged opportunities for leisure but also provided the means to put this time off work to the most diverse uses. Nature is made accessible through the car, now no longer a monopoly of the élite but an artefact in almost everyone's possession. It is the car which, more than anything else, opens up a new world, of the wild, that is refreshingly different from the worlds of the city and the factory. In a curious paradox, this 'most modern creation of industry' becomes the vehicle of anti-industrial impulses, taking one to distant adventures, to 'homey little towns, enchanting fairy tale forests, far from stale routine, functional ugliness or the dictates of the clock'.[26] Here lies the source of popular support for the protection of wilderness in the United States – namely, that nature is no longer restricted to the privileged few, but available to all.

In India, still dominantly a nation of villages, environmentalism has emerged at a relatively early stage in the industrial process. Nature-based conflicts, it must be pointed out once again, are at the root of the environmental movement in countries such as India. These conflicts have their root in a lopsided, iniquitous and environmentally destructive process of development in independent India. They are played out against a backdrop of visible ecological degradation, the drying up of springs, the decimation of forests, the erosion of the land. The sheer immediacy of resource shortages means that direct action has been, from the beginning, a vital component of environmental action. Techniques of direct action often rely on traditional networks of organisation, the village and the tribe, and traditional forms of protest, the *dharna* and the *bhook hartal*.

Northern environmentalism, in contrast, relies rather more heavily on the 'social movement organisation' – such as the Sierra Club or the Friends of the Earth – with its own cadre, leadership and properly audited sources of funds. This organisation then draws on the methods of redressal available in what are, after all, more complete democracies – methods such as the court case, the lobbying of legislators and ministers, the exposure on television or in the newspaper. But the experience of recent years somewhat qualifies this contrast between militant protest in the one sphere and lobbying and litigation in the other. Indian environmentalists (as with the KPL case) are turning increasingly to the courts as a supplement to popular protest, while in America, radicals disaffected by the gentle, incremental lobbying of mainstream groups have taken to direct action – the spiking of trees, for example – to protect threatened wilderness.

In both the North and the South, however, environmentalism has been, in good measure, a response to the failure of politicians to mobilize effectively on the issue of, as the case may be, the destruction of the wilderness or the dispossession of peasants by a large dam. In India, for instance, the environmental movement has drawn on the struggles of marginal populations hill peasants, tribal communities, fishermen, people displaced by construction of dams – neglected by the existing political parties. And as a 'new social movement', environmentalism in the North emerged, in the first instance, outside the party process. Some environmentalists considered themselves as neither left nor right, representing a constituency that was anti-class or, more accurately, post-class.[27] However, over time the environmental constituency became part of the democratic process, sometimes through the formation of Green parties that fight, and even occasionally win, elections.

Origins and political styles notwithstanding, the two varieties of environmentalism perhaps differ most markedly in their ideologies. The environmentalism of the poor originates as a clash over productive resources: a third kind of class conflict, so to speak, but one with deep ecological implications. Red on the outside, but green on the inside. In Southern movements, issues of ecology are often interlinked with questions of human rights, ethnicity and distributive justice. These struggles, of peasants, tribals and so on, are in a sense deeply conservative (in the best sense of the word), refusing to exchange a world they know, and are in partial control over, for an uncertain and insecure future. They are a defence of the locality and the local community against the nation. At the same time, the sharper edge to environmental conflict, and its close connections to subsistence and survival, have also prompted a thoroughgoing critique of consumerism and of uncontrolled economic development.

In contrast, the wilderness movement in the North originates outside the production process. It is in this respect more of a single-issue movement, calling for a change in attitudes (towards the natural world) rather than a change in systems of production or distribution. Especially in the United States, environmentalism has, by and large, run parallel to the consumer society without questioning its socio-ecological basis, its enormous dependence on the lands, peoples and resources of other parts of the globe.[28] It is absorbed not so much with relations within human society, as with relations between humans and other species. Here the claims of national sovereignty are challenged not from the vantage point of the locality, but from the perspective of the biosphere as a whole. This is a movement whose self-perception is that of a vanguard, moving from an 'ethical present' where we are concerned only with nation, region and race to an 'ethical future' where our moral development moves from a concern with plants and animals to ecosystems and the planet itself.[29]

In the preceding paragraphs, I have sketched a broad-brush comparison between two movements, in two different parts of the world, each carrying the prefix 'environmental'. One must, of course, qualify this picture by acknowledging the diversity of ideologies and of forms of action within each of these two trends. In the United States, anti-pollution struggles form a tradition of environmental action which has a different focus from the 'wilderness crusade'. Such, for instance, is the movement for environmental justice in the United States, the struggles of low-class, often black communities against the incinerators and toxic waste dumps that, by accident and frequently by design, come to be sited near them (and away from affluent neighbourhoods). One American commentator, Ruth Rosen, has nicely captured the contrast between the environmental justice movement and the wilderness lovers. 'At best', she writes, 'the large, mainstream environmental groups focus on the health of the planet – the wilderness, forests and oceans that cannot protect themselves. In contrast, the movement for environmental justice, led by the poor, is not concerned with overabundance, but with the environmental hazards and social and economic inequalities that ravage their communities.'[30]

Likewise, the Northern wilderness crusade has its representatives in the Third World, who spearhead the constitution of vast areas as national parks and sanctuaries, strictly protected from 'human interference'. Southern lovers of the wilderness come typically from patrician backgrounds, and have shown little regard for the fate of the human communities who, after parkland is designated as 'protected', are abruptly displaced without compensation from territory that they have lived on for generations and come to regard as their own.[31]

These caveats notwithstanding, there remains, on the whole, a clear distinction, in terms of origins and forms of articulation, between how environmental action characteristically expresses itself in the North and in the South. Take these two episodes of protest, one from California, the other from central India, the last illustrations of this chapter.

In May 1979, a young American environmentalist, Mark Dubois, chained himself to a boulder in the Stanislaus river in California. The canyon where he lay formed part of the reservoir of the New Melones dam, whose construction Dubois and his organisation, Friends of the River, had long but unsuccessfully opposed. In October 1978, the Army Corps of Engineers had completed the dam, and the following April it closed the floodgates. The level of the reservoir started to rise, and it appeared as if the campaign to 'Save the Stanislaus' had failed. But then, in an act of rare heroism, Mark Dubois went into the waters and chained himself to a rock. He chose a hidden spot, and only one friend knew of the location.[32]

Fourteen years later, an uncannily similar strategy of protest was threatened against another dam, on another river and on another continent. In August 1993, with the onset of the Indian monsoon, the vast reservoir of the Sardar Sarovar dam on the Narmada river began filling up to capacity. It now seemed that the decade-long Narmada Bachao Andolan had irrevocably lost its fight. But the leader of the movement, Medha Patkar, decided to drown herself in the waters. Patkar announced her decision to walk into the river on 6 August, with a group of colleagues, but at a place and time not to be disclosed. Fearing detention by the police, Patkar disappeared into the countryside weeks before the appointed date.

I dare say Medha Patkar had not heard of Mark Dubois, but the parallels in their chosen forms of protest are striking indeed. Both formed part of ongoing, popular movements against large dams. It was only when the movement seemed to have failed that Patkar and Dubois decided to throw the last card in their pack, offering their lives to stop the dam. Notably, in both cases the political system was alert (or open) enough not to allow the environmentalists to make this supreme sacrifice. In Stanislaus, the Corps of Engineers stopped filling the reservoir, and sent search parties by air and on land to find and rescue Dubois. In the Narmada valley, Patkar and her band were found and prevailed upon to withdraw their *samarpan dal* (martyrs squad), in return for which the Government of India promised a fresh, independent review of the Sardar Sarovar project.

While the strategies of direct action might have been superficially similar, their underlying motivations were not. Mark Dubois and his colleagues were striving, above all, to save the Stanislaus canyon as one of the last remaining examples of the unspoilt Californian wilderness. As Dubois wrote to the Colonel of the Corps of Engineers prior to entering the river: 'All the life of this canyon, its wealth of archaeological and historical roots to our past, and its unique geological grandeur are enough reasons to protect this canyon *just for itself*. But in addition, all the spiritual values with which this canyon has filled tens of thousands of folks should prohibit us from committing the unconscionable act of wiping this place off the face of the earth'.[33]

In contrast, Patkar and her colleagues hoped not only to save the Narmada river itself, but also (and more crucially) the tens of thousands of peasants to be displaced by the dam being built on the river. When completed the Sardar Sarovar project will submerge a total of 245 villages, with an estimated total population of 66,675 people, most of whom are tribals and poor peasants.[34] True, the dam will also inundate old-growth forests and historic sites, but it will most emphatically of all destroy the living culture of the human communities who live by the Narmada river. It is thus that the struggle of Patkar and her associates becomes – as they put it in a message written on the 42nd anniversary of Mahatma Gandhi's martydom – a move 'towards our ultimate goal of [a] socially just and ecologically sustainable model of development'.[35]

The Stanislaus/Narmada or Dubois/Patkar comparison illustrates a more fundamental difference between two varieties of environmentalism. The action of Mark Dubois, heroic though it undoubtedly was, was quite in line with the dominant thrust of the environmental movement in the North towards the protection of pristine, unspoilt nature: a reservoir of biological diversity and enormous aesthetic appeal which serves as an ideal (if temporary) haven from the urban workaday world. In protecting the wild, it asserts, we are both acknowledging an ethical responsibility towards other species and enriching the spiritual side of our own existence. In contrast, the action of Medha Patkar was consistent with the dominant thrust of the environmental movement in India, which strongly highlights the questions of production and distribution within human society. It is impossible to say, with regard to India, what Jurgen Habermas has claimed of the European green movement: namely, that it is sparked not 'by problems of distribution, but by concern for the grammar of forms of life'.[36] 'No Humanity without Nature!', the epitaph of the Northern environmentalist, is here answered by the equally compelling slogan 'No Nature without Social Justice!'[37]

Chapter 2

From Political Economy
to Political Ecology

... each Federal agency shall make achieving environmental justice part of its mission by identifying and addressing, as appropriate, disproportionately high and adverse human health or environmental effects of its programs, policies, and activities on minority populations and low-income populations in the United States and its territories and possessions...[1] *Clinton '94 Exec order*

INTRODUCTION

The inability of orthodox economics to cope with green issues has given rise to *ecological economics*, which is the study of the compatibility between the human economy and ecosystems over the long term. Because in ecological economics we see the market economy as embedded in a physical–chemical–biological system, the question arises of the value of natural resources and environmental services for the economy. Is it possible to translate environmental values into monetary values? Ecological economists are very sceptical about the possibility of translating or transmuting future, uncertain, irreversible externalities into monetary values.

In ecological economics, the study of distributional issues constitutes a new field of study, which we call 'political ecology'. While political economy (in the classical tradition) studies economic distribution conflicts, a new field of study is emerging, political ecology, which studies ecological distribution conflicts.[2]

There are some differences as regards distributional issues between conventional economics and ecological economics. In the ecological economy, future human generations, and the values attributed to other species, play a role precisely because the time horizon of the ecological economy is much longer, as we take into account slow biogeochemical cycles and irreversible thermodynamics. Moreover, many natural resources and environmental services are not marketable, because they have no owner. Endowment of 'property rights' and inclusion in the market would change both the distribution of income and the pattern of prices in the market economy embedded in the ecological economy.

Economic incommensurability is one main tenet of ecological economics. It arises not only from the fact that prices in actual or surrogate markets depend on the endowment of property rights and on the distribution of income, and from the fact that we must value future costs and benefits without being able to engage in transactions with as-yet-unborn individuals without knowing whether they will be poorer or richer than we are (hence, the arbitrariness of the rate of discount). Economic incommensurability also arises because most environmental resources and services are not and cannot be in the market or in surrogate markets.[3] Instead of focusing on the internalisation of externalities into the price system by means of actual or surrogate markets, this chapter looks at ecological distribution conflicts which operate at local and global levels over the depletion of resources and environmental pollution.

MARXISM AND ENVIRONMENTALISM

Environmentalism is sometimes seen as a product of prosperity, an approach usually known as the 'post-materialist' thesis, but this fails to do justice to the scope of environmental movements today and in history, particularly to the 'environmentalism of the poor' which grows out of distribution conflicts over the use of ecological resources needed for livelihood. Despite the importance of such conflicts, and the robust Marxist intellectual tradition of studying and explaining social conficts, an ecological Marxism has scarcely existed. Indeed, from the Marxist perspective and in general that of the New Left, the first reaction to the explicit social presence of environmentalism in the late 1960s and early 1970s was one of surprise if not repudiation.[4] The rise of the Green party in Germany was met by incomprehension.

With exceptions such as Raymond Williams, most Marxists chose to interpret environmentalism as a frivolous upper-class fad. They only considered the environmentalism of the IUCN, the WWF and the Sierra Club. Some Marxists thought that environmentalism was a dangerous, romantic anti-industrial trend; for instance, they wrongly identified the German Greens with the ideology of *Blut und Boden* (blood and soil). Southern Marxists rejected environmentalist critiques because they thought it was a Western ploy to keep the Third World underdeveloped. They implicitly accepted the thesis which attributes environmentalism to prosperity. They could sometimes understand the struggles against the effluents of affluence, but they certainly did not understand the environmentalism of the poor. This was eloquently expressed much later by Hugo Blanco:

At first sight, environmentalists or conservationists are nice, slightly crazy guys whose main purpose in life is to prevent the disappearance of blue whales or pandas. The common people have more important things to think about, for instance how to get their daily bread. Sometimes they are taken to be not so crazy but rather smart guys who, in the guise of protecting endangered species, have formed so-called NGOs to get juicy amounts of dollars from abroad... Such views are sometimes true. However, there are in Peru a very large number of people who are environmentalists. Of course, if I tell such people, you are ecologists, they might reply, 'ecologist your mother', or words to that effect. Let us see, however. Isn't the village of Bambamarca truly environmentalist, which has time and again fought valiantly against the pollution of its water from mining? Are not the town of Ilo and the surrounding villages which are being polluted by the Southern Peru Copper Corporation truly environmentalist? Is not the village of Tambo Grande in Piura environmentalist when it rises like a closed fist and is ready to die in order to prevent strip-mining in its valley? Also, the people of the Mantaro Valley who saw their little sheep die, because of the smoke and waste from La Oroya smelter. And the population of Amazonia, who are totally environmentalist, and die defending their forests against depredation. Also the poor people of Lima are environmentalists, when they complain against the pollution of water in the beaches.[5]

If, instead of Peru, we consider its immediate neighbours to the South or to the North, similar lists can be compiled for each country. Thus, in Chile, we could ask: Is the poor urban population of Santiago, who repeatedly complained until the stinking waste dump called Lo Errazuriz was closed down, not environmentalist? Are the Huiliche communities of Compu and Güequetrumao, which on Chiloe island confronted a wood-extraction firm, called Golden Spring, not ecologists? And the people of Paipote, who complain about the sulphur dioxide emissions from copper smelting, and therefore are themselves in danger of jeopardising their own sources of wage labour and their incomes? And the ruined olive farmers of Huasco, some of them poor, some better off, all of them in trouble because of emissions of iron particles and other metals from the pellets factory, are they not environmentalists when they protest, even if they would probably refuse the term?

And in Ecuador, is the indigenous poor population of Zámbiza, in a valley to the north-east of Quito, who unsuccessfully complains because

24

everyday more than one million kilogrammes of domestic waste are deposited in this municipal waste dump, not environmentalist? And the people from Salango, on the coast, who complain about pollution from a fishmeal factory, as they also do in so many other places in the Pacific coast of South America: in Chimbote in Peru, in Talcahuano in Chile? Although perhaps still unaware of the existence of the word itself, are the members of the peasant community of Salinas in Bolivar province, who were successful in preventing mining in their community by Rio Tinto Zinc, though they never knew exactly which ore RTZ was to mine, not ecologists? And the indigenous population of Amazonia (the Secoia, the Huorani) who have fought Texaco, and other foreign oil companies, and also Petroecuador? And the black, poor population in Esmeraldas, mainly women, who lead the struggle against the destruction of the mangroves by the shrimp industry?

There has been no lack of ecological distribution conflicts in the history of humankind. However, the Marxist neglect of ecology goes back to Marx's and Engels' own negative reaction to Sergei Podolinsky's attempt in 1880 to introduce human ecological energetics into Marxist economics. Podolinsky had analysed the energetics of life (life systems being open to the input of energy), and applied these ideas to the analysis of the economy. This was a missed opportunity, and the decades of neglect of the study of energy flow by Marxist historiography and economics have continued to this day. Engels' hasty private notes on the Second Law of Thermodynamics, which he found logically contradicted the First Law, were glorified in successive editions of *Dialectics of Nature* (first published in 1925). If Engels had written, as he might well have done, that the First and Second Laws were dialectically complementary, it could have become the orthodox interpretation. Engels' negative comments on Podolinsky's work in letters to Marx of December 1882 were first published in 1919, and were not questioned until the late 1970s, when my own work (together with J.M. Naredo) on Podolinsky's ideas was published.[6] This delay was rather odd because Podolinsky's work had already and explicitly been praised by Vladimir Vernadsky in the 1920s.[7] When *The Entropy Law and the Economic Process* by Georgescu-Roegen appeared in 1971 (see Chapter 9), asserting the relevance for economics of the Second Law of Thermodynamics, there was virtually no response from Marxists for 20 years. Even today one may read astonishing declarations from Marxist authors. For instance, David Harvey proclaims that neither the Second Law of Thermodynamics nor the inherent sustaining power of ecosystems are 'helpful *at all* in explaining the shifting history of human social organisation', an attack on human ecology and ecological economics from a geographer who should know better, if nothing else from reading Patrick Geddes and Lewis Mumford.[8]

Between, say, 1880 and 1980, there was no school of Marxist

environmental–social history combining the study of class conflict with the study of the human impact on the environment. There was Karl Wittfogel, whose theory of Oriental Despotism was closer to deterministic geography than to environmental history. Although Marx and Engels were contemporaries of the physicists who established the laws of thermodynamics in the mid-19th century, Marxian economics and economic history were based on social and economic analysis alone. In the North American context, an entry to ecological history (or that part of ecological history which pays attention to the flow of energy in human societies, to the efficiency of its use, to endosomatic and exosomatic consumption of energy[9]), was provided by Henry Adams' 'Letter to American Teachers of History' in which he proposed a historical law of exponential growth of energy use.[10] As will be shown in Chapter 3, the debate on whether growth of the economy goes together with a parallel growth in the use of energy and materials is still very much alive today. If Henry Adams was right, one could expect an abrupt 'end of history'. However, there are gains in technical efficiency in the use of materials and energy. We are nevertheless sceptical about the possibilities of an 'angelised' economy (to use Herman Daly's expression, which Henry Adams would have appreciated), and tend therefore to worry about 'the effluents of affluence' and the depletion of resources.

Marxists have resisted the introduction of ecology into historical explanation perhaps because of the fear that this could 'naturalise' human history. There has been, of course, no lack of attempts in this direction, from Malthus' law of population onwards. Indeed, ecological concepts, or at least terms such as Lebensraum, for instance, have been used with criminal intent and to devastating effect against fellow human beings. Social Darwinism is still very much alive, as for instance in Garrett Hardin's espousal of 'life-boat ethics'. Sociobiologists have attempted in recent years to provide 'natural' explanations (the 'selfish gene') of women's historical social subjection. Nevertheless, to introduce human ecology into history does not so much naturalise human history as historise ecology.

The direct endosomatic energy intake for human livelihood is indeed genetically determined, even if in today's world some people starve while, through energy-intensive farming and a high intake of meat, the rich indirectly consume many more calories to feed themselves. But human ecology is different from the ecology of other animals in several crucial respects: (1) Humans lack genetic instructions on the exosomatic use of energy and materials. Such exosomatic consumption depends not on 'nature', but on economics, politics and culture, and exhibits large differences between rich and poor, which are certainly not in our genes.[11] The natural sciences allow us to describe such facts of ecological distribution, but they do not provide explanations. (2) As regards demography, although the growth of human populations follows Verhulst's logistic curve, human demography is much more 'self-conscious' than in other species, and it depends on changing social structures.[12] (3) Finally, human territoriality is politically constructed, a fact that is obvious when considering the issue of freedom (or lack of freedom) of migration. Ecologists are able to explain the patterns of migration of birds or other animals, but in order to explain the migration of humans we must resort to economics, politics and law. Ethological analogies are faulty. For instance, migration from Morocco to Spain is almost completely banned, but migration between Sweden and Spain, both member countries of the European Union, is now free.

Introducing ecology into the explanation of human history thus does not imply in the least the *naturalisation* of human history, or the idea that 'capitalism or the market system are natural outgrowths of human propensities'. On the contrary, introducing ecology into history historises ecology. Ecology is not a *longue durée* backdrop to human history; sometimes it changes more rapidly than economic or political systems, as in many regions of America after 1492, and perhaps again today with global warming and mass biological extinction.

DISTRIBUTION, THE DISCOUNT RATE AND INCOMMENSURABILITY

The economy is embedded in the social perception of externalities, which sometimes give rise to social movements. Therefore, from an ecological point of view, the economy lacks a common standard of measurement, because values would depend on the endowment of property rights and on the distribution of income, and they would also depend on the strength of environmental movements and the distribution of power. In the intergenerational context, pricing of environmental resources and services, which depends on the distribution of income and on the problematic endowment of property rights on items of 'natural capital', is further complicated by another issue, i.e. the rate of discount needed to weigh future costs and benefits. We do not know how to give present values to future, uncertain and irreversible contingencies. In order to give present values to future costs and benefits, we need to determine first a rate of discount (which could be zero). But how can this be determined?

One justification for a positive discount rate that is analytically weak and which some economists have dismissed is pure time preference. Another justification for a positive discount rate is the decreasing marginal utility our descendants will obtain from their abundant consumption, on the assumption that they will be richer than we are. From the point of view of ecological economics, there is no reason to believe they are going to be richer, even leaving aside population increase. In fact, a positive discount rate based on such an optimistic view will give rise to the paradox that future consumption will be undervalued, and therefore the present generation will consume more exhaustible environmental resources and services than it would otherwise, leaving future generations poorer.

What further reason is given for a positive discount rate? The productivity of capital, or the opportunity costs of investment. We agree with this argument, and reject the fundamentalist notion of a zero rate of discount, because investment sometimes increases productive capacity. For instance, when in the Andes consumption and/or leisure were sacrificed in order to build terraces and irrigation systems, this increased the capacity to use solar energy for photosynthesis, and crops increased: a genuine investment under the Inca empire. Without a discount rate, i.e. with equal valuation per unit of present consumption (sacrificed) and future consumption (increased), there would be an irrepressible tendency to increase today's investment, ultimately sacrificing the present generation, and in fact bringing all successive generations except the 'last' ones down to the consumption minimum. But when 'investment' consists, as is often the case, not in a genuine increase of *productive* capacity, but in a mixture of production and destruction, then the appropriate rate of discount is in doubt. This may best be defined as the rate at which investment increases *sustainable* production capacity. But to assess how much of the increase in capital produces an increase in sustainable production, and how much produces an increase in destruction of nature, is a *distributional* issue. How is natural capital depreciation to be measured? If so-called natural capital is not even inventoried (for instance, the loss of biodiversity because of timber extraction), or if natural capital has a low price (because it belongs to nobody, or it belongs to poor and powerless people who sell it cheaply), then the destruction of nature is undervalued. Distributional issues thus impinge on the discount rate through the economic measurement of sustainability. The appropriate discount rate would be that determined by the 'sustainable' productivity of capital; but the measure of sustainability depends on the measure of depreciation of natural capital, and the measure of natural capital depends on the endowment of property rights, and on the distribution of income. This point is closely linked to the critiques brought against the purported empirical results of David Pearce and colleagues on 'weak sustainability'.[13]

Sustainability needs to be assessed through biophysical indicators that incorporate consideration of ecological distribution, as captured, for instance, in concepts such as the Ecological Footprint or Appropriated Carrying Capacity or Environmental Space, which estimate the extent to which a region depends on the rest of the world.[14] Similarly, one might also assess the human appropriation of net primary production, which, if calculated for different regions and countries of the world, would show how some populations live beyond their own biomass production, while others are still below their own production.[15]

Ecological economists thus pose the issue of incommensurability, which should be squarely faced.[16] For instance, one kilowatt-hour generated from fossil fuels is not commensurable in money terms with one kilowatt-hour generated by nuclear energy, once externalities are internalised, because we do not know which monetary values to give to such externalities. Much will depend on the time horizon and discount rate, on the uncertainties of future technical change and on the distribution of income. In the case of nuclear energy, the cost of decommissioning nuclear plants will loom larger and larger in the years ahead. Of course, adjourning the decision makes nuclear energy appear cheaper, just by virtue of the discount rate. But we are then compromising the ability of future generations to meet their own needs. The monetary values given to externalities appear therefore as a consequence of political decisions which are themselves often based on spurious economic arguments.[17]

Incommensurability means that there is no common unit of measurement, but it does *not* mean that we cannot compare alternative decisions on a rational basis, on *different* scales of value, as in multi-criteria evaluation. In project evaluation, multi-criteria evaluation, which is applied political ecology, takes precedence over cost-benefit analysis, which breaks down because of incommensurability of values.[18] Incommensurability has been in the tradition of ecological economics since Otto Neurath and William Kapp. In the 1920s, in the context of the debate on economic calculus in a socialist economy, Neurath had asked how a socialist economy could assess preservation of coal reserves for future generation against extra manual work from the present generation. In his idea of a *Naturalrechnung*, an 'economy in kind', Neurath was influenced mainly by the Austrian engineer and social reformer Popper-Lynkeus, who had drawn many energy and material balances for the German economy, anticipating a revolution. Von Mises, from the liberal side in the debate on the socialist economy, was to assert that such an economy would be irrational, because, since the means of production would be socialised, there would be no prices, and therefore there would be no rational means of deciding whether electricity should be generated from coal or from waterfalls. A reply came later from Oskar Lange, arguing for a 'parametric' role of prices (lack of markets would not prevent the authorities from issuing price lists for inputs and outputs, to guide decisions by managers, who would follow the efficiency rule of equalising marginal costs and marginal revenues), and indeed, a socialist economy does not necessarily imply the abolition of actual markets. This debate is well known. It is important, however, to understand Neurath's introduction of ecological issues to the debate, which led him to a conclusion of 'incommensurability' of the elements of the economy.

Should the economy use more coal, and less human labour, or vice versa? asked Neurath. The answer

depends for example on whether one thinks that hydro-electric power may be sufficiently developed or that solar heat might come to be better used, etc. If one believes the latter, one may 'spend' coal more freely and will hardly waste human effort where coal can be used. If however one is afraid that when one generation uses too much coal thousands will freeze to death in the future, one might use more human power and save coal. Such and many other non-technical matters determine the choice of a technically calculable plan ... we can see no possibility of reducing the production plan to some kind of unit and then to compare the various plans in terms of such units.[19]

Or, as Kapp put it half a century later

To place a monetary value on and apply a discount rate (which?) to future utilities or disutilities in order to express their present capitalised value may give us a precise monetary calculation, but it does not get us out of the dilemma of a choice and the fact that we take a risk with human health and survival. For this reason, I am inclined to consider the attempt at measuring social costs and social benefits simply in terms of monetary or market values as doomed to failure. Social costs and social benefits have to be considered as extra-market phenomena; they are borne and accrue to society as a whole; they are heterogeneous and cannot be compared quantitatively among themselves and with each other, not even in principle.[20]

The increased greenhouse effect, and the long–term problems of nuclear power, can be readily brought into this framework. Comparability need not presuppose commensurability. We can rationally discuss sources of energy, transport systems, agricultural policies, patterns of industrialisation and the preservation of tropical rainforests, taking into account both monetary costs (and benefits) and present and future socio-environmental 'costs' (and 'benefits') as they impinge on different groups of people, now and in the future, without an appeal to a common monetary unit of measurement. Such economic incommensurability opens a broad political space for environmental movements.

ECOLOGICAL DISTRIBUTION CONFLICTS

If political economy studies economic distributional conflicts, political ecology would study 'ecological distribution' conflicts. What does *ecological distribution* mean? This refers to the social, spatial and temporal asymmetries or inequalities in the use by humans of environmental resources and services, i.e. in the depletion of natural resources (including the loss of biodiversity) and in the burdens of pollution.[21] For instance, an unequal distribution of land, when coupled with pressure of agricultural exports on limited land resources, may cause degradation by subsistence peasants working on mountain slopes which would be not cultivated so intensively if the land in the valleys were more equally distributed.[22] Other examples are the inequalities in per capita exosomatic energy consumption and in the use of the Earth's recycling capacity for carbon dioxide, and the territorial asymmetries between sulphur dioxide emissions and the burdens of acid rain; the intergenerational inequalities between the enjoyment of nuclear energy (or emissions of carbon dioxide), and the burdens of radioactive waste (or global warming).

Some of these asymmetries are beginning to be classified, but the transfers to which they refer have no agreed prices. For instance, 'environmental racism' in the United States means locating polluting industries or toxic waste disposal sites in areas of Black, Hispanic or Indian population. Again, there is increasing discussion on 'ecologically unequal exchange' and on the 'ecological debt' (with both spatial and temporal aspects). Thus work has been done in the Netherlands on the environmental space, both for procuring resources and for disposal of emissions, really occupied by her heavily populated, rich, and polluting economy. Europeans pay nothing for the environmental space used in order to dispose of carbon dioxide emissions. The Europeans (and also the citizens of other rich countries) vastly exceed their rightful per capita carbon dioxide allowance, and they act as if they owned a sizeable chunk of the planet outside Europe, but (almost) nobody is yet complaining, or trying to charge them a fee.

Environmental Justice in the United States

There have been for a long time two main schools of environmentalism in the United States, (as explained more fully in Chapter 4), identified respectively with John Muir (the preservation of wilderness) and Gifford Pinchot (the conservation of natural resources to be exploited sustainably). Little by little, there arose in the 1960s and 1970s another type of environmental movement, against the effluents of affluence which today has acquired social roots among 'people of colour'. This new environmental justice movement against 'environmental racism' is said to have started in Warren County in North Carolina in 1982.[23] While there are attempts at connecting the environmental justice movement with mainstream 'western' environmental movements,[24] an important political task would be to connect this American movement with the many environmental movements of the poor in other countries, which, in terms of the number of people involved, have far more weight.

One main platform of the environmental justice movement has been the opposition to the incineration of waste because of the risk of dioxines and furans.[25] Many African American, Native American and Latino communities in the United States have depressed economies; these communities offer attractive locations for those who advocate the siting of toxic waste facilities or polluting industries as a means to give employment and increase local economic growth. We have here an application of Lawrence Summers' principle, 'the poor sell cheap.'[26] The market-through willingness to accept compensation, or through so-called 'hedonic prices', i.e. the decrease in value of properties threatened by pollution—would indicate that locations where the poor live are more appropriate than locations where the rich live. The defence of the poor against pollution dangers has come through the organised environmental justice movement, which came into being with the First National People of Color Environmental Leadership Summit in October 1991 in Washington DC, and which does not appeal to an ecologically extended market but to the judicial system or to forms of direct action, often inspired by the Civil Rights movement of the 1960s. Similarly, in India, the environmental movements of the poor resort to forms of civil disobedience inspired by Mahatma Gandhi's national liberation struggles. In the United States, ethnic awareness now serves environmental purposes, but this is scarcely a novelty in world history.

Gender and the Environment

Enriqué Mayer and César Fonseca explain that on one occasion, in Peru,

in the community of Tapuc ... the women, speaking Quechua, were strongly complaining that the eucalyptus trees planted on the *manay* should be pulled off immediately. *Manay* is the fallowed land in the sectoral fallowing system [communally controlled, and with a long rotation period of six or eight years] ... the women insisted on behalf of the community that the land under *manay* had been inherited from the ancestors in order to grow potatoes and other rootcrops, and that they could not feed their children with the leaves of eucalyptus. Moreover, where the eucalyptus tree grows, the soil get poorer, and it becomes useless even for onions.[27]

Eucalyptus (as shown in the previous chapter) is a contentious tree, but one cannot deny its contribution in the Andes to the availability of fuelwood and building materials, and to the control of erosion. However, the question arises, who was right from an environmental point of view: the women who spoke Quechua, or their menfolk and the forest engineers who, in Spanish, were promoting the plantation of eucalyptus trees on the common fallow lands? When natural resources become degraded, and privatised, it is to be expected that women will be in the forefront of resistance. Women have been leaders of environmental movements of the poor much more often than they have been leaders of union struggles. Why should this be so? Bina Agarwal has outlined several reasons for women's participation in and leadership of these movements. First, women are concerned with the provisioning and care of the household, not because of a particular liking for it, but because of a constructed social role. Scarcity and pollution of water and lack of fuelwood, are women's preoccupations. There is no need to postulate an essential biological link between women and nature in order to understand women's role in the material provisioning of the *oikos*, i.e. in the ecological economy as opposed to the money economy. Second, women have a small share of private property, and depend more on common property resources. Third, women often have specific traditional knowledge (in agriculture and medicine) which becomes devalued with the growth of the generalised market system, or the intrusion of the state.[28]

In the environmental justice movement in the United States, the participation of women is remarkably high, and at least the first two reasons offered by Bina Agarwal also apply. Lois Gibbs started the Love Canal struggle against toxic waste, and had for a while a leading position in the environmental justice movement. But the specific social situation is different from that in India or the Andes, in the sense that the environmentalism of the (relatively) poor in the United States may be characterised as a struggle for a better quality of life, against the effluents of affluence, rather than a struggle to keep control over environmental resources and services necessary for livelihood and survival. Indeed, one main purpose of this chapter, and of this book more generally, is to work towards a classification of such different varieties of environmentalism.

Varieties of Environmentalism

Was the concern in Germany for the *Waldsterben* caused by acid rain motivated by an ancestral German love of the forests, or by a post-material interest in landscapes? Might it have been motivated also by the material worry about the loss of forests as sinks for carbon? Environmentalism could be explained by concern for the increasing depletion of material resources and increasing environmental pollution, or increasing expenditures to mitigate pollution. Environmentalism has also been explained, according to the post-materialist thesis of Richard Inglehart and others, in terms of a change in cultural values away from material consumption, towards 'quality of life' issues. The fact that economic distribution conflicts are no longer so acute, leads to a generational shift towards new values, which include an increasing appreciation of environmental amenities because of the declining marginal utility of abundant, easily obtained material commodities. Inglehart's research interests lie mainly with the industrialised countries. We have criticised this thesis on the grounds that there is indeed much evidence for the 'environmentalism of the poor' in many social conflicts in history and at present. Sometimes the contents of such conflicts are immediately identified as 'environmental'; at other times, non-environmental idioms are used. Also, it is easy to find evidence (through opinion polls) for a strong interest in the environment in poor countries as well.[29] Is the contrast then between a post-materialist environmentalism of affluence and a materialist environmentalism of the poor? This is too simple. There exists a materialist environmentalism in rich countries against the effluents of affluence. Sometimes the participants have been relatively poor people but, at other times, as in the anti-nuclear movement in the 1960s and 1970s, the leaders were often middle-class professionals worried about radioactive waste and future generations. Being rich may offer some protection against but certainly not invulnerability to radiation from nuclear wastes. Like radiation, the potential risks posed by depletion of the ozone layer or by climate change are both material in nature and cut across categories of wealth and class: another 'material' reason for being an environmentalist in the North. On the other hand, the environmentalism of the poor is not always materialist in origin. For instance, there have been attempts to explain Southern environmentalism in terms of non-materialist (especially religious) values and also to explain the environmentalism of peasant women in terms of a non-materialist, essentialist identification with nature.[30]

Perhaps the best-known instances of the environmentalism of the poor are Chico Mendes and the *seringueiros* (in Brazil), the Chipko movement and the Narmada Bachao Andolan (in India), and now the Ogoni struggle against Shell in Nigeria. But there are many more. To take some examples from Brazil, there is the ethnic group of ex-slaves of the Trombetas river, which from the mid-1970s has fought hydro-electricity generation and bauxite mining by Brazilian and foreign companies, which threatened to destroy the waterfall Cachoeira Porteira, a place sacred to them. At the same time this group confronted IBAMA, the state environmental agency, which designated the territory occupied by these *negros de Trombetas* as a 'biological reserve', but which is seen as a trick to dislodge them to the benefit of mining corporations. Again, in the region around Santarem a conflict exists between *ribeirinho* fishermen – who fish in the *varzea* lakes which the Amazon leaves behind in the period of low waters, from July to December – and industrial fishermen called *geleiros* (icemen). Attempts are being made to legally institute a system of communal management of the lakes, to the benefit of the resource and the local people. The movement in defence of the babassu palm in Maranhão and neighbouring states, in the Brazilian north-east, based mainly on women (the *quebradeiras de coco*) is also becoming well known. Women who make a living or complement their meagre income by collecting the fruit, breaking it up and and selling the seed   want to preserve the palm trees against landowners. Finally, in various parts of Brazil we can find movements of *atingidos pelas barragens*, struggles of people to be displaced by large dams.[31]

One could travel around the world collecting such cases of the environmentalism of the poor. What an enjoyable research journey that would be! In between journeys (or on the bus and train) research on the environmentalism of the poor as it is manifested in fiction, in Latin America and elsewhere could be done, if fiction is the word. Thus, in the Peru of the 1950s and 1960s, which is described in Jose Maria Arguedas' *Todas las Sangres* ('All Bloods'), we could ask: Were they not environmentalist, the poor neighbours of San Pedro de Lahuaymarca who allied themselves with the Indians of the community, and burned down their own church and killed the main engineer of the mining company of Wisther & Bozart, whom the authorities had allowed to use the maize fields of La Esmeralda to place the slag?

Table 2.1 classifies some varieties of environmentalism. Although the basic typology is sound (the environmentalism of affluence versus the environmentalism of survival; the environmentalism of enhanced quality of life versus the environmentalism of livelihood), some overlapping situations do not easily fit into the table. For instance, there are struggles in poor countries against toxic waste, whether imported or locally produced, while there are struggles in rich countries (Canada, New Zealand, the United States) by native peoples to enforce territorial rights in order to retain access to their own natural resources or to protect themselves against waste dumping. Also, the defence of communities against the state or the market often rests in part on religious values. And certainly there are cases of the 'anti-environmentalism of the poor', for instance, the Amazonian *garimpeiros* who look for gold, and pollute rivers with mercury. The global versus local dimension, not shown in Table 2.1, will be discussed in the next section.

Table 2.1

Some Varieties of Environmentalism

	Materialist	Non–materialist
In affluent countries	Reaction against the increased impact of the effluents of affluence, e. g. the environmental justice movement in the United States, the anti-nuclear movement	Cultural shift to postmaterial 'quality of life' values and increased appreciation of natural amenities because of declining marginal utility of abundant, easily obtained material commodities
In poor countries	The environmentalism of the poor, i. e. the defence of livelihood and communal access to natural resources, threatened by the state or by the expansion of the market	'Biocentric' eastern religions (as distinct from western 'anthropocentric' religions)
	Reaction against environmental degradation caused by unequal exchange, poverty, population growth	Essentialist eco-feminism (poor women intrinsically closer to nature)

INTERNATIONAL EXTERNALITIES

Today's exploitation of nature raises the novel issue of the internalisation of externalities. The value of such externalities is clearly related to outcomes of distributional conflicts. Some examples from Ecuador will be given, but similar cases are found in other countries of the South; for instance, in Peru pollution by sulphur dioxide from the Southern Peru Copper Corporation has given rise to an international court case (*New York Times*, 12 December 1995). There is also a court case against the mining firm Freeport-McMoran in New Orleans for damages in Irian Jaya (*the Economist*, 20 July 1996; *Down to Earth*, 31 July 1996).

What is the true value of a barrel of Texaco oil, a bunch of bananas, or a box of shrimps from Ecuador? It depends on the value of the damages caused. There are no 'true' values. There are no 'ecologically correct' prices, although there might be 'ecologically corrected' prices. The value of the perceived negative externalities is a product of social institutions and distributional conflicts. In principle, if the people damaged are poor (and of future generations), then the externalities will be cheaper, but the internationalisation of environmental conflicts may provide interesting counter-examples.

Texaco was involved in the extraction of oil from the northern part of the Amazonian territory of Ecuador from the early 1970s until 1990. Damages of US$1,500 million have been claimed, arising from oil spills, deforestation, and disruption of the life of local communities. The case is now under consideration by a court in New York.[32] Texaco extracted about 1000 million barrels of oil during that period, so that damages claimed are about US$1.5 per barrel, about 10 per cent of the gross value of sales. The government of Ecuador, which made the original agreement with Texaco, is *not* a plaintiff in the class-action suit in the New York court. On the contrary, the government is pushing for an out-of-court settlement, by which Texaco would pay for the restoration of some damage and would also pay some indemnities – in the form of health centres and the like – to the communities affected. Most of the Indians and other plaintiffs involved have not much experience of the generalised market economy, let alone the US legal system. The out-of-court settlement discussed in 1994–95, by which the government of Ecuador was trying to stop the court case, seemed to imply a payment by Texaco of about US$15 million, one hundred times less than the damages being sought in court. Should the case be eventually heard in New York, the court will be in a position to decide (as would have been the case for the victims of the Bhopal gas tragedy) whether distribution of income should or should not influence the price of externalities. Should Texaco, a US company, pay according to US values or Ecuadorian values? If there is an out-of-court settlement (as happened in the civil case over Bhopal), this would also have interesting implications. Perhaps damages will be paid of only one cent per barrel of oil extracted. This would be another application of the principle 'the poor sell cheap', which I also call 'Lawrence Summers' principle'. Poor people accept cheaply, if not gladly, inconveniences or risks which other people would be ready to accept only if offered large amounts of money. But money is not the relevant standard of comparison for people who are not yet wholly immersed in the generalised market system.

Another case, of smaller dimension, was brought by unions from Ecuador and other countries, in a Texas court against Shell, Standard Fruit, Dow Chemical and others, arising from the pesticide DBCP applied to banana plantations, which has caused male sterility. This case first arose in Costa Rica. In Ecuador, the banana farms are owned by Ecuadorians, but they produce under contract and were induced by the trading firms to use the chemical. How much is a case of male sterility worth? Should it be paid at US prices or those of Ecuadorian banana workers? Will Dow Chemical pay higher indemnities for damages from silicon implants to US women than for damages from DBCP to Ecuadorian men? The *existence* of externalities depends on whether (real or claimed) property rights have been damaged, and in such cases, there is no doubt that people own their own health; however the *value* of the externality depends on the distribution of income. As Lawrence Summers put it, 'the measurement of the costs of health-impairing pollution depends on the foregone earnings from increased morbidity and mortality. From this point of view a given amount of health-impairing pollution should be done in the country with the lowest cost, which will be the country with the lowest wages'.[33] The courts might decide, however, against the logic of the market, and assess damages from DBCP at US 'prices', on the grounds that the damage has been caused by North American firms. Such international cases are good examples of the social and institutional non-market influences on the valuation of externalities. In Ecuador, as in Colombia, there could be similar cases for damage to health in the production of flowers for export.

A third such conflict in Ecuador opposes commercial shrimp or prawn cultivation to the preservation of mangroves in the Pacific coast. Here there is as yet no court case, but possible plaintiffs would be people who used the mangroves sustainably and outside the market, and who are damaged by their destruction by the shrimp industry. These people are mostly poor women and their families, who live sustainably, if poorly, by directly using or selling the products of the mangroves. A strong protest movement against the destruction of mangroves by the shrimp industry arose in 1995 in Esmeraldas, the coastal northern province of Ecuador, led by local people, and environmental activists. Property rights over the mangroves are unclear. Although the demand for shrimps is international, the industry itself is owned by nationals. How much are the externalities involved worth, at present value? Factors to be taken into account are the period of regeneration of the mangroves after being destroyed by shrimp farming, and the discount rate to be applied to the benefits of shrimp farming and the costs of mangrove destruction. Beyond this, pseudo-market valuations of damages in terms of willingness to accept compensation, for instance, would depend on income levels.

Ecologically Unequal Trade?

Some aspects of historical geography which were studied in in the past are currently being studied from a more critical perspective using notions such as *Raubwirtschaft*, which had been forgotten even though the term was coined by geographers and introduced by Jean Brunhes in his classic book

Géographie Humaine.[34] There is also a new discussion of the *staple theory of growth*, a theory that is often attributed to the Canadian historian Harold Innis, in his work on the export of raw materials from Canada and the relation between these exports and economic growth due to different linkages. Later, Innis' critical perspective was forgotten and doctrinaire neo-liberals glorified economic growth based on the extraction of natural resources.[35] As part of the attempt at creating a theory of ecologically unequal exchange, new arguments have been raised against the staple theory of growth.[36] Extractive economies produce poverty at a local level, and an absence of political power, leading to the inability to slow down the rate of resource extraction or to raise the prices. This is, for example, the situation that Algeria presently faces, with its current and future exports of non-renewable resources like oil and gas. Mexico also faces this situation. Which movements and political organisations will defend these resources? What political discourse will they adopt?

Some regions have developed on the basis of extractive enterprises. For example, despite the continuous displacement of coffee plantations in São Paulo due to soil exhaustion, many local economic linkages were created because *fazendeiros* (landowners) and exporters resided in this state. There are many examples that cast doubt on the staple theory of growth and strengthen the theory of underdevelopment as a consequence of dependence expressed as unequal trade. This is not only because of the undervaluation of the labour of the world's poor and the deterioration of the terms of trade expressed in prices; there are also the different 'production times' exchanged when extracted products which can only be replaced over a long period, if at all, are traded for products that can be produced quickly. In the case of mineral resources, it is obvious that exploitation occurs much faster than replacement; often the result is to leave a polluted hole in the ground and a gaping hole in the social fabric of the mining area.[37] Only if agricultural or forestry exports do not outstrip the rate of replacement, and if prices are reasonable, would it appear that they can provide lasting economic benefits. But it is necessary to bear in mind that from the ecological point of view, these are not only exports of the solar energy incorporated without cost by means of photosynthesis, but also of soil nutrients. In the case of fish exports, which in principle also appear to be biologically renewable, the extreme variability of plankton growth must be taken into account. This makes the application of the concept of 'maximum sustainable yield' – first developed by German forestry science and later by Gifford Pinchot in the United States – impossible. In practice we see how one area after another exhausts its fishing resources. The histories of some of these disasters, like that of California, have already been written,[38] while others, such as Peru, still await their historians.[39]

The argument that in exporting non-renewable resources an unequal exchange results, since the market undervalues the necessities of the future, is almost never referred to in international politics. It is an argument that will grow in the Third World in the coming years, although it could have become politically relevant much earlier: for instance, in Andean countries during the 'age of guano', between 1840 and 1880, or throughout the 200 years (since the mid-17th century) of exports of the bark of *Chinchona officinalis*, the quinine tree.

Global and Local Ecological Distribution Conflicts

Until the second half of the 1980s, there were almost no attempts to develop a political ecology linked to political economy, or to theorise an ecological Marxism at local and global levels which could deal with ecological distribution conflicts. Since then, the German economist Elmar Altvater has published several books[40] in which he has developed a spatial and temporal dialectics of capitalism. The capitalist economy continuously attempts *la mise-en-valeur* of new territories, such as Amazonia. The market valorisation of the resources extracted implies a speed of extraction (or a speed of insertion of pollutants) which is quicker than the biogeochemical cycles of nature. To extract means to take out without putting back, and so petroleum and many other natural resources, such as mahogany, have been extracted (rather than produced) and destroyed.[41] The need to pay real interest rates of over 5 per cent per year, or the required rates of profit on capital, contradict the rhythms of nature, and clearly contradict the law of entropy, which Altvater, following Georgescu-Roegen, includes in his analysis, in the steps also of Frederick Soddy's writings of 70 years ago. Economic time in the newly incorporated territories is quicker than biological time, at least for a while, and people who followed the rhythms of nature are dispossessed in the process.

Some neo-Marxist authors such as James O'Connor and Enrique Leff have explained environmental movements as the result of non-internalised externalities.[42] The growth of capitalism, which is still threatened by the exploitation of workers and the exploitation of the peripheral populations of the world – what O'Connor calls the first contradiction of capitalism – is also threatened by a second contradiction, as firms externalise social and environmental costs, which sometimes gives rise to new social movements. Such movements confront not only capitalists but also the state because the state is assumed to provide the conditions of livelihood and production threatened by the growth of the capitalist economy. As the market system has spread over the world it has led to more intensive use of renewable and exhaustible resources, and it has also led to the production of externalities, i.e. losses not measured by market prices, including the loss that resource exhaustion represents for future generations. As the market expands it paradoxically uses or wastes more resources and more environmental services that are outside the market, and precisely because they are outside the marketplace no value is assigned to them. In the same way that unpaid domestic toil is unpaid because of the social structures and conventions that exist, so the conditions of livelihood and production represented by an adequate supply of water, energy, clean air, land and waste disposal are all provided by nature from outside the marketplace.[43] If nature is degraded, the general supposition is that it is the state's responsibility to correct this environmental impact or to find new resources, to the extent of 'oil wars' if necessary, in order to maintain the conditions of production. Thus the role of the state, not just that of the market, means that conflicts over the ecological conditions of livelihood and production soon turn into political conflicts.

In a later chapter we explain how the growth of capitalist agriculture, with an intensive use of fossil fuels and biologically simplified, has produced a movement of self-conscious peasant agroecology which is not at all a post-modern fad but a route towards an alternative modernity based on the defence of agricultural biodiversity and sensible agronomic practices which are threatened by modern, anti-ecological agriculture. This is an example of the second contradiction. The environmental justice movement in the United States is another example, with its mix of race and class. It is easy to find other examples of the second contradiction, but there are also cases in which despite the existence of an acknowledged externality – global warming, destruction of the ozone layer, loss of wild biodiversity – there has *not* been a spontaneous birth of grassroots environmental movements. First, the scientists and, sometimes, the international wilderness movement, have called attention to such externalities before any grass roots movement adopted them as issues. The debate on trade and environment was effectively started by the Worldwide Fund for Nature (with a paper by Arden-Clarke), though if this debate is set in the context of the more general debate on unequal exchange, then the origin is certainly more remote. This absence of grassroots movements contrasts with their presence in other types of environmental conflicts, as for instance sulphur dioxide emissions from power stations or smelters, or the loss of access to common property resources by private enclosures. There is need for scientific warning systems in such cases.

There is then at first sight a gulf between local movements and global issues. However, if we look (as we do in Chapter 6) at the defence of agricultural biodiversity (by CLADES in Latin America, by the Third World Network in India), we notice an interesting phenomenon: the use of global environmental ideas for local struggles. As a response to the attempts through the GATT negotiations to enforce intellectual property rights on 'improved' seeds, when nothing has ever been paid for traditional seeds and traditional knowledge, there were strong movements of protest in India. In fact, an 'agricultural exception' in GATT would make as much or even more sense than the 'cultural exception' demanded by some French and other European film-makers against the free entry of Hollywood products.

The use of global ideas in order to fight for local or national aims is also present in other debates arising in the South. For instance, the lack of action in the North to prevent emissions of carbon dioxide (the main greenhouse gas) far in excess of the ability of the Earth to absorb carbon dioxide through new vegetation or in the oceans will accelerate the debate on the ecological debt, while the proposals for 'joint implementation' – i.e. paying for reforestation projects in the South to offset excessive carbon dioxide emissions in the North – will provoke a general discussion on carbon dioxide emission allowances or on property rights on the absorptive capacity of the Earth, following Agarwal's and Narain's proposals of 1991.[44]

Until about 100 years ago, the social perception of carbon dioxide emissions by humans burning fossil fuels as an externality did not exist, and in fact, until the 1950s, the usual interpretation by scientists was that an increase in temperature would be good. Attempts at cost-benefit analysis of the increased greenhouse effect are not convincing because of the doubts over the type of value appropriate for the valuation of damages such as loss of human life, because many items are not easily measured in physical terms, much less easily valued in money terms.

In this context, we could look at cases of 'joint implementation' in the tropics; as, for example, between FACE (Forest Adsorption of Carbon Dioxide Emissions, a Dutch foundation of electrical firms) and INEFAN, the agency for natural parks and forests in Ecuador. Here we see a typical case of buying a cheap sink for carbon dioxide in the expectation that this will be credited to the account of Dutch carbon dioxide emissions. FACE has projects in several countries of the world. One of them, Profafor, consists of planting 75,000 hectares in the Andes with eucalyptus and pines. The FACE report[45] states that in the Ecuadorian Andes at altitudes between 2,400 and 3,500 metres, 'agriculture is no longer possible, and livestock farming is less profitable' – an arrogant statement, although perhaps one should not expect great expertise in mountain agriculture from a Dutch foundation.

'Joint implementation' is usually praised on the grounds of cost effectiveness. It is cheaper to place carbon dioxide in the growing vegetation of tropical countries than to reduce carbon dioxide emissions in rich countries. Indeed, were it not for the absorption of human-produced carbon dioxide by natural sinks – namely, new vegetation and the oceans – the greenhouse effect would be even more marked. Despite uncertainties over 'missing' carbon sinks (perhaps in Northern forests), there is a consensus that approximately one-half of the carbon dioxide produced by humans burning fossil fuels does not accumulate in the atmosphere, but is placed gratis in such natural sinks. Thus the rich behave as if they were the owners of a disproportionate part of the carbon dioxide absorption capability provided by the new vegetation and the oceans. The remaining carbon dioxide is dumped into the atmosphere as if they owned that too. In this sense, joint implementation – i.e. exporting carbon dioxide to outside sinks, beyond one's own environmental space – has been going on for many decades. What is now being proposed is that, in specific cases amounting to a minute proportion of the excessive emissions of carbon dioxide, a payment will be made for the use of one of the natural sinks, new vegetation. Therefore, such explicit afforestation proposals for joint implementation as exist at the moment put on the table the issue of property rights over the absorptive capability of carbon dioxide. They also raise the issue of the North's ecological debt to the South, given the environmental service of carbon dioxide absorption provided gratis up to now. Countries in a creditor position in the matter of ecological debt could provide a lead, and could lend a sense of urgency to negotiations on climate change. Furthermore, the global discussion on carbon dioxide emissions can be locally linked to campaigns against urban planning in the service of the motor car (from Mexico to Bangkok). There is already an Alliance for Climate (against carbon dioxide emissions) between environmentalists in Northern cities who wish to restrict car traffic and the Amazonian umbrella organisation for indigenous groups, COICA, which wishes to preserve the rainforest against logging, cattle ranching, mining and oil extraction. There is also a growing international organisation, called Oil-Watch, trying to combine the efforts of the many communities of the South endangered by the oil industry – for instance, by Shell in Nigeria, a case made notorious by theexecution of Ken Saro-Wiwa. Shell is also active in extracting oil and gas in Amazonia, and in many other places, including the North Sea and the Brent Spar platform.

Here I shall quote from an Oilwatch report[46] on the consequences of Shell's activities in the Peruvian Amazon in the 1980s.

In the lower Urubamba area of Peru, Shell started a programme of seismic prospecting to evaluate the state of the reserves of natural gas. The group most affected by the programme was the Nahua people. Before 1984, the Nahua had no previous contact with the outside world. The first contacts were often sporadic and often violent; their confrontations with Shell, for instance, caused a number of injuries and put the continuation of the work at risk. The company tried to improve relations with the Nahua, offering them tools, food and other gifts, even taking some of the Nahua to the Shell camps. The initiative was a success and the exploration programme was able to continue. The budding relationship between Shell and the Nahua lead to forestry companies attempting a similar approach, offering gifts in return for wood. Unfortunately, the repeated contact introduced whooping cough and influenza, to which the Nahua had no resistance. The most conservative estimates are that 50 per cent of the population died, and that many others fled to a neighbouring area or to the city of Sepahua, where their culture completely disintegrated, condeming them to begging in the street. Recently, Shell signed a contract with the Peruvian government to exploit the Camisea gas reserves.

Table 2.2 is offered in lieu of a conclusion. It attempts a fairly comprehensive classification of ecological distribution conflicts, both domestic and international. It also includes the related resistance movements. The range of cases it contains constitutes the research agenda of the evolving field of political ecology.

Table 2.2

Ecological Distribution Conflicts and Related Resistance Movements

Name	Definition
Environmental racism	Dumping of toxic waste in locations inhabited by African Americans, Latinos and Native Americans
Environmental justice	Movement against environmental racism
Environmental blackmail	Either you accept LULU (locally unacceptable land use), or you remain jobless
Toxic imperialism	Dumping of toxic waste in poorer countries
Ecologically unequal exchange	Importing products from poor regions or countries at prices which do not take account of exhaustion or of local externalities
Ecological dumping	Selling at prices which do not take account of exhaustion or externalities; it takes place from North to South (farm export from Europe or USA), and from South to North.
Internalisation of international externalities	Law suits against multinationals (Union Carbide, Texaco, Dow Chemicals, Shell, etc.) in their country of origin, claiming damages for externalities caused in poor countries
Ecological debt	Claiming damages from rich countries on account of past excessive emissions (of carbon dioxide, for

Transboundary pollution	instance) or for plundering of natural resources Applied mainly to sulphur dioxide emissions crossing borders in Europe, and producing acid rain
National fishing rights	Attempts to stop open-access depredation by imposing (since the 1940s in Peru, Ecuador, Chile) exclusive fishing areas
Environmental space	The geographical space occupied by an economy, taking into account imports of natural resources and disposal of emissions
Omnivores vs. ecosystem people	The contrast between people living on their own resources, and people living on the resources of other territories and peoples
Ecological footprint or appropriated carrying capacity	The ecological impact of regions or large cities on the outside space
Biopiracy	The appropriation of genetic resources ('wild' or agricultural) without adequate payment or recognition of peasant/indigenous knowledge and ownership (including the extreme case of the Human Genome project)
Workers' struggles for health and safety	Actions (in the framework of collective bargaining or outside it) to prevent damages to workers in mines, plantation or factories
Urban struggles for clean water, green spaces...	Actions (outside the market) to improve environmental conditions of livelihood or to gain access to recreational amenities in the urban context
Indigenous environmentalism	Use of territorial rights and ethnic resistance against external use of resources (e.g. Crees against Hydro Quebec in Canada, Ogoni against Shell in Nigeria)
Social ecofeminism	The environmental activism of women, motivated by their social situation; the idiom of such struggles is not necessarily that of environmentalism/feminism
Environmentalism of the poor	Social conflicts with an ecological content (today and in history) of the poor against the (relatively) rich, not only but mainly in rural contexts

Chapter 3

Poverty and the Environment: A Critique of the Conventional Wisdom[1]

The general proposition that economic growth is good for the environment has been justified by the claim that there exists an empirical relation between per capita income and some measures of environmental quality. It has been observed that as income goes up there is increasing environmental degradation up to a point, after which environmental quality improves... There are... reasons for caution in interpreting these inverted U-shaped curves.[2]

INTRODUCTION

The relationship between wealth (or poverty) and environmental degradation varies with each factor analysed. For instance, emissions of carbon dioxide increase with wealth. Emissions of sulphur dioxide also increase with industrialisation, but diminish when a country becomes richer and filters are installed in power stations or metal smelters. As for water quality, it is lower in poor countries and increases with wealth, but the consumption of water also increases with wealth; hence water reserves are overexploited in some rich countries and suffer salinisation in coastal areas. Finally, the production of domestic wastes increases as living standards increase, and their composition makes them harder to recycle.

By providing the results of a few selected indicators, it can be argued not only that wealth increases appreciation of environmental values but also that wealth itself is good for the environment. The main message of the Brundtland Report was that poverty is the main cause of environmental degradation, and it explicitly recommended an annual growth rate of 3 per cent for the South as well as for the North (to accomodate higher exports from the South). Brundtland's message was that economic growth, renamed 'sustainable development', is a remedy for both poverty and environmental degradation.[3]

The proponents of the 'post-materialist' thesis[4] accept that in the affluent countries there is concern about the deterioration of some environmental indicators, and about the increasing part of GNP which must be spent on 'protective', 'defensive', 'corrective' or 'mitigatory' measures against environmental damage[5], but this school nevertheless emphasises cultural change as the main explanation of environmentalism. It tends to emphasise the purported 'dematerialisation' (and 'de-energisation') of the economy, and would therefore explain the rise of environmentalism as a post-material cultural shift towards appreciation of nature and the amenities it provides. This has also been the consensus among mainstream environmental and resource economists in the United States[6] until challenged by the new ecological economics.[7] Indeed, orthodox environmental economics had proposed that the demand for environmental goods increases with income, and that the poor are 'too poor to be green'. Inglehart[8] describes the environment of the Netherlands as 'nearly pristine', a most optimistic assessment since this is a country with a population density of 400 persons per square kilometre, and nearly as many cows, pigs and cars as humans. This misrepresentation allows him then to attribute Dutch environmentalism mostly to 'post-materialism'. The Scandinavian countries are also classified by Inglehart as 'nearly pristine' environments. They are certainly less populated than the Netherlands. The growth of environmental concern in Scandinavia is once again attributed by Inglehart mostly to 'post-materialism', with no regard to the following facts: their economies are partly based on extraction of natural resources; one country (Sweden) has an excessive number of nuclear power stations relative to its population; the countries have been subject to radiation from Chernobyl and to acidification from external sources. There are certainly enough material reasons to become an environmentalist in Scandinavia.

SUSTAINABILITY AND CARRYING CAPACITY

That wealth provides the means to correct environmental damage, that wealthy people are environmentally more conscious because they can afford to care for quality of life issues, and that poverty is one main cause of environmental degradation, are the politically correct beliefs. However, for many ecologists this constellation of beliefs represents no more than an attempt to blame the victims, and it provokes outrage. In this chapter, indignation is repressed, and the argument that the poor destroy the environment is considered calmly, even when the speaker comes from the South such as the former Finance Minister of India Dr. Manmohan Singh, who justified programmes of trade and market liberalisation on the grounds that they would generate resources for cleaning up the environment.[9]

It may appear that poverty is the cause of environmental degradation only when the number of poor people is large and exceeds the territory's carrying capacity. Let us therefore analyse the concept of *human* carrying capacity. Indeed, the intellectual origin of the notion of sustainable development is the link between *carrying capacity* and *economic development*, as explicitly stated by Jeffrey A. McNeely of the International Union for the Conservation of Nature, which was already using the term 'sustainable development' in 1980:

... future consumption depends to a considerable extent on the stock of natural capital. Therefore, conservation may well be a precondition for economic growth. Conservation is certainly a precondition for 'sustainable development', which unites the ecological concept of carrying capacity with the economic concepts of growth and development.[10]

Without doubt, ecological degradation could be caused by excess population. It could, however, also be due to the pressure of exports on a limited resource base. We therefore start with a discussion of these two concepts: 'population pressure' on resources and 'production pressure' on resources.[11] Once we have clarified this difference, we will consider cases where poverty is the cause of environmental degradation *without it being due* to population pressure on resources or production for export.

Export-Based Economic Growth

Some areas are net exporters of agricultural products and therefore experience a degradation of their cultivated land that is not due to excessive *population* pressure on resources but rather to the pressure of *production* on resources. In some Hispanic countries in the Caribbean, production for local consumption is known as *frutos menores* ('lesser fruits', meaning something insignificant). In parts of the Andes it is called something more suggestive of basic local necessities : *panllevar* ('bread in hand'). This situation of pressure of exports on resources has been known since J. von Liebig, the founder in 1840 of agricultural chemistry, compared small- and large-scale agriculture, praising the former for recycling nutrients more efficiently than it was possible for the large-scale agriculture necessary to supply large cities or foreign markets. In North American economic circles this idea was supported by the protectionist Carey. In Europe, Marx cited Liebig approvingly.

Let us consider some examples of export pressure on resources in Central America. Costa Rica is a fertile country, relatively prosperous and with protected areas. Grazing land for meat production has expanded at the expense of forests, and even at the expense of agroforestry and exclusively agricultural land, although this process is not as rapid now as it was 20 years ago. Coffee and banana exports also put pressure on resources, while both sectors suffer regular price slumps due to excess world supply and European protectionism. Banana cultivation, now expanding in the tropical rainforest of the Atlantic coast, has led to deforestation and an increase in pesticide applications – despite loud protests from the workers exposed – and to damage to river and marine ecosystems. In Costa Rica coffee occupies the highlands and is based on medium and small farmers who are the backbone of Costa Rica's democracy, while bananas are grown in the lowlands by wage-labourers on foreign-owned plantations. Coffee was introduced to the Americas c. 1650, and in different countries has produced different cultural and power structures. In Costa Rica, the population linked to coffee cultivation is of Hispanic origin, the properties are not very large, and commercialisation is under national control. The banana – from South-East Asia, which reached Africa by c. 1500 and the Caribbean by c. 1600 – was established on the Atlantic and Pacific coasts under the supervision of large multinational companies, such as United Fruit, the famous 'Mamita Yunai' in Fallas' novel of this title. In both cases, the products have been exported under conditions of cyclic excess production. There is a further crisis in the conditions of production due to soil exhaustion (as has already happened with the banana, and may yet happen with coffee cultivated without shade on steep slopes) and excessive pesticide use (as has happened with the banana). Seventy years ago the workers on banana plantations spreading insecticides asked for nothing more than a little more pay and a little less work. However, in the 1980s they took the banana and chemical companies to court in the United States and even won a case or two.

The expansion of cattle farming peaked in the 1970s. Economic gains from cattle production have also undermined the conditions of production, as much grazing land was abandoned after a few years because of weed growth, nutrient loss and soil compaction. In Central America the proportion of total meat production for export has diminished, partly due to foot-and-mouth disease. Between 1971 and 1975, exports accounted for 41 per cent of production, dropping to 38 per cent between 1976 and 1980, and later to only 20 per cent,[12] showing the existence of a growing local market. Although consumption per capita is low in comparison with that of the United States, this local market has been growing faster than the population.

Central America as a whole generates a positive balance of trade for products such as meat, fruits and vegetables, sugar, coffee, tea and cocoa. As a result of the current wave of neo-liberal policies, there is now pressure to increase these exports, or promote new exports such as shrimps, at the expense of local production of basic foodstuffs, such as cereals and pulses, and at the expense of the environment. Both production pressure and population pressure on resources – because of a growing population, which leads directly to deforestation by increasing precarious agriculture – could put a country like Costa Rica in an ecological position as perilous as that of Haiti or El Salvador in as little as 20 years. Over the past 20 years there have certainly been widespread protests in Costa Rica against the destruction of the tropical rainforest, threatened by both precarious agriculture and cattle production for export (what is called the Hamburger Connection) or local consumption, as well as by the expanding cultivation of bananas, coffee and other export crops. A countering trend is the growing crop of 'ecotourists' in Costa Rica's national parks, while the sale of bioprospecting services is meanwhile becoming very controversial (as we shall see in Chapter 6). Costa Rica covers 50,000 km² and has three million inhabitants. There are signs of overpopulation, although population density is still much below the European average: for instance, a partly industrialised European region such as Catalonia covers 30,000 km² and has six million inhabitants. In Costa Rica the population is still growing quickly, although the birth rate is fortunately now in decline. Therefore both exports and the local population are exerting pressure on resources.

Turn now to Chile, whose booming economy has been described as 'The Tiger without the Jungle'.[13] What is behind the boom in the Chilean economy? Adjusting for inflation, the value of export earnings more than doubled between the start of the Pinochet regime and the end of the 1980s. Exports increased to a 40 per cent share of gross domestic product and also changed in composition, as shown in Table 3.1.

Table 3.1

Breakdown of Chilean exports, 1970 and 1989

Sector	1970	1989	Main product
Mining	85.8%	55.4%	Copper
Forestry	3.9%	9.5%	Cellulose
Farming	1.5%	9.4%	Fresh fruit
Fishing	2.7%	9.1%	Fishmeal
Others	6.1%	16.6%	Metallurgy

Source: Banco Central de Chile, cited by Mónica Ríos in 'Desarrollo sostenible y reformas económicas: el caso de Chile' (Sustainable Development and Economic Reforms: The Case of Chile), in Olman Segura, ed., Desarrollo Sostenible y Políticas Economcias en América Latina (San José, Costa Rica: DEI, 1992).

Without being overly simplistic, it is plain to see the extent to which the boom is based on the export of exhaustible resources, such as copper, or renewable resources that are perhaps being exploited at unsustainable rates. Many Chileans are aware of the need to restrain exploitation of fishing and forestry resources and are speaking out. Swept along by the neo-liberal tide, the Chilean economy is obviously not a victim of demographic pressure, but perhaps it will fall victim to the pressure on its resources of production for export.

Indeed, the ecological history of South America must be interpreted *not* in terms of population pressure – because of the demographic collapse after 1492 – but as a history of exporting natural capital, a history of 'ecological dependence'. More recently, and both in Africa and Latin America:

the penetration of the South by new agricultural production, marketing, and contract agriculture technologies, has . . . changed agriculture in some areas of America and Africa, substituting greater specialisation and economic dependency for the traditional, ecologically sustainable system. These problems are aggravated by the large external debt of so many African and Latin American countries, forcing them to pay by exporting cash crops or forestry products, etc. Environmental changes in the South must thus be understood in terms of the international division of capital.[14]

In some Latin American countries where there is still a significant indigenous presence, there is a growing pride in non-modern technical knowledge:

Our forefathers had [apparently] less adequate technological resources and made the ecosystems qualitatively and quantitatively productive. They developed appropriate technologies for each habitat. But now, what technology has been transferred has been inappropriately applied, and there has been a change in attitudes and practice towards nature . . . . There is no environmentalist ethic and this has led to Guatemala functioning – at a national and local scale – as an agricultural exports terminal for more developed countries.[15]

This retrospective pride in pre-conquest agricultural achievements is supported by the present awareness that peasant agriculture preserves biodiversity and is also more efficient than modern agriculture in terms of energy use.[16]

However, the distinction between local and export crops (with the latter considered an example of 'production pressure on resources') is sometimes valid, but not always. It is valid in the case of Peruvian production of coca leaf for export, which greatly exceeds local demand and might be another example of an environmental catastrophe due to export pressure. Coca production leads to gully erosion if the terraces have not been built carefully enough. This is because the coca plant requires first deforestation and then complete removal of weeds. In addition there is normally no tree cover. [17] In contrast, sugar and cotton need not be export crops, although this has been their role in the economic history of Peru and other countries. In fact, domestic consumption of sugar in Peru has increased and exports have diminished, and now the question is what health effects the consumption of this cheap calorie source will have. 'Production pressure on resources' gradually turns into 'population pressure on resources' when export crops become subsistence crops.

In general, however, in Latin America, and also in some other regions of the world, pressure on the environment is due not to demographic pressure, but rather to external demands or internal inequalities. This is one of the reasons why the relationship between poverty and the environment is analysed here without resort to the concept of carrying capacity. Another argument against the use of this concept is that agricultural production can increase greatly if inputs are increased. According to the FAO–IIASA study on potential agricultural production[18], not a single Latin American country, not even Haiti, El Salvador or Peru, would face serious problems in securing an adequate supply of food if what the study defines as a 'high level of inputs' were used. But would this be sustainable? The general principle is that discussion of carrying capacity requires the specification of the level of inputs. When these inputs are exhaustible resources, as they are in the industrial and agricultural sectors in high-income countries, then it can be argued that the carrying capacity has already been exceeded, since resources used now will not be available in the future. Anyway, there is always the opposing argument that new technologies may create new resources. Thus, if one believes that environmental problems are caused by excessive physical pressure on resources, by the economy outstripping the productive and regenerative capacity of the environment, orthodox economists may reply that economic decisions taken regarding total pressure on resources are, in the final analysis, choices between present and future use of resources, applying present values to future uses. This means that the ecological discussion of carrying capacity becomes an economic discussion of the current valuation of unknown future phenomena.

Carrying Capacity and Boserup's Thesis

The 'carrying capacity' of a specific area is the maximum population of a given species that can be indefinitely maintained without a degradation of the resource base that might lead to a reduction of the population in the future.[19] Although the poor consume little, if they are numerous a greater burden on the environment is implied. In most countries, birthrates have fallen or are falling, but the population pressure on resources will increase for at least the next 50 years. The world population was about 900 million in 1800 and grew to 1,600 million in 1900. In 2000 it will be about 6,000 million, and will stabilise, we hope, at between 10,000 and 12,000 million before the end of the next century. Clearly human impact on the planet is already excessive in terms of our effects on other species and the availability of natural resources and environmental services. Of course, this impact varies greatly with the economic status of different populations.

Many people are still unaware that from the 16th to the 20th century the greatest demographic expansion was generated by Europeans, both in Europe itself and in the countries to which they emigrated. Shortly after the European conquest of the Americas, the American population plunged. Where it once had comprised 20 per cent of humanity, a century later it made up only 3 per cent of the world's population, including the European migrants.[20] A similar collapse took place in Australia and throughout Oceania a couple of centuries after 1492. Table 3.2 shows the growth of world population from 1800 to 1900. Fortunately, birth control methods began to be used in several European countries in the 19th century. It is in the 20th century, above all in the last decades, that population growth has occurred in poor countries. However, the demographic history of Europe does not allow it to preach to others the virtue of reproductive moderation.

The idea of carrying capacity has been given a statistical definition in order to make it more effective. A model was proposed by Fearnside based on the Amazon, an interesting area to study since population density is low, therefore excess population should not be a problem. In the colonisation process, we find an empirical relationship (shaped like the letter U) between population density (on the horizontal axis) and the colonists' risk of failure. When population density is too low, there is a high chance of failure. When population density exceeds a certain value, the probability of failure is again high, and it is assumed that population exceeds carrying capacity, even though the densities in question are, in relative terms, very low.[21] Carrying capacity obviously also depends on the use of inputs and on the terms of trade with other regions that the colonists can command.

The use of the concept of carrying capacity to study the relationship between demography and resources among *Homo sapiens* could be rejected for several reasons. For one, the inequality in wealth and income among members of the human species leads to much greater variation in energy and material consumption than in other species. Furthermore, the human species is often able to improve its production techniques. Economists who reject the concept of carrying capacity sometimes base their arguments on an incorrect interpretation of a thesis advanced by Ester Boserup.[22] Boserup maintained that population increase can lead to an increase in agricultural production by shortening rotation cycles. Conversely, the depopulation of Africa by the slave trade removed one of the key incentives to agricultural

Table 3.2

Growth and Territorial Distribution of World Population, 1800–1900

	Inhabitants (in millions)		Distribution (%)	
	1800	1900	1800	1900
Africa	90	120	9.9	7.5
North America[1]	6	81	0.7	5.0
Latin America	19	63	2.1	3.9
Asia[2]	597	91○	65.9	56.9
Europe (with Russia)	192	423	21.2	26.3
Oceania	2	6	0.2	0.4
TOTAL	906	1,608	100.0	100.0

[1] North America north of the Rio Grande.
[2] Excluding Asiatic Russia.

Source: A. M. Carr-Saunders, World Population *(Oxford: Oxford University Press, 1936).*

intensification, thus helping to explain the persistence of the shifting agriculture that was so deplored by early colonial administrators. Boserup pointed out that returns diminished for increases in labour inputs within each cultivation system, but she showed that increasing population pressure might lead to shifts in the cultivation system, thus increasing production. These new cultivation systems also show diminishing returns, but the carrying capacity of a territory may increase more than once due to improvements in cultivation, until it reaches a system of multiple crops on irrigated land.

However, the intensification of 'modern' agriculture is not merely through the suppression of the fallow periods; it is also an increase in external agricultural inputs, which can be described as a process of replacing renewable energy with non-renewable energy.[23] This is technically different from Boserup's shifts, which are based on the production of renewable energy through agriculture. Boserup's analysis stops before the introduction of Peruvian guano, Chilean saltpetre and the industrial production of chemical fertilisers, i.e. before 1840. We can define Boserup's shifts as an increase in technological efficiency, in the sense that they increase a given area's production and the amount of the sun's energy that is used advantageously. (However, these changes do not increase productivity per hour of work; this is why only population pressure can make the itinerant agriculturalist take up the plough.) Boserup-type shifts could also be called 'agricultural involution'[24], because they mean you must run faster just to remain (per capita) in the same place.

Modern agriculture uses a technology based on increasing the flow of external energy and materials into the economy, and on decreasing genetic variety. The fact that conventional economics measures this shift as an increase in productivity is only a consequence of the low value it assigns to 'genetic erosion' and to non-renewable resources, and the absence of an assigned value for the effects of pollution. Every year the equivalent of 1,500 litres of petroleum are used to feed each American.[25] The shift to mechanised chemical agriculture cannot be incorporated into Boserup's thesis. Perhaps we are on the threshold of another momentous technical change through biotechnology, but the true cost in terms of complementary inputs and ecological damage is not known. In any case, invoking Boserup's name is not relevant, as she studied agriculture in a pre-industrial context. This means that objections to the use of carrying capacity because it contradicts Boserup's thesis turn out, in fact, to be objections to using the concept of carrying capacity because it implicitly excludes external subsidies to the agricultural economy in question.

The Carrying Capacity of an Open Economy

If the economy receives a free subsidy of energy and materials, there is no limit to its carrying capacity beyond the cost, in energy and material resources, of transporting these external subsidies. That is to say, the idea of carrying capacity may make sense at a global level, but it does not make sense at the regional or national level. Although it is not possible for every country to simultaneously increase its carrying capacity through the use of resources from ecosystems in other countries, they can all simultaneously make *selective* use of some products from other countries, because what is limited in one land may be abundant in another. The carrying capacity of the world as a whole is greater than the sum of the carrying capacities of all its countries.[26] Water is a limiting factor in Mexico but not in Canada, although the resources needed to build a pipeline from one to the other would be great. Tin in Bolivia exceeded local needs, as did petroleum in Romania. Energy and materials appear to have flowed mostly from poor countries to rich ones; the discipline of ecological history will have to investigate this question in more detail.

The carrying capacity of an open economy will be different from that of a closed one. It will probably be greater, although it may be lesser if commerce exhausts the resources of the country in benefit of others. (This relates to the discussion in the previous chapter of 'ecologically unequal trade', one of the sources of the 'ecological debt' the rich owe to the poor). If Haiti has exceeded its carrying capacity and needs to import food, then Japan has most certainly exceeded *its* carrying capacity, as it needs to import both food and petroleum, unless we believe that not only the economic value (in monetary terms) but also the 'ecological value' of Japan's exports equals or exceeds that of its imports. We do not know how to measure 'ecological value'. Energy content is not an adequate measurement. Likewise, the acceptance of prices as a measure of value not only disregards the influence of monopoly and the distribution of income, but also implicitly accepts current prices as an adequate measure of the value of future shortage of resources and of current and future harm from pollution, which is obviously not the case. Oscar Wilde said that a cynic is a person who knows the price of everything and the value of nothing, a remark particularly relevant to ecological economics.

The Use of Fertilisers

If we compare the level of population pressure on resources and the use of fertilisers in different countries, we find that there is a general tendency towards increased use of fertilisers as population increases. However, income levels are also an important factor. Rich countries can afford to use an enormous quantity of fertiliser when population density is very high (leading to serious pollution). Table 3.3 shows that no American country, except the small Caribbean islands (Barbados, etc.), has yet reached levels of cultivated land per capita as low as those of Japan (0.04 hectares), the Netherlands (0.06), Switzerland (0.06), or Belgium (0.08), but that some countries (especially in the Andes, Central America, and the Caribbean) may drop to these alarming levels within 20 or 30 years if current rates of population growth continue. The Latin American countries with figures for average cultivated land per capita below the world average of 0.31 hectares are El Salvador (0.13), Haiti (0.14), Peru (0.19), Colombia (0.20), Venezuela (0.22), Costa Rica (0.23), Guatemala (0.23), the Dominican Republic (0.24), Panama (0.26), Ecuador (0.27) and Mexico (0.31). The average non–weighted use of commercial fertilisers in these countries is only 55 kilograms per hectare (kg/ha) if we include Haiti, and 60 kg/ha if we exclude Haiti, a country that should use more fertilisers but cannot afford them. As already mentioned, no Latin American country would face serious problems securing adequate food supply if a 'high level of inputs' was used.[27] In sharp contrast, the corresponding group of rich countries was per capita cultivation figures below the world average (former West

Germany, 0.12; United Kingdom, 0.13; Austria 0.20; Italy, 0.21; and Norway, 0.21) have an average non-weighted use of fertilisers of 301 kg/ha.

If we now consider the Latin American countries with per capita agricultural land above the world average (Cuba, 0.32; Nicaragua, 0.39; Honduras, 0.41; Chile, 0.46; Uruguay, 0.48; Bolivia, 0.53; Brazil, 0.56; Paraguay, 0.59; and Argentina, 1.18), the average use of fertilisers is only 38 kg/ha including Cuba, and only 21 kg/ha excluding Cuba. In Cuba it is not a question of population pressure on resources but pressure from sugar exports that use a relatively high fertiliser input.

Finally, if we take the remaining high-income countries with more than 0.31 hectares of cultivated land per capita (France, 0.35; Sweden, 0.36; Finland, 0.43; Denmark, 0.51; Spain, 0.53; United States, 0.80; Canada, 1.84; and Australia, 3.10), average fertiliser use is 148 kg/ha. Low population pressure leads then to a relatively low use of fertilisers, but poverty also leads to low use of fertilisers. The use of less fertiliser contributes to the conservation of the world's resources (phosphate deposits, or using energy to manufacture nitrogenous fertilisers) and also avoids certain types of water pollution. On the other hand, the exhaustion of the soil due to a lack of fertiliser is an example of environmental degradation caused by poverty. However, as population and/or production pressure on the land increases, the response may be an increase in fertiliser use, provided the country is not too poor to afford fertilisers, but such intensification of production is very different from Boserup's shifts in cultivation systems, since it implies bringing outside inputs into agriculture.

All this leads to the conclusion that the idea of carrying capacity is therefore not very meaningful unless the level of inputs is specified. If we introduce the condition of 'lack of degradation of the resource base' into the definition of 'sustainable development', then, as Nicholas Georgescu-Roegen repeatedly pointed out, the world's carrying capacity will be the population sustained by an agricultural production system using only the energy of the sun.[28] But orthodox economics will immediately point out that this ignores the possibility of technological advances.

Migration and Carrying Capacity

Can indirect evidence, such as the presence of emigration, tell us whether carrying capacity has been exceeded? The economic history of humanity is a history of international trade, and also of international migration. Migration is normally analysed in terms of factors of attraction or expulsion. Although there may have been migrations due to the outstripping of carrying capacity (for example, Ireland in the middle of the 19th century), factors of attraction are generally more important. Within the

Table 3.3

Cultivated Land per Capita and Fertiliser Use

Latin American countries			Rich countries		
	1	2		1	2
El Salvador	0.13	114	Japan	0.04	435
Haiti	0.14	4	The Netherlands	0.06	787
Peru	0.19	22	Switzerland	0.06	432
Colombia	0.20	59	Belgium	0.08	536
Venezuela	0.22	63	F.R. Germany	0.12	423
Costa Rica	0.23	135	United Kingdom	0.13	368
Guatemala	0.23	46	Austria	0.20	253
Dominican Rep.	0.24	33	Italy	0.21	170
Panama	0.26	42	Norway	0.21	290
Ecuador	0.27	29	France	0.35	308
Mexico	0.31	64	Sweden	0.36	154
Cuba	0.32	172	Finland	0.49	218
Nicaragua	0.39	47	Denmark	0.51	257
Honduras	0.41	15	Spain	0.53	75
Chile	0.46	30	USA	0.80	101
Uruguay	0.48	31	Canada	1.84	49
Bolivia	0.53	2	Australia	3.10	25
Brazil	0.56	35			
Paraguay	0.59	5			
Argentina	1.18	4			

1. Hectares of *arable* land per capita, 1985
2. Fertiliser use in kg/ha, 1983–85

Source: World Resources Institute (with IIED and UNEP), World Resources 1988–1989, (Washington DC: WRI, 1988), Table 17.2.

frontiers of the nation-state, where there is usually freedom of movement, people emigrate from their region in search of employment opportunities and a better standard of living. This was true of the South–North migration in the United States between 1910 and 1950. The number of international migrants would be much greater than it actually is if the frontier police did not stop people emigrating from countries with low per capita consumption of energy and materials and trying to enter countries with a high per capita consumption of energy and materials. What is truly striking, given the difference in 'temperature' between different societies, is how little migration there actually is.

Migration rarely results from insufficient carrying capacity, as the factors of attraction are usually a stronger motive. However, the lack of opportunity to emigrate increases population pressure on resources. As an example, the famine in the Sahel in the 1970s was partly caused by the interruption of migrations. In periods of drought, nomadic groups used to be able to move south, but national frontiers now prevent their free circulation. To this must be added the extension of cash-cropping. Temporary or permanent migratory movements may increase the Earth's carrying capacity considerably, although it may be argued that exportation of excess population may lessen incentives to reduce birth-rates in the countries of both origin and destination.

Thus, in summary, the application of the notion of 'carrying capacity' in a human context requires that the regulations governing emigration and immigration, the group's standard of living, as well as the political and territorial distribution of the population be clearly stated and explained. (Ecology as a 'natural science' is not a suitable tool for explaining these factors.) In the human species, the exosomatic use of energy and materials is not determined genetically but rather is unlimited for each individual. Furthermore, humanity is continually transforming its technology. Although the new technologies mean that resources are used faster than they can be recycled by biogeochemical cycles, many economists continue to doubt that this indicates that we are outstripping carrying capacity, for there is the possibility of introducing substitutes.

It may seem a waste of time to discuss the concept of carrying capacity only to reject it, but it is necessary to clarify this point in order to study how poverty damages (or does not damage) the environment.

IS POVERTY A CAUSE OF ENVIRONMENTAL DEGRADATION?

The main argument of this chapter is that wealth is a greater threat to the environment than poverty. However, it is worth studying impartially the counter-argument that poverty causes environmental degradation. Let us now examine a few cases, mostly taken from studies in the Peruvian and Bolivian Andes.

Although there is external pressure on water and mining resources, the Andean region does not engage in agriculture for export (except for flowers in Ecuador and Colombia). In the Peruvian mountains, there is population pressure on resources, as only 3 per cent of the land is suitable for cultivation, and 27 per cent for grazing. Some traditional agricultural practices have stabilised ecosystems and limited environmental deterioration; this is true for the large number of potato varieties cultivated, and the communally controlled fallow system. Fallow periods allow for the fixation of atmospheric nitrogen, the recovery of the soil and the control of pests. In any case, traditional practices also include excessive grazing in communal areas, even in the former large estates, because of internal and external pressure from peasants.[29]

The privatisation of communal land, not for ecological reasons but as an incentive to production ('the magic of property will turn sand into gold', as Arthur Young, the l8th-century agronomist and traveller, once said), formed part of the European bourgeois revolutions. Social history refers to this event as 'the tragedy of the enclosures'. In the Andes, on the contrary, much land remains outside the marketplace. In fact, the share of land in private hands declined after the agrarian reforms. In Peru, in the case of the large sheep ranches, neighbouring communities had for a long time been demanding the return of their land. To avoid overgrazing, and to protect the (introduced) improved sheep breeds, the agrarian reform of 1969 did not authorise the return of this land, but instead transferred some of the profits obtained by these new SAIS ('agricultural companies of benefit to society') to the communities. The social distance between the administrators of the new SAIS and the indigenous population, together with other factors, led to the disappearance of most SAIS.[30]

Open access to resources for everyone, a free–for–all (when rules for communal management fail and there is no private property either), may lead to overgrazing, the exhaustion of fishing resources, a drop in the water table due to excessive irrigation or overexploitation of forests. In cases where cost is incurred now but the benefit will be enjoyed in the future, it may be expected that communal ownership will manage resources better than private ownership, because the private rate of discount will probably be higher than the communal rate of discount, i.e. the future is less valued under private ownership, because of shorter time horizons of families or firms, as compared to communities. This consideration is relevant when studying land improvements, such as the conservation of terraces and irrigation systems.

It is estimated that in the mountains of Peru there are about one million hectares of terraced land in disrepair, compared with the two million hectares of arable land in the same area. Terraces have also been abandoned in Greece, Italy and Spain, but for different reasons. In the Andes, poverty leads to deterioration of the land. Investment is only significant if it covers large areas, which requires the collaboration of many peasant families under the communal system. To reconstruct terrace systems in the Peruvian mountains, between 300 and 1,000 days' work per hectare are necessary. Other similar improvements include the reconstruction of ridging (*waru-waru*) in the *altiplanos* and of small-scale irrigation facilities. Assuming a day's work to be worth only 10 kg of cereal (or 40 kg of potatoes), and investing 700 days labour per hectare, the annual increase in production would need to be (net of extra fertiliser costs) about 700 kg of cereal or 2,800 kg of potatoes to give an annual return of 10 per cent. The figures available for costs and benefits of terraces in Peru are of this order. Although the peasants may be aware of the long-term advantages of improving the land, improvements cannot be undertaken without co-ordination among numerous families. While communal institutions may help, public funds are necessary to finance the work, which leads to concern about costs and thus to the assessment of land improvement projects by means of a cost-benefit analysis. The results of cost-benefit analysis fundamentally depend on the discount rate adopted, and of course the poor cannot afford to borrow money at high rates of interest. Here we see how poverty is a direct cause of environmental degradation, although we are left with the question of why these indigenous peasants are so poor.[31]

The Use of Firewood and Deforestation

There is a 'natural' and universal hierarchy in the use of domestic fuel. As income increases, wood and charcoal are replaced by kerosene and butane gas or LPG, in bottles which are in turn replaced by piped gas or electricity. Poverty sometimes causes deforestation because the poor are unable to ascend in the hierarchy of domestic fuels. Increasing income can lead to a decrease in the energy used for cooking, as large quantities of firewood are replaced by small quantities of fossil fuel. This may also prevent the depletion of forests in arid areas and reduce competition between forestry and agriculture.

Pricing policies may accelerate this process or slow it down. Appropriate pricing policies favouring the distribution of kerosene or butane may be the most important measures to take in meeting the needs of the poor and the environment. For example, it would be scandalous if a deforestation crisis were to occur in a dry region of a country that exports oil if this were in part because rural families were too poor to buy kerosene or butane.

Demand for fuel destroys forests near villages and towns in many countries. The loss of trees leads to increasing erosion. Where dried dung is used instead of firewood, soil fertility is lost and harvests are reduced. This is less common in Latin America than in Asia or Africa, partly because the contribution of dung and firewood to total energy consumption is lower, and partly because the depletion of forests that would leave the population without firewood is not a problem in the humid tropical regions of the continent. In Latin America, one main threat to the forests is 'colonisation': the forests are being cut down faster than they can regenerate, and the valuable wood is burnt on the spot or left to rot. Other enemies of the forests are cattle ranching and logging – even when only species such as mahogany are extracted, there is indirect widespread devastation, prime examples of export pressure on resources.[32]

Lack of firewood is a problem in only a few parts of Latin America; arid or semi-arid regions like the Andes, the coastal regions of Peru, the *sertões* in Brazil, and parts of Central America and the Antilles. The Peruvian and Bolivian mountains suffer a high risk of becoming deserts with an acute shortage of firewood. In the Andes, after trees like the *Polylepis* and *Buddleia* were wiped out, shrubs like *Lepidophyllum* were cut, and later even *Distichia muscoide*. The last resort was the collection of dung for fuel. It is estimated that in Asia, the Middle East and Africa about 400 million tonnes of dung are burnt per year (each tonne implies the loss of 50 kg of cereal yield), but there are no comparable figures for Latin America.[33] Poverty fosters the destruction of tree cover, in turn affecting the water cycle and leading to soil erosion, while the use of dung as an alternative fuel for cooking or heating promotes the loss of soil fertility. Herdsmen and peasants living in the mountains of Peru and Bolivia cannot afford kerosene or butane and must use dung for fuel.[34] In this case, the economy is closed to external energy flow due to the lack of money to pay for it.

Estimated consumption of firewood is between 750 kg and 900 kg per person per year. Satisfying this need creates great tensions within the relatively dry and densely populated highland ecosystem. A reasonable estimate of firewood use in Guatemala is about one tonne per person per year, part of which comes from pruning the trees providing shade in the coffee plantations, while the rest comes from forestry production or deforestation. Since the energy value of firewood consumed per person is three times greater than the energy consumed as food, this may lead to great pressure on resources in densely populated areas. Like most medium-income regions, there was a tendency in Central America towards the replacement of firewood by kerosene or bottled gas. This was temporarily halted by the rise in oil prices after 1973 and 1979. In Costa Rica, a rainy and mountainous country, cooking using hydroelectricity is common and there is no deforestation problem caused by the collection of firewood for cooking. The causes of deforestation here have been quite different.[35]

In some countries or regions, domestic demand for firewood or dung cannot be satisfied without reducing food or forage production. A higher price for firewood may increase the territory used to grow trees, almost in the same way that a higher price for oil may stimulate exploration for new reserves. However, this territory cannot be increased beyond a certain limit. The World Bank prefers social reforestation and the use of charcoal, produced through improved methods; it also prefers to improve oven efficiency rather than the introduction of oil products. However, according to Gerald Foley,[36] if firewood, charcoal and dung were replaced by oil, the extra demand for oil on the world market would be only about 100 million tonnes a year, that is about two million barrels a day. The quantity of oil necessary is much less than the energy equivalent of the firewood substituted, because stoves that use petrol derivatives are far more efficient. Let us consider some more detailed recent figures. Social preference for butane or kerosene as domestic fuel is undeniable, and is due to cleanliness, the saving in time and effort for the women who cook and the lower amount of domestic pollution (by carbon monoxide, other gases and soot) when compared to firewood, charcoal or dung. If we suppose that annual use is only 500 kg of firewood per person, with an energy content equivalent to 0.35 tonnes of oil per tonne of firewood, and if we take into account the greater efficiency of stoves that use kerosene or gas (compared to modern firewood stoves with an efficiency of 15 per cent or less, kerosene or gas stoves have an efficiency of 40 to 50 per cent), we find that to replace the fuel used by the 3,000 million poor people of the world, about 200 million tonnes of oil a year would be needed. This is a large quantity, but quite feasible; it is equal to about five times Spain's annual consumption of oil, or a quarter of US consumption. Oil at $15 a barrel is so cheap that it can be wasted by rich countries, but too expensive to be used as domestic fuel by the poor. There is then a good environmental argument against fundamentalist neo-liberal dogmas against subsidies: while oil consumption in the rich countries should be taxed, the use of LPG or butane, or kerosene for cooking should be subsidised in poor countries where firewood is becoming scarce, or where dung should rather be used as fertiliser.

It is emphatically *not* in the interests of the rich countries for the poor countries to attain comparable levels of per capita consumption, not only in the kitchen but in all spheres of life, including private transport by car. Using present technologies, this would lead to a dramatic increase in the rate of depletion of oil and gas, and would greatly increase local and global pollution problems. But we are discussing a different problem. The impact on world oil demand if firewood, and dung, were replaced by oil products would be small.

Deforestation is not always caused by poverty or by cooking needs. Deforestation occurs for quite different reasons in the Amazon than in arid regions of Latin America. In the Amazon, one cause is the burning of trees that is part of the shifting agriculture practiced by 'colonists'. Another cause is the expansion of cattle ranching. Logging and mining, including oil extraction, are likely to become the main cause of deforestation in the coming decades in many regions of Amazonia. Similarly, deforestation in the other humid tropical regions of the world has been generated by commercial enterprises, to the detriment of the poor. Thus

In Central America, especially in Costa Rica, Nicaragua, and Honduras, where deforestation was very fast in the 1960s and 1970s, the main reason was land clearance for cattle ranching ... In South-East Asia, rapid deforestation is caused by exporters of tropical hardwoods. The main beneficiaries are the large concessionaries – generally military officials and colleagues of politicians in high government circles – who cornered felling rights as a result of political patronage. Again, the main losers are the poor, including forest dwellers (generally ethnic minorities) who were displaced and the peasants located downstream, whose harvests depend on the hydrological 'sponge effect' of the forests ... as Barraclough and Ghimire show, *accusing poor immigrants of destroying the forests is like blaming poor recruits for the suffering and destruction of war* .[37]

However, in the arid regions of Asia, Africa and Latin America (the *sertões* in Brazil, the coast of Peru, the highlands of the Andes or Central America), the reason for deforestation is the use of firewood or charcoal as fuel by the poor. Recently, the Batán Grande forest in Lambayeque on the north coast of Peru has been declared a Reserve for the Protection of Plants. But in Lambayeque alone, where there are 400,000 hectares of dry woodland, more than 2,000 hectares are lost every year due to lack of employment and poverty: the peasants' only option is to cut down the trees to produce charcoal.[38] As it happens, only a few kilometres away is the oil pipeline from the Peruvian jungle to the coast, and a few hundred kilometres further north is the Ecuadorian pipeline also transporting large quantities of oil from the jungle to the coast, both for export. Charcoal would not be used or sold if people could obtain the little gas they need for cooking at a reasonable price.

Poverty and the Urban Environment

We have seen by examining rural cases how unequal distribution of income and wealth as well as unequal access to resources leads to poverty, and poverty then leads to environmental degradation. Now we shall see the same in an urban context. Environmental degradation leads to disease. One of the main causes of death in low-income countries are diseases of faecal origin, which cause a quarter of all deaths in children under five.[39] The quality of drainage and sewage services has an inverse relation to income. Additionally, paying rents that are high in comparison to income leads to crowding, an important factor in promoting the spread of tuberculosis. The lack of water makes the poor even poorer, and obliges them to abuse the environment. Trachoma and scabies result from a lack of water for personal hygiene; cholera, diarrhoea, typhoid and hepatitis are aggravated by a lack of water to eliminate waste. These are examples of the connection between poverty and environmental degradation, in both urban and rural contexts, and where neither population pressure on resources nor production pressure on resources are direct causes of environmental degradation.

Illnesses are not always related to poverty; on the contrary, those related to consumption of tobacco, alcohol and animal fats increase with income. However, some urban environmental problems are caused by poverty. Poor people in a city have less water, even less than proportional to their income: they have to pay more for water because they do not have water connections. In Lima at the beginning of the 1970s, the shanty-town inhabitants bought water from lorries and used about 25 litres per person per day. In houses with water connections, inhabitants used about 150 litres per person per day. The poor paid, in total, three times more for their water, that is, about 18 times more per litre.[40] This is parallel to the problem of cooking for street-dwellers in India: even if, in the cities, it is cheaper to cook using kerosene than using firewood brought from far away, it is first necessary to have a stove that uses kerosene, and then a place to keep it.[41] People who have less water because they are poor suffer more from illnesses related to its low quality, and from lack of water for personal hygiene, washing of clothes, and elimination of excrement. Some public health experts emphasise these environmental issues, while others with a more clinical approach propose massive vaccination programmes, oral rehydration, etc., because they are cheaper than general preventive hygiene programmes. But both schools agree that increasing income eliminates threats to health by ensuring an abundant supply of cheap water. There is a similar relation for other diseases that are not associated with lack of water. Reducing poverty may lead to the installation of insect netting, for example.

ECOLOGY AND 'ADJUSTMENT' PROGRAMMES

Alongside programmes to alleviate the effects of stabilisation policies on the 'poorest of the poor' (and also alongside the suppression of the 'IMF revolts', such as the terrible massacre in Venezuela in March 1989), programmes to avoid environmental damage could also be implemented.[42] This is because the temporary increase in poverty caused by adjustment policies may have effects on the environment, just like 'structural' poverty does. The relationship between 'adjustment' and ecological damage arises from the need to produce a surplus in order to bring external trade payments into balance, including debt and interest payments. This surplus may be obtained by means of low salaries or better terms of trade, or by an increase in technical efficiency that does not increase the flow of energy and materials in the economy. A fourth method of increasing the size of the surplus is exploiting the environment; in other words, externalising costs and undervaluing future needs. In order to escape from the poverty caused by 'adjustment' programmes, one remedy is to increase the use of renewable or non-renewable resources – as is happening, for example, in Brazil.[43] This also explains the unrestrained oil export policies of Venezuela, Ecuador and Mexico. When interest rates are high, there is a tendency to discount long-term problems, e.g. environmental ones, in favour of the most pressing ones. Conversely, if long-term problems of pollution and depletion of resources are given a low current value, then the current exploitation of resources increases. This point, relevant to the ecology of debtor countries, was pointed out long ago by the Oxford Nobel Prize chemist and ecological economist Frederick Soddy. Unlike real wealth, which is subject to the laws of thermodynamics, debts (i.e. financial wealth, or as Soddy put it, 'virtual wealth') do not decay with time. On the contrary, debts increase at a compound interest rate.

During the 1980s, exploitation of resources in low-income countries increased in order to cover the balance of payments, including debts, and a deterioration of the terms of trade due to increased supplies of raw materials. If Mexico had reduced oil exports, whether independently or in line with OPEC policy at the beginning of the 1980s, this might not only have contributed to the conservation of non-renewable resources and to reduce carbon dioxide emissions (by maintaining higher oil prices). It might also have meant greater net oil revenue for Mexico. This line of argument will become more common as the ideas of ecological economists spread. In any case, if 'adjustment' programmes were less harsh, or if they also addressed redistribution of income, their negative effects on the poor and the environment would be less.

Let us suppose that the South does in fact need lessons from the IMF and the World Bank on the financial stabilisation of their inflationary economies, and let us also suppose (although reality shows us the opposite) that the ecological dangers and social injustice inherent to adjustment programmes can be avoided. Should we also accept that the North is in a position to give lessons on *ecological adjustment* and to impose an environmental conditionality on loans? The consensus of international agencies is that the poor are enemies of the environment and this is sometimes accepted by official circles in the South. Southern governments and even left-wing parties, whether due to self-interest or ignorance, accept that ecology came to the South not in the form of the Chipko movement, or Chico Mendes and their countless predecessors and contemporary counterparts, but in the form of recent intellectual influences from Europe or the United States. They are not aware of the ecological content of historical and modern national and social conflicts because these movements did not express themselves in the language used by environmentalists in the North.

Ecological movements are a thing of the North, they say in the South; the poor are a danger to the environment, they say in the North. Wonderful! The situation is now ready for the imposition of ecological 'adjustments' by the North, as well as financial ones. What this boils down to is the imposition of an environmental conditionality that the South must fulfil if it is to obtain loans or access to the markets of the North.[44] Will the South tamely accept this new conditionality? Will it be accepted by countries that export and have exported natural resources, including oil and gas, cheaply without any type of ecological price correction? Will it be accepted by the many countries sacrificing their ecological subsistence farming by importing the North's agricultural surpluses based on processes that are ecologically damaging, and products that may also be?

The idea of environmental conditionality might be rejected on the basis of two different lines of reasoning. The first is rather silly but quite common: 'The bloody gringos are meddling in our affairs again, blocking the entry of our bananas (our tuna-fish, our tropical hardwoods, or our Amazonian gold extracted by the *garimpeiros* (individual prospectors) in Yanomani territory) ... and to cap it all they refuse to give us loans unless we give in to all that stupid environmental impact assessment nonsense.' The second, more intelligent, position takes for granted that ecology is a stronger idea in the South than in the North. Southern goverment officials might come to believe that the greatest threat to the environment comes from the overdeveloped economies of the North. These are the beneficiaries of unfair terms of trade which are the basis for their current levels of per capita consumption of energy and materials, levels which are extravagant and cannot be copied. Rather than imposing a unilateral environmental conditionality on countries of the South, the North should also adjust its financial economy to its 'productive' economy, and its productive economy – which is highly polluting and contaminating – to its own environmental space as well as to the global ecosystem. The question would then be: who is going to bell the cat of imposing ecological adjustments on the North? In general, this will not take place through pressure on loans. For who is going to refuse financing US deficits for ecological reasons? Ecological adjustment could be imposed, to some extent, on the North by ecologically corrected increases in prices or by restrictions on trade, the responsibility of an international trade organisation controlled by a democratic and ecological United Nations – GATT was not, and the new World Trade Organization is unlikely to be.

PROTECTIVE EXPENDITURE AND INCOME LEVELS: LEIPERT'S LAW

The thread running through this chapter is its critique of the conventional wisdom that generalised economic growth (called 'sustainable development') is a remedy for both poverty and environmental degradation. Our criticism accepts that poverty can be a cause of environmental degradation, as we have seen in the previous sections, but we believe that generalised economic growth may increase, rather than diminish, environmental degradation. It is true that wealth allows people to allocate more resources to protecting the environment from the effects of this wealth. Rich countries are cleaner, but this does not mean that they are any more ecological.

We shall use the term 'protection' (or defence or mitigation) for those activities that protect the population or the environment from the effects of production. In 1970, William Kapp pointed out that 'the traditional measures of growth and production in terms of GNP are becoming more and more inadequate as measures of growth and production, as ever greater quantities and proportions of expenditure are allocated to protecting and maintaining the fabric of our environment'.[45] The public purse pays many of these protective costs, but not all. What is now called 'Green capitalism' is the commercial economic activity that aims to repair the ecological damages caused by other enterprises. Some chemical industries ruin the environment, and others try to restore it, and this is all counted as production! The growing proportion of GNP dedicated to these costs in Germany has been documented by Christian Leipert. There is now a debate on whether such costs should be counted not as income in the national accounts, but as intermediate costs to be deducted from the added value.

Some forms of waste depend on 'exosomatic' consumption', i.e. on cultural and lifestyle preferences, rather than human biology. Others (excretion, for example) depend on 'endosomatic' consumption, and are independent of income levels (although vegetarian diets produce more solid wastes). Overall, the poor produce fewer wastes. Wealth, however, produces large amounts of wastes: what we might call the *effluents of affluence*. Experts on health and the elimination of wastes in low-income countries are aware that poor communities produce less liquid and solid wastes than relatively richer ones, and the wastes of the poor are more suitable for composting. As an example, in Mexico in 1985, daily production of solid domestic wastes was about 32,600 tonnes, which only represents about 500 g per person per day, much less than in high-income countries.

Mexican babies tend not to use disposable nappies. However, the Mexican landscape is much dirtier than, say, the French landscape, even though Mexicans live in a larger country and produce less rubbish. It has been estimated that about 15,000 tonnes of this waste is not collected but is just disposed of by the roadside, or down the drains, or on open land. Those who live in poor urban districts often complain about inadequate storm drainage; however, without adequate elimination of solid wastes, storm drainage is impossible because the drains are blocked. In poor countries it is also normal to dump solid wastes on tips or heaps that serve as open-air incinerators.[46]

Poor urban areas are noisier and more polluted than high-income urban areas. However, this is not due to greater waste production but to lower protective, or mitigating, expenditure. The relationship between poverty and environmental degradation also holds for industrial illnesses, for example, those related to asbestos; how to diminish pollution in the industrial cities of middle-income countries, like São Paulo, has long been a problem.[47] Normally, in rural areas environmental risks related to pesticides and fertilisers first grow and then diminish as income increases, stricter standards are imposed for workers, and protective expenditure is undertaken. For the population at large, however, intensive agriculture and cattle raising in rich countries continues to represent a large environmental burden that is *not* corrected – for instance, nitrites in the water, or ammonia and methane from cattle, as in the Netherlands.

As a general rule, poverty – and this means low public expenditure, specifically a low level of local public expenditure – prevents environmental protection. In a rural zone with a very low level of income, some forms of pollution do not exist. They increase very rapidly with urban development and increased income, much more rapidly than protective costs increase. The tendency is reversed at high income levels.

ECOLOGY AND POSITIONAL GOODS

Although, as we have seen, there are cases in which alleviating poverty may lead to reduced environmental damage, the idea that generalised economic growth is 'good' for the environment is unacceptable. Some forms of wealth can never become universal unless economic growth is uncoupled from pollution and resource exhaustion. As an example, a world with a stable population of 10 billion people and a density of cars equivalent to that in North America would have about 4 billion cars, about 10 times the current number. Cars with combustion engines will not become items of mass consumption, due to their need for fossil fuels and their environmental impact, but kerosene or butane stoves could become mass-consumption goods.

Can economic growth be uncoupled from a parallel increase in the use of energy and natural resources? The close correlation between per capita income and use of commercial energy supports the argument that they cannot be separated.[48] However, another school of thought identifies the large potential for increasing energy efficiency in low-income countries and eastern Europe, and the real increase in energy efficiency in the OECD countries after 1979.[49] Sometimes, changes in intensity of energy use in the economies of specific countries or regions may be deceptive, because they result from changes in the composition of trade in energy-intensive products. For instance, the energy used to smelt the aluminium that the Japanese import from Brazil (e.g. the hydroelectricity from Tucurui in Pará, sold at about one cent per kwh) is not included in the statistics for Japan's energy consumption. In addition, the increases in energy and material efficiency may stimulate further use (as Jevons already noted for coal in Britain in the mid-19th century).

In order to study the compatibility of economic growth and good environmental management, we can use the concept of 'positional goods' introduced by Fred Hirsch. In his book *The Social Limits to Growth*[50] Hirsch tried to explain the persistence of distributive conflicts in the high-income countries during the 1960s. As salaries increased together with increased productivity, the availability of mass-consumption goods increased. However, there was dissatisfaction, one of the causes being precisely the 'positional' nature of certain goods and services. According to Hirsch, the satisfaction derived from 'positional goods' diminishes if many people possess them. Thorstein Veblen's category of conspicuous consumption includes one type of positional good, the 'exclusive' product bought for its snob value. But Hirsch's concept is much wider. Satisfaction is negatively affected by general use when the sum of the individual decisions to buy these goods imposes social costs. If everyone has a car, or if everyone wishes to be very highly educated in order to get a well-paid job, or if everyone wants a yacht or a house in the country, then possession of the good changes the social situation, due to traffic congestion, the lack of clean air, the lack of well-paid jobs, or the agglomeration of country houses or yachts which makes possession of them less attractive. Hirsch paid more attention to congestion on European motorways and beaches during the summer holidays than to an ecological analysis of the economy, and for this reason he discussed social limits to economic growth rather than ecological ones. He wrote, 'An acre of ground used for food production can, in principle, increase two, ten, or a thousand-fold as technology advances . . . but, on the contrary, an acre of ground used for the enjoyment of a single family cannot increase its initial productivity in this use'.[51] Since Hirsch did not understand the ecological costs of modern agriculture and of the economy in general, the relevance of his idea of positional goods is even greater than he supposed.

According to Hirsch, there is a difference between a 'material economy' and a 'positional economy' when 'material economy' is defined as production subject to continuous increases in productivity per unit of labour. The British economist Roy Harrod had given this the name of 'democratic wealth' in opposition to 'oligarchic wealth'. From the ecological point of view, however, the 'material economy' is also a 'positional economy' that imposes costs on present or future generations. This is because the increased productivity per unit of labour that has generalised 'democratic wealth' by means of massive consumption of goods has been achieved at the cost of exhausting resources, polluting the environment, and extinguishing biological diversity.

Krutilla's Criterion and Inglehart's Thesis

The definition of 'sustainable development' – development that covers present needs without prejudicing the ability of future generations to cover their own needs – implies a development model characterised by the production of non–positional goods, perhaps a 'Fordism without Fords'. Cars cannot become a mass-consumption good, nor can a consumption of 70 kg of meat per person per year become a norm. Now that the public is aware of the threat of global warming, even burning firewood in an isolated village in Karnataka or in the mountains of Guatemala, or burning coal in a power station in China where most villages do not have electricity, must be considered a 'positional good' imposing costs, not only in the future but in the present. Much carbon dioxide was released into the atmosphere by industrialisation, and there was much deforestation in high-income countries and their colonies, before scientists began to worry about the negative effects of the enhanced greenhouse effect. There may be more positional goods than we think.

Hirsch's ideas about these two types of goods had been anticipated in discussions of environmental policy. In the 1950s and 1960s, a famous North American environmental economist, John Krutilla, sought ways to preserve the landscapes threatened by hydroelectric dams. The landscapes doomed on the basis of cost–benefit analysis. Krutilla introduced an overvaluation of the recreational value of the landscape and an undervaluation of electricity, using the interesting argument that electricity would be cheaper in the future due to technical progress in the form of nuclear power (electricity as 'democratic wealth'). Incomes, meanwhile, would continue to increase as would the demand for mountain landscapes due to their contribution to the quality of life – an unconscious echo of the Trevelyan

Thesis discussed in the Introduction. These landscapes would then acquire scarcity value, because their supply could not be increased by technical progress; we should say that this is 'oligarchic' wealth, or a 'positional' good. The increasing scarcity of the recreational or aesthetic services provided by nature in relation to manufactured goods justified attaching greater value to nature's services by giving them a price greater than the current market value. This is not a bad idea, except that the distinction between commodities that can be produced in abundance without ruining the environment and amenities that are provided by nature and which are becoming scarcer and scarcer with respect to demand is not very convincing if we consider the history of nuclear power, the acid rain produced by the burning of coal for electricity, and the escalation of the greenhouse effect. In fact, Krutilla's idea exaggerated the ease with which the material goods of the human economy could be obtained without reliance on nature and anticipated Inglehart's interpretation of environmentalism as a social phenomenon characteristic of rich 'post-materialist' societies more worried about the quality of life than livelihood.[52]

THE SOCIAL ECOLOGY OF THE POOR

There is a point which deserves further analysis before bringing this chapter to a close. Often, poor people who have little or no property of their own rely on common property resources, and there is a presumption that a 'tragedy of the commons' might occur. There has been considerable confusion about the impact of different forms of ownership on resource conservation: open access, communal property, state property and private property.[53] Garrett Hardin's well known article 'The Tragedy of the Commons' (1968) explained the problems of pollution and resource exhaustion as the results of the conflict between, on the one hand, marginal private gains that accrue exclusively to the person using a communal resource – e.g. introducing an additional sheep – and, on the other hand, the marginal social costs in the form of degradation of the pasture, which must be shared by all, including also future generations. Hardin's article had great repercussions, and now global ecological problems are discussed under the title 'The Global Commons.' But the atmosphere and the oceans are not communal goods with management rules established by legislation or ancestral customs: they are in fact resources with open access for all, as demonstrated by whaling until treaties regulated it, or the use of the atmosphere, the oceans and new vegetation to dump carbon dioxide; a free for all, to the benefit of the rich who act as if they had property rights on all three sinks. In fact, fishing often demonstrates the conflict between the logic of free access and the logic of communal management, regulated by fishermen's guilds or associations, for example. There are also national and ecological conflicts, such as the ones between Great Britain and Iceland ('the Cod Wars') and between Spain and Morocco, and Spain and Canada (over fish stocks which straddle the 200 miles limit), and we can understand efforts to impede open access. As an example, in 1947 Peru extended its exclusive fishing rights to 200 miles through legislation passed under the presidency of Bustamante y Rivero. We do not mean to say that fishing is presently well regulated. For instance, regulations governing mesh size in nets have been counterproductive. Nets that permit small fish within, say, the cod population to escape are applying selection pressure in favour of fish that are small, leading to reduction of average size at breeding age. But nevertheless, *open access* is *not* the *commons*.

European social history – as in the classic works of Marc Bloch, R. H. Tawney, Karl Polanyi and others – has focused on the 'tragedy of the enclosures' rather than on the 'tragedy of the commons'. This is because the privatization of communal lands in modernising Europe, and elsewhere, left the poor without any way of making a living and turned them into a proletariat. One of the most spectacular processes of privatisation of land in human history has occurred over the last 30 years in the Amazon, with serious ecological consequences, partly due to the system of subsidies for meat production on new pastureland created by burning forests. The popular response, exemplified by the movement led by Chico Mendes, is a reaction against the tragedy of the enclosures for its social *and* ecological consequences.

The study of water management is particularly interesting in this context, as there is not normally a simple 'rule of capture', except in the case of underground reserves, ie. a 'first come, first served' rule. Civil society has created complex institutions to deal with the contradiction between private gain and social costs. As mentioned earlier in the Andean context, other aspects of social and ecological reality, such as soil conservation by terracing, collective systems of agricultural rotation, and to some extent the rules governing use of grazing, show that communal management can be an excellent means of preserving the environment. In southern Europe and northern Africa, a skilful comparative analysis by John McNeill in *Mountains of the Mediterranean*[54] shows the influence of different factors on the management of the land. In the Rif in Morocco, population pressure and the pressure of exports on the land is still increasing, while in other areas of the Mediterranean the land is now deteriorating because of depopulation. Deforestation is relatively recent in many Mediterranean areas. It was driven in the 19th century by three factors: population pressure, the outside pressure on the forest for logging or charcoal (for mines, for instance) and the evolution of the property system towards privatisation.

Ownership systems have important effects on forest management and on the use of firewood and charcoal. A social and ecological history could be written that would comprehend robbery and other social conflicts after the private appropriation of the forests (the sale of church land and communal land in so many countries in the 19th century), and that would explain the role of these communally used resources in the human ecosystems privatised during the liberal wave at the end of the 18th and 19th centuries.[55] In the ecological history of India, the communal management of woodlands has had to resist the enroachment of state ownership, rather than private ownership. Forest degradation was not due to abuse by the poor, but to state ownership under British colonial exploitation for short-term gain, in particular the production of railway sleepers. There has been a confrontation between two positions. On one side the colonial state and its republican successor, and on the other side tribal and peasant communities, with their own rules governing access to and use of the forest. This is a clear example of the 'environmentalism of the poor', as these communities use these resources less intensively, because they are guided by use value rather than pecuniary value. Thus, Guha and Gadgil conclude there is conflict between, on one hand, state control and commercial exploitation which is anti-ecological, and, on the other, community use and the moral economy of the poor. Guha and Gadgil adopt the analytical categories developed by E. P. Thompson and James Scott to analyse different types of social struggles in defence of forest rights, from the mid-19th century down to the celebrated Chipko movement of the present day.[56]

Another famous ecological–social conflict, which has already lasted 20 years, is taking place in India between traditional fishing and industrial fishing with trawlers. The tendency is toward the displacement of the traditional fishermen and the exhaustion of their resources due to export pressures. The conflict was previously was over shrimp, and now is over cuttle-fish and squid. The coast of the state of Kerala is only 600 kilometres long, but its traditional fishermen used to produce a third of all the fish in India. Since the 1950s there have been attempts to modernise the methods of fishing, giving trawlers to fishing co-operatives, but in the end it has been outside proprietors who have come in with industrial methods. There are now two social sectors with distinct perspectives: those who fish for their living and those who fish for their earnings. Apart from the incidents of violence between the two groups, the traditional fishermen have also gained the support of the authorities in imposing temporary closed seasons during the season of the monsoons (July and August), when several species reproduce. The trawlers' nets graze the bottom of the sea and impede reproduction. While the fishermen's unions may succeed in having a closed season called, the authorities – who are in fact enthusiastic about the increase in exports – do not necessarily enforce it effectively. This is a classic case of the environmentalism of the poor.[57]

We have focused mainly on rural movements, but we certainly would also find a similar popular ecological awareness in some non-rural contexts. How would this ecological awareness have been expressed? We may interpret many social conflicts in industry and mining as ecological conflicts, for health and safety in the workplace, or against industrial diseases. We may also consider some urban struggles as ecological struggles, for example, struggles against high rents which lead to overcrowding, and in turn to tuberculosis, or struggles for adequate water supplies, which reduce diarrhea and cholera. There have also been struggles for the protection and enhancement of green spaces in cities of the North and the South. This is not to say that these historical movements have utilised the terminology of scientific ecology. They have rather used their own distinctive discourse – political, popular, indigenous, or even religious as the case may be.

CONCLUSION

Chapters 1 and 2 suggested that some radical social movements that struggle against poverty should also be considered ecological movements. In this chapter, we have compared the environmentalism of the poor – which insists on ecological and economic redistribution – to mainstream environmental management, which insists that economic growth is the chief remedy for both poverty and environmental degradation. We have considered if poverty is the cause of environmental degradation, whether through deforestation, soil erosion or inadequate urban sanitation. If poverty arises, or is thought to arise, from unequal economic and ecological distribution, then we may expect that social movements against the rich will also be ecological movements. A classification of social movements based on ecological criteria, as was attempted in the previous chapter, may then be helpful in advancing the study of the relationship between poverty and environmental degradation. The conventional wisdom maintains that economic growth is, in general, good for the environment. The illusion of continued economic growth is encouraged by the world's rich in order to maintain peace among the poor. But the truth is that unchecked economic growth leads to the exhaustion of resources and to pollution, and this harms the poor. There is thus a conflict between the destruction of nature to make money and the conservation of nature in order to live. Popular struggles against the forces of privatisation to maintain land and natural resources under communal control are well known throughout history. These struggles by the poor reveal an implicit ecological awareness. The survival of the poor is not guaranteed by the expansion of the market system; on the contrary, their survival is threatened by its expansion. In the past and in the present, many agrarian protests – regardless of the way in which they have expressed their grievances – have had an ecological aspect because they have tried to maintain environmental resources outside the marketplace. In our view, we should also see as ecological, the struggles of indigenous and peasant groups who organise themselves against ranching interests, large hydro-electric projects, and mining, and also many urban conflicts, even when the people themselves, or their leaders, do not know of or even reject the label 'ecologist' or 'environmentalist'. Chico Mendes was for 10 years a union leader of rubber collectors, fighting against deforestation and cattle ranches in Acre, in the remote western tip of Brazil's Amazonia; he learnt that he was also an ecologist only a couple of years before his death.

Chapter 4

Towards a Cross-Cultural Environmental Ethic

The human world interests me more than the world of nature; maybe it is a heresy to say such a thing in America.

(Czeslaw Milosz)

AMERICAN DEBATES ON ENVIRONMENTAL ETHICS

Discussions on environmental ethics have reached their high-water mark in the United States, whether measured in terms of column inches of print space, enrolments in college courses or – the surest indicator – the intensity of the debate. With the setting aside of wild areas being regarded as the best gauge of an ecological conscience, the development of environmental ethics has been closely linked to the growth of the American wilderness movement. Battles over the creation, preservation and extension of wilderness areas form the backdrop against which the environmental community has examined and re-examined its ethical responsibilities towards nature.

Apart from the wilderness crusade, three factors seem to have given a major impetus to modern debates on environmental ethics. In a famous essay first published in 1967 (and relentlessly anthologized since), the California historian Lynn White located the 'historical roots of the ecologic crisis' in the Judeo–Christian belief that man was meant to dominate nature. The part played by different religious traditions in annihilating (or safeguarding) the integrity of the natural world now came under close scrutiny. White's attack led many Christians to look towards reviving traditions of stewardship that had been suppressed within their own religion; others, abandoning Christianity altogether, enthusiastically embraced non-Western religions believed to be more in harmony with nature.[1]

A second major influence has been a guilt complex rather more specific to the United States. In resisting the equation of a dollar sign with their culture, Americans have pointed increasingly to their remarkable system of national parks. John Muir's life-work, wrote one of his early admirers and supporters, was to help the American people throw off the 'two shackles which retard our progress as a nation – philistinism and commercialism – and advance with freedom towards the love of beauty as a principle.'[2] Sixty years later, a new biographer of Muir suggested that the wilderness movement was articulated from 'a deep stratum of the national experience which was surely as American as those of Joseph Coors and Union Carbide'.[3]

Christian anxiety and American insecurity notwithstanding, equally significant in moulding the contemporary debate on environmental ethics has been a factor which relates to nature rather than to culture. As compared to tropical ecologies, temperate ecosystems are both more benign and more amenable to scientific exploitation for utilitarian ends. For the city dweller, the temperate forest is more welcoming than the tropical forest; in this sense Aldous Huxley was right – even without his poems, one can imagine Wordsworth in the Lake District, but scarcely in northern Borneo. At the same time, the relative simplicity of temperate ecosystems, and their greater ability to recover from disturbance, have inspired radical programmes of environmental modification. The ecological environment in temperate climates, therefore, facilitates both the conquest and worship of nature. This paradoxical situation is reflected in the two classic polarities of environmental ethics – the opposition of utilitarian to preservationist, and of anthropocentric to biocentric attitudes towards nature.

This triple heritage of Christianity, anti-philistinism and a benign ecology has given the debate on environmental ethics a distinctively North American stamp. A particular feature of this debate has been its rather narrow focus on individual attitudes towards nature, a focus perhaps not unrelated to what Donald Worster once called the 'Protestant roots of American environmentalism'. In the United States, environmentalism has been overdetermined by the Calvinist imprimatur, such that both leaders and followers (and analysts, too) have come to believe that the original sin of separation from nature can be redeemed only through a wholesale *personal* identification with it. This juxtaposition of singular Man to singular Nature gives rise to a series of binary oppositions, around which the history of environmental ideas is then written. Thus Donald Worster's magisterial history of ecological ideas in the West is woven around the opposites of *arcadian* and *imperial* atitudes towards nature. Likewise, both Roderick Nash and Stephen Fox have tried to rewrite the history of American environmentalism as a struggle between *preservationists* who wish to preserve nature and wild species for their own sake and *utilitarians* who, with the help of science and rational management, transform nature into useful commodities, working towards 'the greatest good of the greatest number for the longest time'. And for today's deep ecologists, the only two admissible attitudes are *anthropocentric* and *biocentric* respectively. In such cases, the story of environmental ethics is reduced to a Manichean struggle between one set of good ideas (arcadian, preservationist, biocentric) and another set of evil ones (imperial, utilitarian, anthropocentric).[4]

This chapter[5] tries to see the American debate on environmental ethics from within broader perspectives that may enrich it. To circumvent its idealist and individualist tenor, I intend to recast the environmental debate as a debate about social utopias. For every theory of nature is itself embedded in a larger theory of society. As Raymond Williams warned us many years ago, 'if we talk only of singular Man and singular Nature, we can compose a general history, but at the cost of excluding the real and altering social relations'. The 'idea of nature contains an extraordinary amount of human history', and 'what is often being argued . . . in the idea of nature is the idea of man; the idea of man in society, indeed the ideas of kinds of societies.'[6]

Environmental Philosophies of History

In the modern marketplace of ideas, environmentalism occupies the broad space between two sharply opposed views of the human predicament: the utopian vision of the economist, and the profoundly pessimistic or dystopian vision of the biologist. Human beings everywhere, says the neo-classical (i. e. orthodox) economist, are irremediably selfish, each working to maximise his own welfare. It is only the invisible hand of the market which, somehow, transforms a welter of competitive individual actions into the best of all possible worlds. This buoyant view of the human prospect rests on two complementary assumptions: an infinitely expanding technological frontier (which assumes that any resource shortage or crisis shall be overcome by the discovery of new substitutes), and the rejection of any physical limits to economic growth (which assumes that the rest of the world will come to enjoy the lifestyle characteristic of a middle- or upper-class American).

The economist's mystical belief in the magic of the market as an instrument of human welfare is in vivid contrast to the biologist's equally mystical belief in the human propensity for collective suicide through overbreeding. Biologists also practice methodological individualism, and promote with equal passion a view of human nature as essentially selfish, but in this view human beings live not to maximise their economic welfare but their 'inclusive fitness', the prospects of survival for themselves and their closest relatives. With no market to fall back upon, and with an awareness of ecological limits, this perspective on selfishness can only forecast doom, as an expanding human population exceeds the 'carrying capacity' of its habitat. From Malthus through Darwin to Garret Hardin, there has been a long line of doomsday prophets who believe that this conflict between individual selfishness and collective well-being does not admit of any rational solution.

If the economist acknowledges no natural limits to growth, the biologist is obsessed only with such limits. What the two have in common is their scepticism of purposive action for the common good: in the one case it is not needed as the market shall take care of all our problems; in the other case it is probably too late.

These two traditions of social thought serve us here only as a point of departure. Our concern rather is with the vast middle ground they have left uncolonized, into which step varieties of environmentalism which do not view humans as being essentially selfish. Compared to the dominant schools in economics and biology, most environmentalists take a more subtle view of the human prospect. They acknowledge that 'Spaceship Earth' does set certain limits to economic expansion, but argue that it is only at certain times and in certain places that environmental degradation is of sufficient magnitude to threaten the future of a society. However, like neo-classical economics and Malthusian biology, ecological consciousness might also be viewed as a distinctive response to the growth of industrial society. Within the environmental movement, there have been three generic responses to industrialisation. The three environmental philosophies of our time are *agrarianism*, *wilderness thinking*, and *scientific industrialism*, respectively. At one level, of course, these are simply three perspectives on the human–nature relationship. Scientific industrialism and wilderness thinking are the two old antagonists parading under new names: one advocating the conquest of nature, the other human submission to natural processes. Agrarianism is nothing but the search for a golden mean of stewardship and sustainable use.[7] However, each of these perspectives on nature also forms part of a larger philosophy of social reconstruction. They all offer distinct theories of history which outline where society is coming from, where it seems to be heading, and in what direction it should go. These philosophies are all utopian, for their critique of the existing social order has as its point of reference an idealised society free of all blemish.

Agrarianism

The grain-based civilisations of Europe and Asia were the apogee of human history for agrarianism. The agrarian views with disfavour both tribal

80

society – where life is believed to be nasty, brutish and short – and industrial society, where humans have wholly succumbed to the pursuit of wealth. His ecological and social ideal is peasant society, where technology is on the human scale and the bonds of community are strong. The political programme of agrarianism, therefore, is to resist the onslaught of commercialism and industrialism where they have not yet made inroads, and where they have, to turn one's back resolutely on modern society and go 'back to the land'.

As a social response to industrialisation, agrarianism has usually invoked the traditions of a society staring defeat in the face. In his great book on the making of the modern world, Barington Moore, Jr., rather cynically remarked that the peasant rebellions of early modern Europe represented the 'dying wail of a class over whom the wave of progress is about to roll'.[8] The memories of these peasant movements, however, were kept alive by a galaxy of poets and writers whose moral, and indeed ecological, indictment of industrial capitalism has been brilliantly analysed, in the English case, by Raymond Williams.[9] But even as the industrial economy of the North is transforming itself into a post-industrial one, in other parts of the world agrarianism continues to exercise a compelling appeal.

Later in this chapter, I will refer to the heritage of the best known American agrarian, Thomas Jefferson, while a later chapter in this book is devoted exclusively to the best known Indian agrarian, Mahatma Gandhi. For a succinct statement of the agrarian ideal, we might turn to Gandhi's close contemporary, the poet and novelist Rabindranath Tagore, the first Asian to win the Nobel Prize for literature. In an arresting analogy, Tagore observes that

Villages are like women. In their keeping is the cradle of the race. They are nearer to nature than towns, and in closer touch with the fountain of life. They possess a natural power of healing. It is the function of the village, like that of women, to provide people with their elementary needs, with food and joy, with the simple poetry of life and with those ceremonies of beauty which the village spontaneously produces and in which she finds delight. But when constant strain is put upon her, when her resources are excessively exploited, she becomes dull and uncreative. From her time-honoured position of the wedded wife, she then descends to that of a maid-servant. The city, in its intense egotism and pride, remains unconscious of the hurt it inflicts on the very source of its life, health and joy.

In medieval civilisation, or what Tagore calls the 'natural state', the 'village and the town have harmonious interactions. From the one flow food and health and fellow being. From the other return gifts of wealth, knowledge and energy.' But this balance is rudely shattered by the growth of industrialisation. Now, 'greed has struck at the relationship of mutuality between town and village.' For 'modern cities feed upon the social organism that runs through the village. They appropriate the life stuff of the community and slough off a huge amount of dead matter, while making a lurid counterfeit of prosperity.' Indeed, cities today 'represent energy and materials concentrated for the satisfaction of that bloated appetite which is the characteristic symptom of modern civilisation.'[10]

Wilderness Thinking

This environmental philosophy is firmly implanted in American soil. There is a widespread agreement within the wilderness movement on the need to protect fully and if possible expand the system of national parks; there is, however, no such consensus on a philosophy of social reconstruction based on the wilderness ethic. One school, among whose influential spokesmen is Roderick Nash, views nature appreciation as an indication of a culture's maturity. Here, wilderness is not counterposed to civilisation, but is in fact the surest indicator of the flowering of civilisation. In this perspective, automobiles and national parks, free-flowing rivers and power plants, universities and trails, can and must coexist.

Of more interest to the present discussion is the radical strand in wilderness thinking, which we may call pre-agrarianism or primitivism. This believes that an original state of human harmony with nature on the North American continent was rudely shattered by the white man: B.C. may as well stand for 'Before Columbus'. The founder of the Wilderness Society, Robert Marshall, claimed that before the arrival of Columbus the whole continent was a wilderness, and 'over billions of acres the aboriginal wanderers still spun out their peripatetic careers, the wild animals still browsed in unmolested meadows and the forests still grew and moldered and grew again precisely as they had done for interminable centuries'.[11] For the primitivist, the victory of agriculture signals a precipitous fall in ecological wisdom, as with the discovery of iron human history entered a downward spiral. Industrialism only further accentuates the separation of humans from nature, a partial brake on its excesses being provided, belatedly and ineffectively, by the movement to set aside areas of forest and wilderness as national parks.

The primitivist theory of history has inspired truly radical proposals – for example, the reduction of the human population of the world by 90 per cent to allow the recovery of wilderness areas and of species threatened with extinction. In pursuance of the principle of biocentric equality they hold dear, so-called deep ecologists,[12] perhaps the leading edge of primitivism, turn their back on both agricultural and industrial society. Only hunting and gathering, they believe, can satisfy essential human needs without sacrificing the rights of non-human species. A return to pagan, pre-Christian origins is therefore a precondition for restoring the harmony in nature. This return to origins would allow even white society to recover its humanity. To quote the Native American thinker Vine Deloria, Jr., 'the white man must drop his dollar-chasing civilisation and return to a simple, tribal, game-hunting, berry-hunting life if he is to survive. He must quickly adopt not only the contemporary Indian worldview but the ancient Indian worldview to survive.'[13]

The primitivist theory of history is in essence a theory of *de–development*, a steady fall from the natural high of hunter–gatherer society. For primitive humans were literally reared in the womb of nature. Exposed from birth to the sights, smells and sounds of the natural world, hunter–gatherers were at one with their surroundings, feeling themselves to be the 'guests rather than masters' of nature. This unity was disrupted by civilisation, which in the words of the California ecologist Paul Shepard 'increased the separation between the individual and the natural world as it did the child from the mother . . . '. Significantly, agriculture rather than industry is held to be the original culprit, fostering a duality of humans and nature in which 'wild things are enemies of the tame; the wild other is not the context but the opponent of "my" domain'.[14]

Scientific Industrialism

What distinguishes this philosophy is that of the three environmental philosophies considered in this chapter, it alone looks ahead. Here human salvation lies in the future, not in the return to an agrarian or pre-agrarian past. The task is to tame industrialism and temper its excesses, not to turn one's back on it. As a philosophy of *resource use* – the term abhorrent to agrarian and primitivist alike – scientific industrialism seeks to replace the anarchy of the market with a rational programme of state control. Industrial capitalism may be ecologically wasteful, but scientific expertise, if backed by legislation and an activist state, can assure the sustained yield of natural resources so crucial for human welfare.

Like agrarianism and wilderness thinking, scientific industrialism too has a distinctive three-stage interpretation of human history. Two remarks of the 19th-century geologist and explorer John Wesley Powell pithily summarise how the scientific conservationist views the past, which he abhors, and the present, which he seeks to direct and control. Powell writes that

In savagery, the powers of nature are feared as evil demons; in barbarism, the powers of nature are worshipped as gods; in civilization, the powers of nature are apprenticed servants.

And again, that

In savagery, the beasts are gods; in barbarism, the gods are men; in civilization, men are as gods, knowing good from evil.[15]

The victory of good over evil, men over gods, rational control over nature versus blind submission to it, was not, however, always quick or painless. The long and sometimes lonely struggle of the scientific industrialist was well described by the pioneering German–American forester Bernhard Fernow. In an essay on the 'battle of the forest' (and the forester) published in 1894, Fernow starts – in an interesting twist to primitivist narratives – with the process of ecological succession. The process of glaciation is followed by the formation of the soil, the gradual emergence of plants and then trees, culminating at last in what we know as the virgin forest. This painfully slow and by no means unidirectional process is the 'unwritten history of the battle of the forest', a 'product of long struggles extending over centuries, nay thousands of years'. But the hurdles of nature are nothing compared to the threats posed by humans. For pre-industrial society in general, but especially the farmers and herdsmen, take 'sides against the forest' – through 'willful or careless destruction' they have 'wasted the work of nature through thousands of years by the foolish destruction of the forest cover'. They have 'accomplished in many localities utter ruin . . . and turned them back into inhospitable deserts as they first were before the struggle of the forest had made them inhabitable.' Scientific forestry inaugurates a more hopeful stage, but the habits of many lifetimes die hard. Fernow leaves us with a picture of the forester heroically battling the uneducated citizen, with the result very much in the balance: 'The battle of the forest in this country is now being fought by man, the unintelligent and greedy carrying on a war of extermination, the intelligent and provident trying to defend the forest cover.'[16]

The world over, scientific industrialists have seen themselves as bringing civilisation to barbarians, science to the superstitious, progress and well-being to the half-starved and half-clothed – all by the simple expedient of substituting, for earlier and allegedly wasteful economic methods, the new sciences of forestry and water management. A British colonialist with many years of experience in Asia once remarked that

Man himself modifies nature, and, before he has evolved a scientific civilisation, nearly always injuriously; and it is not simply because the temperature of Northern Europe is milder than that of Central Asia and Southern Europe that it is greener than these regions, but because it has not been so long subjected to the corroding influences of the presence of barbarous and semi-civilised humanity. Under these influences India was being gradually reduced, during the decline of the [Mughal]

84

Empire, to the blighted condition of Central Asia, and was only saved from this impending doom by the British conquest. Similarly, were extended irrigation and scientific forestry introduced into Khiva, Bokhara and Samarcand, their pristine and verdure would gradually be restored to them; and it would at last be found that in the apparently purposeless subjugation of these countries Russia had fulfilled her highest destiny.[17]

Women in Society

Although our three philosophies of history do not always address themselves to the place of women in society, I shall end this section with some speculations on the subject. The ideal role of women in the life of the village is vividly illustrated in the extracts from Tagore. In her 'time-honoured position of the wedded wife' she keeps the family and household going, and in the community at large women are the symbol of continuity, the conduit by which traditions are passed on from one generation to another. From one point of view, the role of women is here stable, secure and well defined; from another point of view, severely circumscribed. Primitivists tend to believe the latter, suggesting that it is only among hunter–gatherers that we find a relative equality of the sexes; this is ascribed to the absence of private property in land and to the fact that women, as the primary gatherers of food, play a far more important role in economic life. Respect for women in primitive society, it is further argued, goes hand in hand with the 'feminine principle' in nature. Finally, scientific industrialists would argue that modern science enormously expands opportunities for both men and women. Only in modern society are women not barred from professional careers, while city life frees them from the petty tyrannies and superstitions of the village.

ENVIRONMENTAL PHILOSOPHIES IN TWO CULTURES

Thus far, I have sketched the broad outlines of three environmental philosophies of history (a graphic summary is also provided in Figure 4.1). How are these contending philosophies articulated in practice? I now examine their articulation in two different contexts, India and the United States. Not only are these the two cultures I know best, but they also make a fascinating study in contrast. They are both large and complex democracies, but with strikingly different religious traditions and economic systems. One is the most powerful country in the industrial world, now moving towards a post-industrial economy and 'post-material' society; the

Figure 4.1

Environmental Philosophies: A Graphic Summary

AGRARIANISM

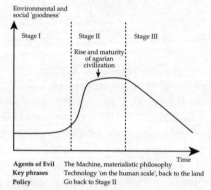

Agents of Evil	The Machine, materialistic philosophy
Key phrases	Technology 'on the human scale', back to the land
Policy	Go back to Stage II

PRIMITIVISM

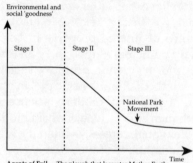

Agents of Evil	The plough that lacerates Mother Earth: the white man
Key phrases	Pristine /primordial/virgin/unspoilt nature, the equality of sexes and of all species
Policy	Go to back to Stage I (eliminate 90% of the human population if necessary?)

SCIENTIFIC INDUSTRIALISM

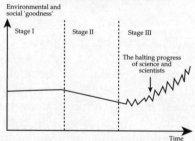

Agents of Evil	Illiterate, prescientific humans (especially peasants)
Key phrases	Efficiency, sustained yield, science, expertise
Policy	Leave it to the experts

other is a populous and largely agricultural country seeking desperately to industrialise as rapidly as possible.

What stands out, in any such comparison, is that while the dominant environmental philosophy in India is agrarianism, in the United States it is wilderness thinking. As Chapter 1 documents, the Indian environmental movement bases itself on the traditions of an agrarian culture while invoking a more recent history of peasant movements against British colonialism, led by Mahatma Gandhi. Four decades after Indian Independence, agrarianism is enjoying a remarkable revival, as economic planning for industrialisation has devastated the country's natural endowment without making a significant dent in the problem of poverty. The rhetoric of the environmental movement is greatly influenced by Gandhi's anti-industrial philosophy, and its more vocal sections call for a return to the Mahatma's vision of a village-centred economic order.

Of course, agrarianism has also been a powerful current in American cultural and political history. Its most famous statement, Thomas Jefferson's *Notes on Virginia*, is, like Mahatma Gandhi's pamphlet *Hind Swaraj* (Indian home rule), in the main a manifesto for social reconstruction based on the susbsistence farm. There are, however, two important ways in which American agrarianism differs from its Indian counterpart. While Gandhi, and Gandhism, invokes the spirit of community believed to be intrinsic to traditional peasant culture, the yeoman farmer of Jefferson's imagination is a figure of sturdy independence. In the Jeffersonian vision private proprietorship of land is a *sine qua non* of the individualist spirit, which is in turn the bedrock of democracy. And while Gandhian agrarianism is acutely aware of ecological limits (as elaborated in Chapter 8), the American version has as its premise the ecological abundance of a sparsely settled continent.

Their occupation of a seemingly endless continent was, indeed, a source of great comfort to early American agrarians like Jefferson and St. Crevecouer. In Europe, limitations of space may have forced the working poor to accept the miseries of city life, but on the new continent, virgin land, the precondition for a society of independent yeoman farmers, 'had been given to Americans in extreme, almost unbelievable abundance'.[18] This optimism was shared by the most famous of Jefferson's 20th-century followers, the co-signatories of the Nashville manifesto *I'll Take My Stand*. The most eloquent of these Southern agrarians, the poet John Crowe Ransom, claimed that the unemployment problem of the 1930s was a direct consequence of industrialisation and the shift of population from the country to the city. Advocating the return of the unemployed to the land, Ransom observed: 'So far as America is concerned, there always was land enough for [the farmer] to till; there was no such problem as overpopulation' – and even as he wrote, 'the land is still with us, as patient and nearly as capable as ever'.[19]

In our own time, there have been some interesting attempts to recast the Jeffersonian ideal along ecological lines, for example by Wendell Berry.[20] This is, however, a marginal strand in the American environmental movement, whose core is undoubtedly the wilderness ethic.[21] In fact, wilderness lovers are in the main quite hostile to agriculture. Evidently, going back to nature does not imply going back to the land. That sage among contemporary ecologists, Raymond Dasmann, once confessed that for many years he had been interested only in the 'extremes of land use, the city and the wilderness'. The country in between – farm, rangeland, pasture, shrub jungle – had been to him 'just space to be passed through as quickly as possible'.[22]

What Dasmann ignored his compatriots have more actively deplored over the years. One recalls John Muir's characterization of sheep as 'hoofed locusts'[23] and this prejudice against farming and farm animals is very widespread indeed. Coming from the cities, lovers of the wilderness condescend to the farmer and 'take for granted the dependence of both city and country on the agricultural base'.[24] Some wilderness thinkers, themselves urbane and cosmopolitan, deplore the farmer for his uncouth ways, like the early editor of *Harper's Magazine* who wrote that 'if a man perspires largely in a cornfield on a dusty day, and washes hastily in a horsetrough, and eats in shirt-sleeves that date their cleanliness three days back, and loves fat pork and cabbage neat, he will not prove the Arcadian companion at dinner'.[25] Others fear the farmer for his impact on 'virgin' nature. Muir, for instance, wrote of a farmer he knew that he had

a call to plow, and woe to the daisy sod or ozalea thicket that falls under the savage redemption of his keen steel shares. Not content with the so-called subjugation of every terrestrial bog, rock, and moorland, he would fain discover some method of reclamation applicable to the oceans and the sky, that in due calendar time they might be bought to bud and blossom as the rose ... Wildness charms not my friend ... and whatsoever may be the character of his heaven, his earth seems only a chaos of agricultural possibilities calling for grubbing-hoes and manners ...[26]

Nor is this hostility restricted to the American farmer and shepherd. Touring Africa in 1957, one prominent member of the Sierra Club strongly attacked the Masai for grazing cattle in African wildlife sancturies. He held the Masai to be illustrative of a larger trend, wherein 'increasing population and increasing land use', rather than industrial exploitation, constituted the main threat to the world's wilderness areas. The Masai and 'their herds of economically worthless cattle', he said, 'have already overgrazed and laid waste too much of the 23,000 square miles of Tanganyika they control, and as they move into the Serengeti, they bring the desert with them, and the wilderness and wildlife must bow before their herds'.[27] Even more plaintive are the wilderness biologists working in the tropics, one of whom complained: 'Where will be taxonomists and evolutionists when cows and corn dominate this earth?'[28]

Here again, India provides an illuminating contrast. While it has an even greater diversity of ecological regimes than the United States, the movement for the protection of wild areas has not enjoyed much popular sanction. Support for the national park movement in India comes mainly from international conservation organisations, and from a class of big game hunters turned preservationists (who include many former Maharajahs). Furthermore, the designation of parks and sanctuaries has been heavily biased towards the preservation of large mammals such as the tiger, the rhinoceros and the elephant – that is, what the biologist Michael Soule terms 'metacharismatic megavertebrates'. The establishment of huge sanctuaries for their protection has led to the uprooting of villages situated within their boundaries, while the protected species themselves are often a threat to the lives and livelihood of human communities living adjacent to wilderness areas. The management of national parks is, therefore, a subject of quite some controversy, though it is fair to say that within the environmental movement, the burden of opinion is ranged against wildlife management – as it is presently practiced – for its neglect of the interests of peasants and tribals.[29]

We have therefore a curious symmetry: the dominant environmental tradition in the United States, wilderness thinking, is hostile to agriculture, whereas the dominant tradition in India, agrarianism, is not favourably disposed to lovers of the wild. What then of the third of our philosophies, scientific industrialism? This is an environmental tradition that is truly transcultural, moving itself with effortless ease across the world. In India and the United States, as indeed in China and Brazil, Germany or Indonesia, forestry experts and irrigation engineers uphold an identical vision of large-scale, centralised and expert-controlled resource management.[30]

Associated with the state and with state power, scientific industrialism has come to be the common enemy of the popular environmental movement in the North and in the South. In the United States, free-flowing rivers and natural forests are cherished by environmentalists for their beauty and ecological value, but coveted by resource managers for the millions of cubic feet or kilowatt-hours they might yield. This is the classic dilemma, preservationism versus utilitarianism, that underlies a good part of American environmental history and environmental conflict. In India, however, conflicts over water and forests more sharply highlight the question of *alternative uses* – subsistence versus commerce, local versus national, peasants versus industry. Thus large dams and eucalyptus plantations, to cite but two examples of scientific conservation at work, are criticised both for their diversion of resources from centre to periphery and for the trail of environmental destruction they leave in their wake.

These conflicts are vividly represented in the symbols and slogans of the environmental movement. A focal point of the American movement has been the struggle – over men, minds and materials – between scientific industrialism and wilderness thinking, while in India scientific industrialism opposes agrarianism. Not surprisingly, scientific conservationists loom large in the demonology of environmentalists everywhere. If the great icon of the American environmentalism is John Muir, himself a product of the 'university of the wilderness', its demon is indisputably Gifford Pinchot, the founder of the United States Forest Service. Likewise, Indian environmentalists like to contrast Mahatma Gandhi, the prophet of a village-centred economic order, and Jawaharlal Nehru, the long-serving Prime Minister who initiated and guided the programmes of industrial development that have devastated the countryside and the human communities who live there.

All social movements need their symbols of good and evil, their icons and their demons. These representations of John Muir and Gifford Pinchot, Mahatma Gandhi and Jawaharlal Nehru, are indicative only of the ferocity of the debate between the three great environmental philosophies of our time. It is ironic that scattered throughout Muir's writings are warm references to Pinchot's programmes for the takeover and rational management of the American forests. After having read and heard a great deal about the Muir-Pinchot divide, I visited the Muir woods outside San Francisco, to find a splendid redwood named – the Gifford Pinchot Tree! And Nehru was, after all, a close associate and political colleague of Gandhi over many decades – indeed, his chosen political heir, the man to whom the Mahatma left India 'in safe hands'.

SOCIAL ECOLOGY OR ECOLOGICAL SOCIALISM?

The three environmental visions outlined in this chapter are all *utopias* in the quite specific sense that none can be realised in full. The claims of scientific industrialism notwithstanding, there are ecological limits to the global spread of the consumer society; despite the deep ecologist's deepest yearnings, a return to our hunter–gatherer origins is quite out of the question; and in much of the Third World, the world of stable subsistence farming so beloved of the agrarians is rapidly giving way to a more thrusting, individualistic and market-oriented way of life.

Perhaps the debate between proponents of these three philosophies has in fact run its course. I like to believe that we are on the threshold of a new phase in the development of environmental ethics, with a fresh synthesis coming to take the place of these three contending philosophies. This synthesis would take from primitivism the idea of *diversity*, from peasant cultures the ideal of *sustainability*, and from modern society in general, rather than from scientific conservation in particular, the value of *equity*. One of the remarkable turn abouts in our time has been the retreat from the monocultural view of society and nature – the remaking of the world in the image of Europe – and for this new appreciation of diversity, biological as well as cultural, we have largely to thank wilderness thinking and the anthropologists and activists working in defence of indigenous people. Likewise, the ideal of sustainability provides a powerful antidote to another core ideal of industrial society – that of economic growth and consumption without limit – and it is quite easy to trace this idea to peasant cultures, which used land and nature wisely, well, and with a view to the long term. Finally, while scientific industrialism may have ended up as a movement of experts, it was fired, in the first instance, by a passion for equality and democracy, by the urge to bend science, and nature, to make the fruits of economic growth widely accessible.[31] In the modern world, and nowhere else, have challenges to principles of social hierarchy gained moral currency. In pre-modern times, uprisings of peasants, slaves, women and workers had always to contend with a dominant ideology – monarchism, absolutism, theocracy, patriarchy, or caste – that legitimated, justified and strictly enforced inequalities of race and sex, caste, class and religion. Only since the French Revolution have social movements been able to draw sustenance from the wider acceptability of equity as a value.

Diversity, sustainability and equity: these are the building blocks of the environmental ethic in the making. We could call this emerging philosophy *social ecology*, as does the anachist and life-long environmentalist Murray Bookchin, though some would prefer to call it *ecological socialism*. Even more than a name – and despite my jesting about the iconography and demonology of environmentalism – this philosophy needs a patron saint, or preferably, saints. Three likely candidates, from three different parts of the world, are duly celebrated in Part 2 of this book.

Chapter 5

Radical American Environmentalism and Wilderness Preservation: A Third World Critique

Even God dare not appear to the poor man except in the form of bread.

(Mahatma Gandhi)

INTRODUCTION

The respected radical journalist Kirkpatrick Sale has celebrated 'the passion of a new and growing movement that has become disenchanted with the environmental establishment and has in recent years mounted a serious and sweeping attack on it – style, substance, systems, sensibilities and all.'[1] The vision of those whom Sale calls the 'New Ecologists' – and what I refer to in this chapter as deep ecology – is a compelling one. Decrying the narrowly economic goals of mainstream environmentalism, this new movement aims at nothing less than a philosophical and cultural revolution in human attitudes towards nature. In contrast to the conventional lobbying efforts of environmental professionals based in Washington, it proposes a militant defence of 'Mother Earth', an unflinching opposition to human attacks on undisturbed wilderness. With their goals ranging from the spiritual to the political, the adherents of deep ecology span a wide spectrum of the American environmental movement. As Sale correctly notes, this emerging strand has in a matter of a few years made its presence felt in a number of fields: from academic philosophy, as in the journal *Environmental Ethics*, to popular environmentalism, for example, the group Earth First!.

In this chapter I develop a critique of deep ecology from the perspective of a sympathetic outsider. My treatment of deep ecology is primarily historical and sociological in nature, rather than philosophical. Specifically, I examine the cultural rootedness of a philosophy that likes to present itself in universalistic terms. I make two main arguments: first, that deep ecology is uniquely American, and despite superficial similarities in rhetorical style, the social and political goals of radical environmentalism in other cultural contexts (e.g. Germany and India) are quite different; second, that the social consequences of putting deep ecology into practice on a worldwide basis (what its practitioners are aiming for) are very grave indeed.

THE TENETS OF DEEP ECOLOGY

While I am aware that the term *deep ecology* was coined by the Norwegian philosopher Arne Naess, this chapter refers specifically to the American variant.[2] Adherents of the deep ecological perspective in the United States, while arguing intensely among themselves over its political and philosophical implications, share some fundamental premises about human–nature interactions. As I see it, the defining characteristics of deep ecology are fourfold.

First, deep ecology argues that the environmental movement must shift from an anthropocentric to a biocentric perspective. In many respects, an acceptance of the primacy of this distinction constitutes the litmus test of deep ecology. A considerable effort is expended by deep ecologists in showing that the dominant motif in Western philosophy has been anthropocentric (i.e. the belief that man and his works are the centre of the universe), and conversely in identifying those lonely thinkers (Leopold, Thoreau, Muir, Aldous Huxley, Santayana, etc.) who, in assigning man a more humble place in the natural order, anticipated deep ecological thinking. In the political realm, meanwhile, establishment environmentalism (shallow ecology) is chided for casting its arguments in human-centred terms. Preserving nature, the deep ecologists say, has an intrinsic worth quite apart from any benefits preservation may convey to future human generations. The anthropocentric/biocentric distinction is accepted as axiomatic by deep ecologists, it structures their discourse, and much of the present discussion remains mired within it.

The second characteristic of deep ecology is its focus on the preservation of unspoilt wilderness – and the restoration of degraded areas to a more pristine condition – to the relative, and sometimes absolute, neglect of other issues on the environmental agenda. I later identify the cultural roots and portentous consequences of this obsession with wilderness. For the moment, let me indicate three distinct sources from which it springs. Historically, it represents a playing out of the preservationist (read radical) and utilitarian (read reformist) dichotomy that has plagued American environmentalism since the turn of the century.

93

Morally, it is an imperative that follows from the biocentric perspective; other species of plants and animals, and nature itself, have an intrinsic right to exist. And finally, the preservation of wilderness also turns on a scientific argument, namely the value of biological diversity in stabilising ecological regimes and in retaining a gene pool for future generations. Truly radical policy proposals have been put forward by deep ecologists on the basis of these arguments. The influential poet Gary Snyder, for example, would like to see a 90 per cent reduction in human populations to allow a restoration of pristine environments, while others have argued forcefully that a large portion of the globe must be immediately cordoned off from human beings.[3]

Third, there is a widespread invocation of Eastern spiritual traditions as forerunners of deep ecology. Deep ecology, it is suggested, was practiced both by major religious traditions and at a more popular level by 'primal' peoples in non-Western settings. This complements the search for an authentic lineage in Western thought. At one level, the task is to recover those dissenting voices within the Judeo–Christian tradition; at another, to suggest that religious traditions in other cultures are, in contrast, dominantly if not exclusively 'biocentric' in their orientation. This coupling of (ancient) Eastern and (modern) ecological wisdom seemingly helps to consolidate the claim that deep ecology is a philosophy of universal significance.

Fourth, deep ecologists, whatever their internal differences, share the belief that they are the 'leading edge' of the environmental movement. As the polarity of the shallow/deep and anthropocentric/biocentric distinctions makes clear, they see themselves as the spiritual, philosophical and political vanguard of American and world environmentalism.

TOWARDS A CRITIQUE

Although I analyse each of these tenets independently, it is important to recognise, as deep ecologists are fond of remarking in reference to nature, the interconnectedness and unity of these individual themes.

Shift to a Biocentic Perspective

Insofar as it has begun to act as a check on man's arrogance and ecological hubris, the transition from an anthropocentric (human-centred) to a biocentric (humans as only one element in the ecosystem) view in both religious and scientific traditions is only to be welcomed.[4] What is unacceptable are the radical conclusions drawn by deep ecology, in particular, that intervention in nature should be guided primarily by the need to preserve biotic integrity rather than by the needs of humans. The latter for deep ecologists is anthropocentric, the former biocentric. This dichotomy is, however, of very little use in understanding the dynamics of environmental degradation. The two fundamental ecological problems facing the globe are (1) overconsumption by the industrialised world and by urban elites in the Third World and (2) growing militarisation, both in a short-term sense (i.e., ongoing regional wars) and in a long-term sense (i.e. the arms race and the prospect of nuclear annihilation). Neither of these problems has any tangible connection to the anthropocentric/biocentric distinction. Indeed, the agents of these processes would barely comprehend this philosophical dichotomy. The proximate causes of the ecologically wasteful characteristics of industrial society and of militarisation are far more mundane: at an aggregate level, the dialectic of economic and political structures, and at a microlevel, the lifestyle choices of individuals. These causes cannot be reduced, whatever the level of analysis, to a deeper anthropocentric attitude toward nature; on the contrary, by constituting a grave threat to human survival, the ecological degradation they cause does not even serve the best interests of human beings. If my identification of the major dangers to the integrity of the natural world is correct, invoking the bogey of anthropocentrism is at best irrelevant and at worst a dangerous obfuscation.

Focus on the Preservation of Wilderness

If the above dichotomy is irrelevant, the emphasis on wilderness is positively harmful when applied to the Third World. If in the United States the preservationist/utilitarian division is seen as mirroring the conflict between the 'people' and the 'interests', in countries such as India the situation is very nearly the reverse. Because India is a long-settled and densely populated country in which agrarian populations have a finely balanced relationship with nature, the setting aside of wilderness areas has resulted in a direct transfer of resources from the poor to the rich. Thus Project Tiger, a network of parks hailed by the international community as an outstanding success, puts the interests of the tiger ahead of those of poor peasants living in and around the reserve. The designation of tiger reserves was made possible only by the physical displacement of existing villages and their inhabitants; their management requires the continuing exclusion of peasants and livestock. The initial impetus for setting up parks for tigers and other mammals such as the rhinoceros and elephant came from two social groups: (1) a class of ex-hunters turned conservationists belonging mostly to the declining Indian feudal élite, and (2), representatives of international agencies, such as the World Wildlife Fund (WWF) and the International Union for the Conservation of Nature and Natural Resources

(IUCN), seeking to transplant the American system of national parks on to Indian soil. In no case have the needs of the local population been taken into account, and as in many parts of Africa, the designated wildlands are managed primarily for the benefit of rich tourists. Until very recently, wildlands preservation has been identified with environmentalism by the state and the conservation élite; in consequence, environmental problems that impinge far more directly on the lives of the poor (e.g. fuel, fodder, water shortages, soil erosion, and air and water pollution) have not been adequately addressed.[5]

Deep ecology provides, perhaps unwittingly, a justification for the continuation of such narrow and inequitable conservation practices under a newly acquired radical guise. Increasingly, the international conservation elite is using the philosophical, moral and scientific arguments used by deep ecologists in advancing their wilderness crusade. A striking but by no means atypical example is the recent plea by a prominent American biologist for the takeover of large portions of the globe by him and his scientific colleagues. Writing in a prestigious scientific forum, the *Annual Review of Ecology and Systematics*, Daniel Janzen argues that only biologists have the competence to decide how the tropical landscape should be used. As 'the representatives of the natural world', biologists are 'in charge of the future of tropical ecology', and only they have the expertise and mandate to 'determine whether the tropical agroscape is to be populated only by humans, their mutualists, commensals, and parasites, or whether it will also contain some islands of the greater nature – the nature that spawned humans, yet has been vanquished by them.' Janzen exhorts his colleagues to advance their territorial claims on the tropical world more forcefully, warning that the very existence of these areas is at stake: 'if biologists want a tropics in which to biologise, they are going to have to buy it with care, energy, effort, strategy, tactics, time, and cash'.[6]

This frankly imperialist manifesto highlights the multiple dangers of the preoccupation with wilderness preservation that is characteristic of deep ecology. As I have suggested, it seriously compounds the neglect by the American movement of far more pressing environmental problems in the Third World. But perhaps more importantly, and in a more insidious fashion, it also provides an impetus to the imperialist yearning of Western biologists and their financial sponsors, organisations such as the WWF and IUCN. The wholesale transfer of a movement culturally rooted in American conservation history can only result in the social uprooting of human populations in other parts of the globe.

Eastern Spiritual Traditions

I come now to the persistent invocation of Eastern philosophies as antecedent in time but convergent in their structure with deep ecology. Complex and internally differentiated religious traditions – Hinduism, Buddhismm and Taoism – are lumped together as holding a view of nature believed to be quintessentially biocentric. Individual philosophers such as the Taoist Lao Tzu are identified as being forerunners of deep ecology. Even an intensely political, pragmatic, and Christian-influenced thinker such as Gandhi has been accorded a wholly undeserved place in the pantheon of deep ecology. Thus the Zen teacher Robert Aitken Roshi makes the strange claim that Gandhi's thought was not human-centred and that he practiced an embryonic form of deep ecology which is 'traditionally Eastern and is found with differing emphasis in Hinduism, Taoism and in Theravada and Mahayana Buddhism'.[7] Moving away from the realm of high philosophy and scriptural religion, deep ecologists make the further claim that at the level of material and spiritual practice 'primal' peoples subordinated themselves to the integrity of the biotic universe they inhabited.

I have indicated that this appropriation of Eastern traditions is in part dictated by the need to construct an authentic lineage and in part a desire to present deep ecology as a universalistic philosophy. Indeed, in his substantial yet quixotic biography of John Muir, Michael Cohen goes so far as to suggest that Muir was the 'Taoist of the [American] West'.[8] This reading of Eastern traditions is selective and does not bother to differentiate between alternative (and changing) religious and cultural traditions; as it stands, it does considerable violence to the historical record. Throughout most recorded history the characteristic form of human activity in the 'East' has been a finely tuned but none the less conscious and dynamic manipulation of nature. Although mystics such as Lao Tzu did reflect on the spiritual essence of human relations with nature, it must be recognised that such ascetics and their reflections were supported by a society of cultivators whose relationship with nature was a far more *active* one. Many agricultural communities do have a sophisticated knowledge of the natural environment that may equal (and sometimes surpass) codified 'scientific' knowledge, yet the elaboration of such traditional ecological knowledge – in both material and spiritual contexts – can hardly be said to rest on a mystical affinity with nature of a deep ecological kind. Nor is such knowledge infallible; as the archaeological records powerfully suggest, modern Western man has no monopoly on ecological disasters.

In a brilliant article, the Chicago historian Ronald Inden points out that this romantic and essentially positive view of the East is a mirror image of the scientific and essentially pejorative view normally held by Western scholars of the Orient. In either case, the East constitutes the Other, a body wholly separate and alien from the West; it is defined by a uniquely spiritual and non-rational 'essence', even if this essence is valorised quite differently by the two schools. Eastern man exhibits a spiritual dependence with respect to nature – on the one hand, this is symptomatic of his pre-scientific and backward self, on the other, of his ecological wisdom and deep ecological consciousness. Both views are monolithic, simplistic, and have the characteristic effect – intended in one case, perhaps unintended in the other – of denying agency and reason to the East and making it the privileged orbit of Western thinkers.

The two apparently opposed perspectives have then a common underlying structure of discourse in which the East merely serves as a vehicle for Western projections. Varying images of the East are raw material for political and cultural battles being played out in the West; they tell us far more about the Western commentator and his desires than about the 'East'. Inden's remarks apply not merely to Western scholarship on India, but to Orientalist constructions of China and Japan as well:

Although these two views appear to be strongly opposed, they often combine together. Both have a similar interest in sustaining the Otherness of India. The holders of the dominant view, best exemplified in the past in imperial administrative discourse (and today probably by that of 'development economics'), would place a traditional, superstition-ridden India in a position of perpetual tutelage to a modern, rational West. The adherents of the romantic view, best exemplified academically in the discourses of Christian liberalism and analytic psychology, concede the realm of the public and impersonal to the positivist. Taking their succour not from governments and big business, but from a plethora of religious foundations and self-help institutes, and from allies in the 'conciousness industry', not to mention the important industry of tourism, the romantics insist that India embodies a private realm of the imagination and the religious which modern, western man lacks but needs. They, therefore, like the positivists, but for just the opposite reason, have a vested interest in seeing that the Orientalist view of India as 'spiritual', 'mysterious' and 'exotic' is perpetuated.[9]

The Radicalism of Deep Ecology

How radical, finally, are the deep ecologists? Notwithstanding their self-image and strident rhetoric (in which the label 'shallow ecology' has an opprobrium similar to that reserved for 'social democratic' by Marxist–Leninists), even within the American context their radicalism is limited and it manifests itself quite differently elsewhere.

To my mind, deep ecology is best viewed as a radical trend within the wilderness preservation movement. Although advancing philosophical rather than aesthetic arguments and encouraging political militancy rather than negotiation, its practical emphasis – that is, preservation of unspoilt nature – is virtually identical. For the mainstream movement, the function of wilderness is to provide a temporary antidote to modern civilisation. As a special institution within an industrialised society, the national park 'provides an opportunity for respite, contrast, contemplation, and affirmation of values for those who live most of their lives in the workaday world'.[10] Indeed, the rapid increase in visits to the national parks in post-war America is a direct consequence of economic expansion. The emergence of a popular interest in wilderness sites, the historian Samuel Hays points out, was 'not a throwback to the primitive, but an integral part of the modern standard of living as people sought to add new "amenity" and "aesthetic" goals and desires to their earlier preoccupation with necessities and conveniences'.[11]

Here, the enjoyment of nature is an integral part of the consumer society. The private automobile, and the life style it has spawned, is in many respects the ultimate ecological villain, and an untouched wilderness the prototype of ecological harmony; yet, for most Americans it is perfectly consistent to drive a thousand miles to spend a holiday in a national park. Americans possess a vast, beautiful and sparsely populated continent and are also able to draw on the natural resources of large portions of the globe by virtue of their economic and political dominance. In consequence, America can simultaneously enjoy the material benefits of an expanding economy and the aesthetic benefits of unspoilt nature. The two poles of 'wilderness' and 'civilisation' mutually coexist in an internally coherent whole, and philosophers of both poles are assigned a prominent place in this culture. Paradoxically as it may seem, it is no accident that Star Wars technology and deep ecology both find their fullest expression in that leading sector of Western civilisation, California.

Deep ecology runs parallel to the consumer society without seriously questioning its ecological and socio-political basis. In its celebration of American wilderness, it also displays an uncomfortable convergence with the prevailing climate of nationalism in the American wilderness movement. For spokesmen such as the historian Roderick Nash, the national park system is America's distinctive cultural contribution to the world, reflective not merely of its economic but also of its philosophical and ecological maturity. In what Henry Luce called the American century, the 'American invention of national parks' must be exported worldwide. Betraying an economic determinism that would make even a Marxist shudder, Nash believes that environmental preservation is a 'full stomach' phenomenon that is confined to the rich, urban, and sophisticated. None the less, he hopes that 'the less developed nations may eventually evolve economically and intellectually to the point where nature preservation is more than a business'.[12]

The error which Nash makes, and which deep ecology in some respects encourages, is to equate environmental protection with the protection of wilderness. This is a distinctively American notion, borne out of a unique social and environmental history. The archetypal concerns of radical environmentalists in other cultural contexts are in fact quite different. The German Greens, for example, have elaborated a devastating critique of industrial society which turns on the acceptance of environmental limits to growth. Pointing to the intimate links between industrialisation, militarisation and conquest, the Greens argue that economic growth in the West has historically rested on the economic and ecological exploitation of the Third World. Rudolf Bahro is characteristically blunt:

The working class here [in the West] is the richest lower class in the world. And if I look at the problem from the point of view of the whole of humanity, not just from that of Europe, then I must say that the metropolitan working class is the worst exploiting class in history ... What made poverty bearable in eighteenth- or nineteenth-century Europe was the prospect of escaping it through exploitation of the periphery. But this is no longer a possibility, and continued industrialism in the Third World will mean poverty for whole generations and hunger for millions.[13]

Here the roots of global ecological problems lie in the disproportionate share of resources consumed by the industrialised countries as a whole and the urban élite in the Third World. Since it is impossible to reproduce an industrial monoculture worldwide, the ecological movement in the West must begin by cleaning up its own act. The Greens advocate the creation of a 'no-growth' economy, to be achieved by scaling down current, and clearly unsustainable, consumption levels.[14] This radical shift in consumption and production patterns requires the creation of alternate economic and political structures – smaller in scale and more amenable to social participation – but it rests equally on a shift in cultural values. The expansionist character of modern Western man will have to give way to an ethic of renunciation and self-limitation, in which spiritual and communal values play an increasing role in sustaining social life. This revolution in cultural values, however, has as its point of departure an understanding of environmental processes quite different from deep ecology.

Many elements of the Green programme find a strong resonance in countries such as India, where a history of Western colonialism and industrial development has benefited only a tiny elite while exacting tremendous social and environmental costs. The ecological battles presently being fought in India have as their epicentre the conflict over nature between the subsistence and largely rural sector and the vastly more powerful commercial–industrial sector. Perhaps the most celebrated of these battles concerns the Chipko movement, a peasant movement against deforestation in the Himalayan foothills. Chipko is only one of several movements that have sharply questioned the non-sustainable demand being placed on the land and vegetative base by urban centres and industry.

These include opposition to large dams by displaced peasants, the conflict between small-scale-artisan fishing and large-scale trawler fishing for export, the countrywide movements against commercial forest operations, and opposition to industrial pollution among downstream agricultural and fishing communities.[15]

Two features distinguish these environmental movements from their Western counterparts. First, for the sections of society most critically affected by environmental degradation – poor and landless peasants, women, and tribals – it is a question of sheer survival, not enhancing the quality of life. Second, and as a consequence, the environmental solutions they articulate strongly involve questions of equity as well as economic and political redistribution. Highlighting these differences, a leading Indian environmentalist stressed that 'environmental protection *per se* is of least concern to most of these groups. Their main concern is about the use of the environment and who should benefit from it.'[16] The Indian movements seek to wrest control of nature away from the state and the industrial sector and place it in the hands of rural communities who live within that environment but are increasingly denied access to it. These communities have far more basic needs, their demands on the environment are far less intense, and they can draw on a reservoir of co-operative social institutions and local ecological knowledge in managing the 'commons' – forests, grasslands and the waters – on a sustainable basis. If colonial and capitalist expansion has both accentuated social inequalities and signaled a precipitous fall in ecological wisdom, an alternative ecology must rest on an alternate society and polity as well.

This brief overview of German and Indian environmentalism has some major implications for deep ecology. Both German and Indian environmental traditions allow for a greater integration of ecological concerns with livelihood and work. They also place a greater emphasis on equity and social justice – both within individual countries and on a global scale – on the grounds that in the absence of social regeneration environmental regeneration has very little chance of succeeding. Finally, and perhaps most significantly, they have escaped the preoccupation with wilderness preservation so characteristic of American cultural and environmental history.[17]

A HOMILY

In 1958, the economist J.K. Galbraith referred to overconsumption as the unasked question of the American conservation movement. There is a marked selectivity, he wrote, 'in the conservationist's approach to materials consumption. If we are concerned about our great appetite for materials, it is plausible to seek to increase the supply, to decrease waste, to make better use of the stocks available, and to develop substitutes. But what of the appetite itself? Surely this is the ultimate source of the problem. If it continues its geometric course, will it not one day have to be restrained? Yet in the literature of the resource problem this is the forbidden question. Over it hangs a nearly total silence.'[18]

The consumer economy and society have expanded tremendously in the four decades since Galbraith wrote these words, yet his criticisms are nearly as valid today. I say 'nearly', for there are some hopeful signs. Within the environmental movement several dispersed groups are working to develop ecologically benign technologies and to encourage less wasteful lifestyles. Moreover, outside the self-defined boundaries of American environmentalism, opposition to the permanent war economy is being carried on by a peace movement that has a distinguished history and impeccable moral and political credentials.

It is precisely these – to my mind, most hopeful – components of the American social scene that are missing from deep ecology. In their widely read book, Bill Devall and George Sessions make no mention of militarisation or the movements for peace, while activists whose practical focus is on developing ecologically responsible life styles (e.g., Wendell Berry) are derided as 'falling short of deep ecological awareness'.[19] A truly radical ecology in the American context ought to work towards a synthesis of the appropriate technology, alternative lifestyles, and peace movements.[20] By making the (largely spurious) anthropocentric/biocentric distinction central to the debate, deep ecologists may have appropriated the moral high ground, but they are at the same time doing a serious disservice to American and global environmentalism.[21]

POSTSCRIPT: DEEP ECOLOGY REVISITED

The preceding pages first appeared as an article in *Environmental Ethics*, volume 11, number 1, 1989. They were written at the end of an extended period of residence in the United States, after several years of research on the origins of Indian environmentalism. That background might explain the puzzlement and anger which, in hindsight, appear to mark the chapter. To my surprise, the article evoked a variety of responses, both pro and con. The veteran Vermont radical Murray Bookchin, himself engaged in a polemic with American deep ecologists, offered a short (three-line) letter of congratulation. A longer (30-page) response came from the Norwegian philosopher Arne Naess, the originator of the term 'deep ecology'. Naess felt bound to assume responsibility for the ideas I had challenged, even though I had distinguished between his emphases and those of his American interpreters. Other correspondents, less known but no less engaged, wrote to praise and to condemn.[22] Over the years, the essay has appeared in some half dozen anthologies, as a voice of the 'Third World', the token and disloyal opposition to the reigning orthodoxies of environmental ethics.[23]

The article having acquired a life of its own, I felt it prudent to include it here without any changes. This postscript allows me to look at the issues anew, to expand and strengthen my case with the aid of a few freshly arrived examples.

Woodrow Wilson once remarked that the United States was the only idealistic nation in the world. It is indeed this idealism which explains the zest, the zeal, the almost unstoppable force with which Americans have sought to impose their vision of the good life on the rest of the world. American economists urge on other nations their brand of energy-intensive, capital-intensive, market-oriented brand of development. American spiritualists, saving souls, guide pagans to one or other of their eccentrically fanatical cults, from Southern Baptism to Moral Rearmament. American advertisers export the ethic of disposable containers – of all sizes, from coffee cups to automobiles – and Santa Barbara.

Of course, other people have had to pay for the fruits of this idealism. The consequences of the forward march of American missionaries include the undermining of political independence, the erosion of cultures and the growth of an ethic of sheer greed. In a dozen parts of the world, those fighting for political, economic or cultural autonomy have collectively raised the question whether the American way of life is not, in fact, the Indian (or Brazilian, or Somalian) way of death.

One kind of US missionary, however, has attracted virtually no critical attention. This is the man who is worried that the rest of the world thinks his country has a dollar sign for a heart. The clothes he wears are also coloured green, but it is the green of the virgin forest. A deeply committed lover of the wild, in his country he has helped put in place a magnificient system of national parks. But he also has money, and will travel. He now wishes to convert other cultures to his gospel, to export the American invention of national parks worldwide.

The essay to which these paragraphs are a coda was one of the first attacks on an imperialism previously reckoned to be largely benign. After all, we are not talking here of the Marines, with their awesome firepower, or even of the World Bank, with its money power and the ability to manipulate developing country governments. These are men – and, more rarely, women – who come preaching the equality of all species, who worship all that is good and beautiful in nature. What could be wrong with them?

I had suggested in my essay that the noble, apparently disinterested motives of conservation biologists and deep ecologists fuelled a territorial ambition – the physical control of wilderness in parts of the world other than their own – that led inevitably to the displacement and harsh treatment of the human communities who dwelt in these forests. Consider in this context a recent assessment of global conservation by Michael Soulé, which complains that the language of policy documents has 'become more humanistic in values and more economic in substance, and correspondingly less naturalistic and ecocentric'. Soulé seems worried that in theory (though certainly not in practice!) some national governments and international conservation organizations (ICOs) now pay more attention to the rights of human communities. Proof of this shift is the fact that 'the top and middle management of most ICOs are economists, lawyers and development specialists, not biologists'. This is a sectarian plaint, a trade union approach to the problem spurred by an alleged 'takeover of the international conservation movement by social scientists, particularly economists'.[24]

Soulé's work, with its talk of conspiracies and takeover bids, manifests the paranoia of a community of scientists which has a huge influence on conservation policy but yet wants to be the sole dictator. A scholar acclaimed by his peers as the 'dean of tropical ecologists' has expressed this ambition more nakedly than most. I have already quoted from a paper published by Daniel Janzen in the *Annual Review of Ecology and Systematics*, which urges his fellow biologists to raise cash so as to buy space and species to study. Let me now quote from a report he wrote on a new National Park in Costa Rica, whose tone and thrust perfectly complements the other, ostensibly 'scientific' essay. 'We have the seed and the biological expertise: we lack control of the terrain', wrote Janzen in 1986. This situation he was able to remedy for himself, by raising enough money to purchase the forest area needed to create the Guanacaste National Park. One can only marvel at Janzen's conviction that he and his fellow biologists know all, and that the inhabitants of the forest know nothing. He justifies the taking over of the forest and the dispossession of the forest farmer by claiming that 'Today virtually all of the present-day occupants of the western Mesoamerican pastures, fields and degraded forests are deaf, blind and mute to the fragments of the rich biological and cultural heritage that still occupies the shelves of the unused and unappreciated library in which they reside'.[25]

This is an ecologically updated version of the White Man's Burden, where the biologist, rather than the civil servant or military official, knows that it is in the native's true interest to abandon his home and hearth and leave the field and forest clear for the new rulers of his domain. In Costa Rica we only have Janzen's word for it, but elsewhere we are better placed to challenge the conservationist's point of view. A remarkable book on African conservation has laid bare the imperialism, unconscious and explicit, of Western wilderness lovers and biologists working on that luckless continent. I cannot here summarise the massive documentation of Raymond Bonner's *At the Hand of Man*, but will simply quote some of his conclusions:

Above all, Africans [have been] ignored, overwhelmed, manipulated and outmaneuvered – by a conservation crusade led, orchestrated and dominated by white Westerners.

Livingstone, Stanley and other explorers and missionaries had come to Africa in the nineteenth century to promote the three C's – Christianity, commerce and civilization. Now a fourth was added: conservation. These modern secular missionaries were convinced that without the white man's guidance, the Africans would go astray.

[The criticisms] of egocentricity and neo-colonialism ... could be levelled fairly at most conservation organizations working in the Third World.

As many Africans see it, white people are making rules to protect animals that white people want to see in parks that white people visit. Why should Africans support these programs? ... The World Wildlife Fund professed to care about what the Africans wanted, but then tried to manipulate them into doing what the Westerners wanted: and those Africans who couldn't be brought into line were ignored.

Africans do not use the parks and they do not receive any significant benefits from them. Yet they are paying the costs. There are indirect economic costs – government revenues that go to parks instead of schools. And there are direct personal costs [i. e., of the ban on hunting and fuel-collecting, or of displacement].[26]

Bonner's book focuses on the elephant, one of the half dozen or so animals that have come to acquire 'totemic' status among Western wilderness lovers. Animal totems existed in most pre-modern societies, but as the Norwegian scholar Arne Kalland points out, in the past the injunction not to kill the totemic species applied only to members of the group. Hindus do not ask others to worship the cow, but those who love and cherish the elephant, seal, whale or tiger try to impose a worldwide ban on its killing. No one, they say, anywhere, anytime, shall be allowed to touch the animal they hold sacred even if – as with the elephant and several species of whale – scientific evidence has established that small-scale hunting will not endanger its viable populations and will, in fact, save human lives put at risk by the expansion, after total protection, of the *Lebensraum* of the totemic animal. The new totemists also insist that their species is the 'true, rightful inhabitant' of the ocean or forest, and ask that human beings who have lived in the same terrain, and with the animals, for millennia be sent elsewhere.[27]

To turn, last of all, to an ongoing controversy in my own bailiwick. The Nagarhole National Park in southern Karnataka has an estimated 40 tigers, the species toward whose protection enormous amounts of Indian and foreign money and attention has been directed. But Nagarhole is also home to about 6,000 tribals, who have been in the area longer than anyone can remember, perhaps as long as the tigers themselves. The state Forest Department want to expel the tribals, claiming they destroy the forest and kill wild game. The tribals answer that their demands are modest, consisting in the main of fuelwood, fruit, honey and the odd quail or partridge. They do not own guns, although coffee planters living on the edge of the forest do; maybe it is the planters who poach big game? In any case, they ask the officials, if the forest is only for tigers, why have you invited India's biggest hotel chain to build a hotel inside it while you plan to throw us out?

Into this controversy jumps a 'green missionary' passing through Karnataka. Dr John G. Robinson works for the Wildlife Conservation Society in New York, for whom he oversees 160 projects in 44 countries. He conducts a whistle-stop tour of Nagarhole, and before he flies off to the next project on his list, hurriedly calls a press conference in the state capital, Bangalore. Throwing the tribals out of the park, he says, is the only means to save the wilderness. This is not a one-off case but a sacred principle, for in Robinson's opinion 'relocating tribal or traditional people who live in these protected areas is the single most important step towards conservation'. Tribals, he explains, 'compulsively hunt for food', and compete with tigers for prey. Deprived of food, tigers cannot survive, and 'their extinction means that the balance of the ecosystem is upset and this has a snowballing effect'.[28]

One does not know how many tribals Robinson met – none, is the likely answer. Yet the Nagarhole case is hardly typical. All over India, the management of parks has sharply posited the interests of poor tribals who have traditionally lived there against those of wilderness lovers and urban pleasure seekers who wish to keep parks 'free of human interference' – that is, free of other humans. These conflicts are being played out in the Rajaji sanctuary in Uttar Pradesh, in Simlipal in Orissa, in Kanha in Madhya Pradesh, and in Melghat in Maharashtra.[29] Everywhere, Indian wildlifers have ganged up behind the Forest Department to evict the tribals and rehabilitate them far outside the forests. In this they have drawn sustenance from American biologists and conservation organisations, who have thrown the prestige of science and the power of the dollar behind the crusade to kick the original owners of the forest out of their home.

Specious nonsense about the equal rights of all species cannot hide the plain fact that green imperialists are possibly as dangerous and certainly more hypocritical than their economic or religious counterparts. For the American advertiser and banker hopes for a world in which everyone, regardless of colour, will be in an economic sense an American – driving a car, drinking Pepsi, owning a fridge and a washing machine. The missionary, having discovered Jesus Christ, wants pagans also to share in the discovery. The conservationist wants to 'protect the tiger (or whale) for posterity', yet expects *other* people to make the sacrifice.

Moreover, the processes unleashed by green imperialism are very nearly irreversible. For the consumer titillated into eating Kentucky Fried Chicken can always say 'once is enough'. The Hindu converted to Baptism can decide later on to revert to his original faith. But the poor tribal, thrown out of his home by the propaganda of the conservationist, is condemned to the life of an ecological refugee in a slum, a fate, for these forest people, which is next only to death.

The illustrations offered above throw serious doubt on Arne Naess' claim that the deep ecology movement is 'from the point of view of many people all over the world, the most precious gift from the North American continent in our time'.[30] For deep ecology's signal contribution has been to invest with privilege, above all other varieties and concerns of environmentalism, the protection of wild species and wild habitats, and to provide high-sounding, self-congratulatory but none the less dubious moral claims for doing so. Treating 'biocentric equality' as a moral absolute, tigers, elephants, whales etc. will need more space to flourish and reproduce, while humans – poor humans – will be expected to make way for them.

The authors of this book by no means wish to see a world completely dominated by 'human beings, their mutualists, commensals and parasites'. We have time for the tiger and the rainforest, and also wish to protect those islands of nature not yet fully conquered by us. Our plea rather is to put wilderness protection – and its radical edge, deep ecology – in its place, to recognise it as a distinctively North Atlantic brand of environmentalism, whose export and expansion must be done with caution, care, and above all, with humility. For in the poor and heavily populated countries of the South, protected areas cannot be managed with guns and guards but must, rather, take full cognisance of the rights of the people who lived in, and oftentimes cared for, the forest before it became a National Park or a World Heritage Site.[31]

Putting deep ecology in its place is to recognise that trends it derides as 'shallow' ecology might in fact be varieties of environmentalism that are more apposite, more representative, and more popular in the countries of the South. When Arne Naess says that 'conservation biology is the spearhead of scientifically based environmentalism'[32] we wonder why 'agroecology', 'pollution abatement technology' or 'renewable energy studies' cannot become the 'spearhead of scientifically based environmentalism'. For to the Costa Rican peasant or Ecuadorian fisherman, the Indonesian tribal or slum dweller in Bombay, wilderness preservation can hardly be more 'deep' than pollution control, energy conservation, ecological urban planning or sustainable agriculture.

Chapter 6

The Merchandising of Biodiversity[1]

Many indigenous groups are suspicious of corporate bioprospecting activities. In a statement read to the Plenary of the Convention on Biological Diversity meeting last November [1995] in Jakarta, the Indigenous Peoples' Biodiversity Network stated: 'What you call bioprospecting we call biopiracy...'[2]

INTRODUCTION

In many poor countries of the South, a *positive* environmental good has been provided by poor people, in the form of agricultural genetic resources. Here the poor do not only sell cheap, they have given away such genetic resources gratis. *In situ* agricultural biodiversity, which is not yet properly investigated and recorded, will lose its potential for coevolution as traditional agroecology disppears. The International Convention on Biodiversity, established in Rio de Janeiro in June 1992 but not yet ratified by the US Congress, abolished the idea of genetic resources being the common patrimony of humankind. The Convention gives countries sovereignty over them, and leaves questions of ownership to national legislation. Who are now the owners of agricultural genetic resources, and also of wild genetic resources? Such questions are not theoretical. A few years ago, the Uruguay Round of GATT negotiations tried to impose upon India the acceptance of intellectual property rights to commercial agricultural seeds. The North American Free Trade Agreement (NAFTA) may yet be the final blow to traditional agriculture in southern Mexico, despite *neo-zapatista* resistance by indigenous peasants in Chiapas and other provinces. These two events raise general questions about the conservation of wild and agricultural diversity. This chapter focuses mainly on agricultural biodiversity and considers proposals for implementation of FAO-sponsored Farmers' Rights as well as other recent proposals.

At present, the International Undertaking on Farmers' Rights of the Food and Agricultural Organization (FAO) and the International

Convention on Biodiversity signed in Rio will probably produce a very small international fund for *in situ* conservation of plant genetic resources.[3] However, the main reason for *in situ* conservation is its potential for coevolution of plant genetic resources. This will not be fulfilled by a limited programme of eco-farming, the setting up of *in situ* ethnobotanical stations or museums in a few chosen regions of the world to complement *ex situ* conservation programmes. This late in history, it might be appropriate for Europe, but not for the South of the planet. Current FAO proposals, instead of being based on a general defence of agroecology, boil down to a policy of a few reserves of traditional farmers, inappropriately applying the theory of optimal portfolio of assets to the conservation and coevolution of agricultural biodiversity. Thus in Southern Mexico agroecological maize growing will disappear, submerged by the inflow of maize from the United Sates-produced with Mexican genetic resources, and cheap Mexican oil. Perhaps some money will be available, under the Fund for Farmers' Rights, for the preservation of a few samples of *milpa* agriculture around San Cristobal de las Casas, for the ecotourists to see.[4] It would be a pity if all the struggle for agricultural biodiversity and Farmers' Rights would yield at the end only a small fund managed by the World Bank and the CGIAR (the consultative body which manages a chain of international agronomic research institutes), consisting of a few traditional farming *in situ* conservation areas in the world. There is a clear parallel here with debates on the protection of wild biodiversity: need we just a sample of habitats, or should we keep as much territory as possible under protection? But there is also a clear difference: the conservation of wild biodiversity (cf. Chapter 5) sometimes enters into conflict with the immediate interests of local groups of poor people, while providing incentives for the conservation of agricultural biodiversity could help some hundreds of million of people who are among the poorest of the world.

Since time immemorial indigenous groups have been accumulating an enormous body of knowledge about biological diversity, and peasant farmers have been selecting and improving seeds. However, this knowledge of natural biological diversity and the conservation of agricultural diversity *in situ* have rarely been valued in economic terms. The fact that genetic resources have not been appropriated and treated as merchandise is, according to some, the reason for the 'genetic erosion' that is taking place, since things without an owner or a price are treated as worthless. It is now being proposed that access to natural genetic resources should have an economic price (as in the controversial agreement between Merck and INBio of Costa Rica, discussed later in this chapter), and that the conservation work of farmers should also be rewarded in monetary terms.

This chapter considers indicators of 'genetic erosion', and asks the following questions: Should biological diversity be defended through ecologically extended markets in which new property rights to genetic resources are sold? Or through broad ecological movements that seek to impose the maintenance of biological diversity a priori, and only then to calculate economic costs? Who would pay these costs? There is a growing popular ecological movement to defend agricultural biodiversity that aims to act not through the market, where the poor are weak and future generations are not represented, but instead through political and social movements favouring ecological agriculture.

GENETIC EROSION

The general opinion regarding modern agriculture, which is based on the improvement of varieties through non-traditional techniques, increased production per hectare, and high fossil fuel energy input, has gradually changed over the last 30 years. There undoubtedly had been previous critical judgements, but the milestones in this discussion have been:

- Rachel Carson's book attacking chemical pesticides (1962).[5]
- D. Pimentel's studies of energy flow in agriculture (1973) and similar studies by G. Leach (1975) and other authors, such as Naredo and Campos in 1980, who acted on a suggestion from Howard Odum and showed that modern agriculture was inferior in terms of energetic efficiency.[6]
- Negative assessments of the 'green revolution' of the 1960s and 1970s, which was based on the introduction of new wheat and rice varieties, leading to a drastic biological simplification of agriculture and forming part of an agricultural production system which requires more chemical inputs and more energy input from fossil fuels.

I have specifically studied the history of the debate about agriculture as a system for converting energy,[7] but it would also be useful to undertake investigation into the debate about agricultural diversity since Vavilov's times or before.[8] Vavilov was the geneticist from Leningrad (St. Petersburg) who in the 1920s identified the so-called centres of diversity of agricultural plants in the various regions of the world where the initial 'agricultural revolutions' took place. But when was the first time that the loss of genetic resources was discussed? Knowledge, like ignorance, is socially constructed.

What are the reasons for the success of modern agriculture in the North and in a few areas of the South? High-yielding varieties – more accurately termed high-response varieties – need greater external agricultural inputs, but direct more energy from photosynthesis into producing the rice or wheat grain; they do this by reducing the height of the plant. This may represent an overall gain for the farmer if lower straw production is not an important economic loss. The defenders of ecological agriculture often refer to the imposition of high-response varieties by government bodies, and it is true that state extension services have often been mere appendages of the commercial interests of companies linked to the inappropriately named 'green revolution'. However, the truth is that the spread of modern agriculture, of which the green revolution is only a single episode, has been largely spontaneous. In North American or European agricultural economics, it is difficult to find any attempt at the economic valuation of, or the construction of indexes for, the loss of agricultural biodiversity. The introduction of new varieties has been considered an undeniable technical progress, greater production more than compensating for the monetary costs of greater agrochemical input. Recent criticism is based on ecological economics. A study by Renée Vellvé[9] shows that in Europe, modern agriculture also leads to biological impoverishment by replacing diversity with uniformity and security with vulnerability. In order to escape the contradiction between apparent increases in agricultural productivity and destruction of the genetic resource base, what action should be taken to save genetic resources? These resources are falling to an increasing extent into the hands of multinational industrial companies, and the efforts of public institutions to store them *ex situ* in gene-banks run into many problems. Fortunately a third party has been involved, not only in the countries of the South, which have the greatest biological diversity, but also in Europe. The most important tasks of conservation have been carried out, whether by farmers, individuals, or local groups, as a popular, ecological initiative that is as yet inadequately financed and without social recognition.

Although round figures are often used (FAO has asserted that 75 per cent of plant genetic resources have disappeared over the past decades),[10] it is difficult to construct indicators of genetic erosion. Often the names of varieties used in traditional agriculture have not been recorded, and the extent of farmers' reutilisation of seeds is unknown. Therefore it is not easy to ascertain the number of varieties which occupy a given share of crop in a given territory. Moreover, the genetic distance between varieties is not indicated by their commercial or ethnic names, and this is precisely what would be of interest. But despite the lack of accurate indicators, the alarm over genetic erosion has grown.

What are the reasons for genetic erosion in agriculture? Is the extension of the market the main culprit? Or, on the contrary, would the extension of the market be a solution? Some will argue that an ecologically extended market can incorporate ecological costs into its prices. Some will suggest that conflicts can be solved by ensuring that the products of ecological agriculture obtain higher prices in a different, specialised market. Others, like myself, argue that the important question rather is: which social agents can best express the conflict between ecological reasoning and market-based reasoning? Or, put more simply, the movement for ecological agriculture can perhaps become a political ideology capable of mobilising peasants convinced of their ancient technical superiority over modern agriculture in terms of sustainability and their skill in using biological resources – soil, water, and solar energy.

PEASANT STRUGGLES TO CONTROL SEEDS

Biological diversity was one of the most important questions at the Earth Summit in Rio in 1992, but only now are people in poor countries becoming aware of its value. Some of these countries include Vavilov's centres of origin for agricultural diversity. In these countries there are still poor farmers who are experts in the traditional selection and improvement of plants, and who practise agriculture with few external inputs, using hundreds of local varieties.[11] The threat to this agricultural diversity comes, above all, from the extension of the market and the fact that decisions relating to production are taken to a greater and greater extent on the basis of priorities indicated by prices.

If profit in the market increases with the introduction of modern agricultural techniques and the so-called high-yield varieties, then the varieties that have been improved by traditional methods have no future. However, a new consensus is arising in the South. The commercial firms that sell improved seeds can protect their intellectual property rights not by patent systems but by the international UPOV[12] system, which nevertheless lets farmers produce and exchange outside the marketplace seeds obtained from commercial varieties. Therefore the so-called 'Farmers' Rights', which value the work by traditional farmers in the creation and conservation of agricultural genetic resources, should be recognised and possibly paid for. How many traditional agriculturalists, with their complex agroecosystems of still unknown genetic wealth, should be preserved and adequately compensated? One billion, including their families? Half a billion? After opening up the Pandora's box of agricultural biodiversity, pro-peasant groups are not to be intellectually and politically pacified by an international fund of US$50 million or $100 million per year (about 10 cents per farmer's family member), which has been estimated as the cost of actually implementing Farmers' Rights.

It is not only the current implementation which is under discussion. There are also historical aspects to Farmers' Rights, connected to the increasing discussion of the ecological debt the North owes to the South. Let us imagine the case of a group of humans, say an indigenous group, which is outside the generalised market system and which has ancient and proven healing methods, part of their vast repertory of botanical and zoological medicinal knowledge. This knowledge is not built up in a single generation, nor is it static. There is always experimentation and improvement.[13] Let us now suppose that this knowledge is transferred to an outside group along with the relevant materials without anything being given in exchange. This could occur by means of scientific research, missionaries of another religion, or by simple political and economic exploitation, whether public or private. This outside group translates and absorbs this knowledge into its own culture and manipulates the materials so that it can apply them in its own system of medicine. Furthermore, through direct political imposition or generalised incorporation into the market, the group responsible for this exploitation ensures that the indigenous group pays hard cash for the re-elaborated materials and medicinal knowledge, with the result that they are effectively banned from using and spreading their own ancient and proven curative methods. This is exactly what has been happening in the medical and pharmaceutical industries. We could accept the superiority of modern medicine and at the same time accept the description above, and understand that something similar has been taking place in the case of agricultural seeds, due in part to the GATT negotiations, which include Trade-related Intellectual Property (TRIP).

In India, the Karnataka Rajya Raitha Sangha, a peasant organisation, in co-operation with the Third World Network, organised in 1993 and 1994 a variety of mass actions against transnational seed companies. The actions were in protest against the possibility that the Indian state, as a consequence of the GATT negotiations, might establish powerful systems of intellectual property rights to 'improved' seeds. In that case, the farmers would no longer be able to produce these seeds and trade them among themselves. As it is, they have never received anything in exchange for their work in conserving and improving their own seeds over many generations. One action was the destruction of Cargill Seeds' installations in Sirivara, Bellary District, Karnataka. There was also strong opposition to W. R. Grace & Co.'s project to set up an installation to manufacture biological pesticides based on the seeds of the *Neem* tree (*Azadirachta indica*), long used by peasants as insecticides. The question here is, who does biological diversity belong to, who does indigenous agricultural knowledge belong to? Can it be acquired without payment by the North and then returned in the form of patented seeds and pesticides? Even if a pesticide with the properties of the *neem* seed is chemically synthesised, making it unnecessary to gather the seeds in India, has this traditional Indian knowledge no value at all? With respect to agricultural seeds in general, and *neem* seeds in particular, the discussion about biological diversity (which until a few years ago was limited to a few experts who sympathised with the Third World or the activists of a few NGOs such as CLADES or GRAIN)[14] has become a matter of interest to newspapers and the cause of widespread social concern.[15]

In India there are tens of thousands of varieties of rice, many in danger of being lost. Some varieties were collected without payment by gene banks, in particular the Philippine International Rice Research Institute (IRRI, part of the CGIAR), where the rice varieties used in the green revolution originated. These plant collections are now at risk of being patented for the benefit of international seed companies, like others held at CIAT in Colombia, CIP in Peru, and CIMMYT in Mexico (each part of the CGIAR). The emerging ecological movement supporting agricultural diversity thus raises two issues.[16] The first is Farmers' Rights to the genetic resources that they have conserved and improved *in situ*. The second is that of favourable, if not free, access to the varieties that have been conserved and improved *ex situ*, based on the reasoning that the precursor genetic materials originated within traditional agriculture and were never paid for. At the same time the governments of the South are waking up. The precursor genetic resources were, until recently, 'world heritage' but now several states are moving quickly to declare them state property on the basis of their interpretation of the Rio de Janeiro Biodiversity Convention. But it is doubtful whether ownership by the state will actually favour poor farmers or indigenous communities.

AGRICULTURAL BIODIVERSITY AS 'CULTIVATED NATURAL CAPITAL'?

Poor people's ethnobotanical knowledge of diversity has been praised within a general argument in support of ecological agriculture based on continually developing indigenous and peasant knowledge.[17] The question now is whether genetic resources in general – wild resources, improved traditional varieties, modern varieties, and genetically engineered varieties – should be commercialised or whether they should continue to be 'world heritage'. So far, the genetic resources produced by traditional selection and improvement of plants and then collected from cultivation have not been paid for, whereas the companies that sell modern improved seeds insist on being paid. Likewise, the products of genetic engineering will not only be sold but will also enjoy a monopoly as a result of the patent system. The Biodiversity Convention signed in Rio recognises that it is peasants and indigenous peoples who have used and conserved these genetic resources since time immemorial, but the Convention does not ensure their ownership and management rights to these resources. It also fails to include in its ambit a critical section of the planet's biological diversity: the part held by national and international gene banks. This omission resulted from pressure exerted by the United States at the preparatory meeting in Nairobi on 22 May 1992. The inclusion of germplasm held by genebanks within the scope of the biological diversity treaty would have forced the signatory industrialised countries to share the profits made from these seeds or germplasm with the poor countries, thus challenging the commercial interests of the big seed companies.[18] Modern, so-called improved varieties cannot function without a continuous supply of new genetic resources to confront new pests and new environmental conditions. But modern agricultural varieties are more profitable in a monetary sense. Thus, the increase in production for the market spoils the very condition necessary for this production, agricultural biodiversity, and a new ecological movement arises to fight the degradation of the environment.

Among economists open to ecological matters, the value of wild biological diversity has been considered in the following terms. Its conservation has an immediate use as a genetic resource for chemical and pharmaceutical industries as well as seed companies. It also has a possible future use called an 'option value'. Finally, it has an 'existence value', exemplified by the membership fees that members of Greenpeace pay to save the whales. They do this not so that people can kill the whales to extract the oil and flesh, nor to conserve a stock for future exploitation, but to protect an endangered species with a right to survive. Some fervent neo-liberals propose that the way to save the whales is to bring them into the market by way of well-defined property rights; thus, if the members of Greenpeace and the World Wildlife Fund paid more (to the world organisation owning the whales, or to their private owners) than Japanese or Norwegian fishermen were willing to pay, they would save the whales through the functioning of the market. In the same way, entomological societies would have to pay to prevent the disappearance of insect species. However, in the marketplace he who pays the piper calls the tune, and future generations are not present to bid, nor, of course, are the threatened species or varieties in question.

The main aim of organisations like the World Wildlife Fund (now renamed the Worldwide Fund For Nature) has been to conserve natural biological diversity; this has also received more attention than agricultural or agroforestry diversity in the strategy of the International Union for the Conservation of Nature.[19] But there is a complementary relationship between wild and agricultural biological diversity. Agricultural genetic resources could be called 'cultivated natural capital'. They cannot be fully substituted by the capital goods, including 'improved' seeds, used in modern agriculture. This cultivated natural capital must be complemented by natural capital, the wild relatives of cultivated plants.[20] Nevertheless, I am not in favour of using the concept of 'natural capital'. Among the natural resources of orthodox economics there are resources that are neither merchandise nor produced like merchandise – the genetic resources of traditional agriculture, or wild biological diversity – while others are not produced as merchandise but are sold or rented as merchandise, such as land. Giving the name natural capital to all natural resources may betray the intention to consider them all as merchandise.

The market, or surrogate markets, cannot give convincing values to future events, which are uncertain and irreversible. Sometimes it is argued that a negative externality has a value equal to the cost of repairing the damage. For example, the price of chemical pollution, to which the market does not assign value, would be the cost of restoring the contaminated site to its former condition. Naturally, if we try to value the loss of biological diversity using this criterion we come up against the problem that the loss is irreversible. The criterion could be modified as follows: the price of biological diversity is what it would cost to maintain it, not only in terms of the costs actually incurred, but also in payment for tasks that until now have been unpaid, and in terms of opportunity costs and benefits – that is to say, the cost of a lower level of agricultural production, or the cost of not destroying the rainforest, which will at the same time have beneficial effects on the climate. First we make the decision to conserve biological diversity, and then we calculate how much it costs. This is not the same as creating legal rights to biological diversity and then organising a market in these rights, and it is not the same as a cost–benefit analysis in present–value terms of the conservation of biodiversity.

'FARMERS' RIGHTS'

Nowadays, pride is growing in traditional ecological agriculture, an excellent example of a 'clean' technology, at a time when there is much discussion of technology transfer. This pride is accompanied by awareness of the fact that little was paid for traditionally improved varieties. (A minimal price was paid in the peasant markets where the seed was collected for the *ex situ* gene banks, and nothing at all was paid for the collection of genetic material under cultivation). Nor was anything paid for the medicinal plants discovered and cared for by indigenous cultures, later used and developed by pharmaceutical companies that charge prices, or even royalties, for medicines protected by trademarks and patents. Unlike medicines, modern improved commercial seeds have as yet not been patented, and protection against their duplication has been achieved by the

117

UPOV system, or by the sale of hybrid seeds that do not breed true. But the new legal framework demanded by the biotechnology industry will allow the patenting of life-forms, including agricultural genetic resources. This is the reason why GATT is imposing the international recognition of patents (or their equivalents) on 'new' genetic resources in the same way that it has always tried to enforce the recognition of patents on medicines.

Activists in favour of ecological agriculture are against the patenting of life forms, as are many ecologists who are afraid that the development of biotechnology, with all its promises and threats, will be subject only to the logic of the marketplace. Specifically, those in favour of ecological agriculture believe that the CGIAR's agricultural research centres should not patent their genetic resources. In general they are against intellectual property rights, because they do not believe it to be the way to defend and reward agricultural diversity. They do not even agree with the payment of 'Farmers' Rights' (recognised by the FAO, but without practical effects), a payment that would not buy the right to exclusive use of genetic resources. Farmers' Rights are not the equivalent of intellectual property rights, but rather more like fees for professional services. Another analogy: patents, copyrights, trademarks and intellectual property rights in general are the monopoly of their creators and inventors as a stimulus to their creativity and as a reward for the time and money invested. However there are other ways of rewarding inventions, such as prizes and honours.[21] Farmers' Rights belong in this category and should serve to give the necessary incentive to ensure the conservation and development of agricultural diversity. Rather than paying royalties for traditional seeds, it would be better to consider *all* genetic resources as 'world heritage'. At the same time social and legal obstacles should be introduced to dangerous or absurd applications of biotechnology (like increasing resistance of plants to pesticides instead of to pests). Economic compensation should be established *by means of product prices* (or income transfers) for ecological agriculturalists using clean technologies and few inputs, to give them incentives to maintain and develop diversity.

Should genetic resources become merchandise so that an ecologically extended marketplace will conserve them? However, future generations cannot participate in this market. In addition, market values depend to some extent on the current distribution of power and income. Who would receive these Farmers' Rights if they were sold in the market? The farmers' organisations? The individual farmers? The governments? What price will be put on them? *The truth is that peasants and indigenous groups would sell their hypothetical Farmers' Rights cheap*, not because they have (until now?) attributed a low value to their work and agricultural knowledge, nor because they attribute little value now to the benefits of biological diversity for future generations, but basically *because they are poor*. If the poor sell cheap, then there is no reason to trust that prices in an ecologically extended market will be an effective instrument of environmental policy. There is a need for environmental policies based on popular social movements, going beyond an ecologically extended market.

THE INBIO-MERCK DEAL

An example of the poor selling cheap is the agreement that INBio (Instituto Nacional de Biodiversidad, National Biological Diversity Institute) of Costa Rica and the pharmaceutical company Merck reached in 1991.[22] What is being sold is not agricultural genetic resources, but wild ones; however, the case is relevant to my argument. What INBio is selling is a service, the collection and preparation of a large number of samples of biological diversity, samples of the plants, insects and micro-organisms to which INBio has access in the conservation areas of Costa Rica. INBio, a private organisation with close links to the state, has free access to these resources and only pays the cost of collection by 'parataxonomists' (who possess their own knowledge, which they sell cheap), and the cost of preparing the samples. INBio does not pay the direct costs of establishing and guarding the natural parks, nor the cost of maintaining these wildlife reserves. The World Resources Institute typically praised this 'recent agreement between a major pharmaceutical company and Costa Rica which deserves to be widely copied'.[23] However, the agreement caused uneasiness in Latin America, among other reasons because Costa Rica shares many of these genetic resources with neighbouring countries. The agreement implies the recognition of rights to genetic resources ('wild' ones, in this case), but it does not guarantee that traditional wisdom and conservation of biological diversity, as such, can compete with other forms of land use that are more profitable in the marketplace. Under the terms of the agreement, Merck pay just over US$ 1 million dollars over two years for rights to chemical screening of a large number of samples prepared by INBio from a large area of Costa Rica that is protected. In addition, Merck will pay royalties on profits from any commercial products. Without further costly conservation measures to complement the local population's interest in conservation, such as legal regulation and supervision of the sites paid for by the Costa Rican authorities or other bodies, the limited monetary incentive provided by Merck would be insufficient to prevent deforestation and genetic erosion. Merck is a commercial company, with a relatively short-term outlook, extending at most to a few decades. Besides, it is to be expected that Costa Rica will sell cheaply. Why has Costa Rica, the classic banana republic, sold bananas cheap to United Fruit, Standard Fruit, or Del Monte?

Because it wanted to? Of course not! If Costa Rica cannot get a good price for bananas, how can it get a good price for biological diversity? An analogy: workers in poor countries have always had a right to their own health. Nevertheless, once they are dispossessed of their lands and livelihoods, they are forced to sell their labour and their health cheaply, if not gladly, in order to get some sort of employment in mines or plantations, including banana plantations. The poor sell cheap. But future human generations, and other species, cannot even come to the market.

THE DEFENCE OF AGROECOLOGY OUTSIDE THE MARKET

The environmental effects of modern agriculture – loss of genetic resources, destruction of non-renewable energy from fossil fuels – make it doubtful that it is really more productive than its predecessor(s). Increases in outputs (per hectare or per hour of work) are measured by subtracting the inputs from what is produced, and then dividing the result by the quantity of the input whose productivity we are measuring. But the prices of production and inputs are inadequately measured because they do not include externalities and do not include the destruction of the conditions necessary for agricultural production.

At this point, there are two possible paths. The first, which is easier to follow to begin with but which may soon become extremely narrow, attempts to reconcile pecuniary reasoning with ecological reasoning. For example, by means of a Green Label, the products of ecological agriculture may obtain higher prices, so long as there is a demand for these differentiated products. Víctor Toledo has expressed this idea as follows:

Ecological agriculture does not aim for a romantic (and unviable) return to pre-industrial forms of production. What it seeks is to set in motion a strategy to modernise farming on the basis of an adequate management of nature and the recognition (rather than destruction) of the rural heritage ... What is most surprising (and encouraging) is that this proposal, which has not formed part of either official policies or the debate among local experts, is taking place as a result of commercial transactions, the result of connecting the growing demand for new organic products in the first world with the ecologically orientated production of traditional Mexican communities. There is the case of some indigenous organisations in Oaxaca and Chiapas that have started to supply organic coffee to the demanding markets in Germany, Italy, Denmark, Holland and other industrial countries. This is because their traditional systems (shade–grown coffee, in mixed farming systems that do not use agrochemicals) managed to survive the policy of modernization. A further example is the consortium of more than a dozen Chinanteca communities who have managed to cultivate vanilla ... or the producers (and exporters) of sesame ... .[24]

In fact, Green consumers in Frankfurt and Amsterdam bought organic coffee produced by the Sandinistas in Nicaragua, and there are worthy efforts to organise alternative channels of international trade in support of self-managing groups practising ecological agriculture. Would it be possible to commercialise, at higher prices, Andean ecological *quinua* in Berlin or San Francisco? One would hope it can be done, but one may doubt, as would Víctor Toledo, whether differentiating products in specialised expensive markets is really the most effective method of defending ecological agriculture. Furthermore, in cases like vanilla production, competition is already presented by the new biotechnology industries.

A problem arises when ecological agriculture cannot compete in the wider market with the products of modern agriculture. When an insoluble conflict arises between ecology and the market, as generally happens when ecological agriculture and modern agriculture clash, then a second option appears. Which social agents will make an ecological economy their political cause? Peasants in the South, who still practice ecological agriculture, seem to be the obvious candidate for this.

Traditional peasants, if they have rights to the land, also have access to the sun's energy and to at least the rainwater that falls on their land, and control a 'fourth resource', the seeds from their harvest. Unlike peasants, modern farmers depend on external energy from fossil fuels, contaminate more, and have lost control over this fourth resource. (This is the terminology used by Henk Hobbelink, the founder of GRAIN.) This raises the following paradox: in rich countries the generalisation of the market led to large but overlooked losses of genetic resources which are not yet mentioned in textbooks on agricultural history, but perhaps in poor countries the extension of the market will ensure adequate pricing of genetic resources and thus prevent genetic erosion. For example, the development of hybrid maize 50 years ago and its dissemination in the United States has led to biological impoverishment and requires a continuous input – either free or badly paid – of genetic material from areas where these new, uniform F–1 hybrid varieties are still not cultivated. There has been no research into free pollination varieties, which with time would have permitted yields as high as those of hybrid maize in the United States, with the seed controlled by the farmer rather than by the seed company.[25] The economics of technological change took as one of its classic examples the rate of return on the research and development of hybrid maize, carried out in the United States 50 years ago.[26] The complementary inputs for this monoculture were simply accounted for on the basis of their market price, without any accounting for externalities from the agrochemicals or fossil fuels used, from increased soil erosion, or from the loss of biological diversity. The development of hybrid maize and later high-yield varieties of wheat and rice, really instigated the current process of genetic erosion within an agricultural system based on mechanisation and in-field monoculture.

The ideology of peasant resistance has been called 'agrarismo' (as in Mexico) or narodnism (as in eastern Europe from 1870 onwards), or 'pro-peasant populism'. Mariátegui (1894–1930), the best-known Latin American Marxist of his generation, who wished to conserve indigenous peasant communities and believed they would play an important role in future Andean socialism, was rightly considered a somewhat populist Marxist.[27] However, in the long history of political ideologies based on peasant resistance and their accompanying economic ideas, there have rarely been explicitly ecological elements, until very recently. Of course, peasants have always had good ecological practice, as shown by their conservation and creation of genetic resources, their soil, water and forest management systems and their use of renewable solar energy, a source that cannot be taken away unless they are evicted from their land. But the explicit ideological link between narodnism, agrarismo or pro-peasant populism (all of which are synonyms), and ecology, is recent.[28] There has been no generalised social awareness of the peasants' ecological virtues, even among those who were on their side. Now there has arisen an international ecological and agrarianist movement that has stressed the peasantry's role in the development of genetic resources. There is also alarm about the unknown social and ecological effects of the new biotechnologies. This awareness has more chance of flourishing in poor countries for two reasons. While the countries of the North are poor in genetic resources, some poor countries in the South contain not only the current genetic wealth of the tropical rainforests, but also, in agricultural terms, the centres of diversity of many agricultural plants. Furthermore, these countries still have traditional farmers using mixed farming systems with low external inputs, capable of creating and maintaining agricultural diversity and making the most of their own, or their neighbours', genetic resources as well as wild varieties. This international movement formed by NGOs is not only struggling to provide an ideological defence for ecological agriculture and those who practice it, but also spreading new skills and experience independently of governments and commercial companies. Once a word as innocent as *compost* has spread internationally and forms part of peasants' everyday language, it may provide a mental defence against salespeople who are always men from fertiliser factories. Once traditional practices are known by the internationally recognised term of *integrated pest control*, they acquire a new legitimacy, even if pesticide use has rendered them obsolete.

Consider also Pat Mooney's proposed substitution of the term *landrace*, which he considers derogatory, by the term *folkseeds*, since plant varieties do not come from the land alone.

In addition to governmental intervention through extension services and subsidies to agricultural chemicals and mechanisation, the market also tends to favour the (partial) triumph of high-yield varieties and related agricultural technology. If they prevailed in the North, how could they not have prevailed in the South? Obviously, labour is much cheaper, yet high-yield varieties are not grown because they save labour, but because they increase production per unit area. Perhaps these increases are not sustainable in the long-term, but the fact is that they basically spread through commercial channels. The typical modern agricultural extension worker, in Europe and the United States, as well as in poor countries, is a salesman for companies selling agricultural inputs, whether directly or through endorsements from already convinced farmers. Where is the equivalent salesperson (man or woman) for ecological agriculture? Why must this task be performed by non-profit-making (or non-profit-motivated) NGOs? Does the market advantage of modern agriculture depend only on direct subsidies for commercial seeds, agricultural chemicals, mechanisation and irrigation pumps? Or would it be more accurate to say that this advantage is due to the market's failure to consider the long-term costs and benefits?

The spread of ecological agriculture was a result of the peasants' own process of learning. The spread of modern agriculture to a large extent also happens this way. In India, for example, direct transfer between farmers has been the main means of spreading 'green revolution seeds', which have remained in the public domain rather than with legal monopolies. The process of exchanging traditional varieties could be made easier, as Mario Tapia has suggested for the Andes, by means of 'seed fairs'. It is the poor farmers who must, every season and on every site, decide whether to conserve traditional varieties or to adopt commercially improved varieties. The farmers are influenced by a variety of considerations relating to livelihood and use value, as well as commercial considerations.

If only ecological agriculture were profitable in the market-place! Although there are cases in which this is so, I do not consider it to be true in general. If it were, the commercial sector would be actively present in the production and sale of ecological agricultural products, but in fact this sector is almost exclusively limited to NGOs and traditional farmers from the South. But those who wish to encourage ecological agriculture have a different argument. An adequate accounting of externalities, correcting prices and removing subsidies to agricultural chemicals, commercial seeds and mechanisation ought to manage to conserve or impose ecological agriculture. Rational decisions on whether to support ecological agriculture or not should not be based on narrow market-based reasoning or even based on extended market reasoning with a necessarily arbitrary valuation of externalities. I believe that the discussion should develop along more directly political lines. What is needed is the social disgrace of modern agriculture as a source of negative externalities – genetic impoverishment, energy wastage, chemical contamination – that we do not know how to translate into updated monetary values, but which would be prudent to avoid.

Once it has been decided that it is necessary to protect and encourage ecological agriculture, once the question has been argued from the perspective of long-term ecological economics taking into account uncertainties and the irreversible nature of some events, once it has obtained enough political force along other lines of reasoning – for instance, in the Ecuadorian, Peruvian and Bolivian Andes the defence of ethnic culture is a factor, as in many other areas of the world – only then will we be able to calculate the cost (in money, in resources, in hours of labour) of protecting and encouraging ecological agriculture. That is not to say this will always be profitable in the short term, but it is a cost that it is perhaps worth paying, even though there is no guarantee it will be recovered in the marketplace.[29]

What costs are we willing to pay for ecological agriculture? What benefits will we obtain? At the moment the only thing that is paid for is the *ex situ* conservation system, but *in situ* conservation and coevolution have been paid for by the traditional peasantry. We are dealing with a typical case of comparison of short-term costs (lower apparent production per hectare and per hour of labour, for example) and uncertain and diverse benefits in the long term (the creation and conservation of biological diversity *in situ*, lower contamination, savings in fossil fuels). Conventional economics does not help us when it comes to making this decision. The international movement in favour of ecological agriculture should therefore not be concerned with short-term economic considerations. It should be a political movement that appeals to ecological-economic reasoning, and to other lines of reasoning, such as the defence of peoples whose ethnic identity is threatened, along with their farming systems.

NAFTA: Petroleum and Maize

To conclude, let us consider how the defence of agricultural diversity might be raised in Mexico nowadays, in the light of what has been stated so far. In the United States, petroleum is relatively cheap, although the country is one of the major petroleum importers. In order to conform to the benevolent sentiments expressed in the Earth Summit about the increasing greenhouse effect, the Clinton–Gore administration considered the introduction of an 'eco-tax,' the BTU tax, but it was not implemented. From the Mexican point of view, the situation is paradoxical. Mexico exports cheap petroleum to the United States. It is 'cheap' because it does not take into account the ecological costs of extraction in the Campeche and Tabasco areas, nor the costs of carbon dioxide (and SO_2 and NO_x) emissions, and in addition the price implicitly undervalues Mexico's future demand for petroleum. Putting an ecological tax on petroleum in the United States, rather than in Mexico would lead to a distributive conflict. As matters stand now, within the framework of the North American Free Trade Agreement, Mexico cannot levy taxes on its exports. It will thus export cheap petroleum to the United States, and it will import products, such as maize, that are in part produced using cheap Mexican petroleum. This American maize is of little genetic interest, and (in part) requires a continuous supply of Mexican genetic resources, which have so far been given free. United States maize exports are subsidised and will continue to be, at least to the extent that their price does not include any accounting entry corresponding to ecological costs. These exports will damage peasant maize production in Mexico, which is more efficient in terms of low fossil energy use and biologically more attractive. In other words, United States agriculture has lax environmental standards in comparison with Mexican peasant agriculture. Thus, assessing the economic impact that liberalisation of maize imports would have in Mexico must include some estimate of environmental costs and benefits.[30]

What would be the environmental costs of a boom in some parts of the Mexican economy due to NAFTA? North American ecological groups paid great attention to the export of Mexican tuna to the United States, because the tuna was caught by methods leading to the death of dolphins. These groups have also paid attention to the potential effects of NAFTA on increasing sweatshop production just over the border, as well as other economic activities, such as strawberry production, which are subject to less strict environmental regulation in Mexico than in the United States. These are without doubt important issues, as is the possible export of domestic and industrial (including nuclear) waste from the United States to Mexico. But crucial points in the ecological-economic discussion, because of their sheer quantity, should be the environmental costs of cheap petroleum exports from Mexico and the threat to its ecological farming system and food security.

The conclusion of the first negotiating round of NAFTA in the summer of 1992 was well received by US maize (and pork) producers who anticipate a large rise in exports to Mexico. It was correctly said[31] that Mexican barriers to the import of maize have prevented US farmers from dominating the

Mexican food market and ruining hundreds of thousands of farmers in southern Mexico. Now, as a result of NAFTA, Mexico must immediately allow the tariff-free importation of 2.5 million tonnes of cereals a year, and the tariffs on imports exceeding this figure will be gradually reduced to zero over 15 years. It is said that this free-trade policy would benefit both countries, as US maize is produced more efficiently than Mexican maize, but how can we talk of efficiency without previously agreeing on a measure of agricultural productivity that takes into account fossil fuel use and the loss of biological diversity in modern agriculture? Perhaps the best system would be to combine the ecological superiority of traditional Mexican *milpa* agriculture, which is without doubt excessively based on hard human labour, and the market superiority of US agriculture, which does not take into account the negative externalities it produces. Ecological criticism of conventional agricultural economics leaves a lot of room for different political points of view, because the ecological critique shows that the current prices are incorrect, but is unable to determine what the ecologically correct prices should be in order to fully internalise the updated externalities.

One cannot condemn this ecological critique as if it were an excuse for obstinate nationalist protectionism, nor in my opinion does it make sense to defend from an ecological perspective the idea of 'bioregional' units *totally* closed to foreign products (and citizens). In ecology, the distinction is made between 'vertical transport' (e.g. of nutrients from the soil up the roots of a tree) and 'horizontal transport' (e.g. soil eroded, down a river to the sea). One could argue that horizontal transport of elements present in abundance in one territory, but limiting factors (in Liebig's sense) in another, will increase the joint capacity to support life. Of course, horizontal transport of oil and minerals is not without costs, but an argument for trade based on Liebig's law is different from an argument for trade based on absolute or comparative economic advantages.[32]

Ecological opposition to NAFTA should be based above all on the fact that no charge is made for environmental costs in export prices, whether petroleum from Mexico or maize from the United States. But this does not mean that we have discovered a magic method of establishing the 'total environmental costs' of those economic activities with future ecological consequences that are irreversible and unknown. There are no ecologically correct prices in the sense that they convincingly internalise all externalities, but *prices may be ecologically corrected* to take environmental externalities into account: by putting a tax on Mexican petroleum in Mexico, and by putting taxes in the United States on agricultural production using modern technology, trade flows would then be based on comparative or absolute advantages that have been ecologically corrected. But these taxes would be in opposition to the free trade ideology expressed in NAFTA and are not on the United States political agenda because of the distributive effects they would have. The United States may consider a tax on exports of Mexican petroleum, but to be paid in the United States, not in Mexico, and awareness of the fact that US agriculture uses dirty technologies with negative environmental impacts is still not widespread. These taxes may well become a subject for political discussion in Mexico.

One could ask, in Mexico, which are the social groups capable of using such a strategy of confrontation against its Northern neighbour? This neighbour considers petroleum imports not only in terms of (falsely computed) comparative advantage, but also in terms of 'national security', which justifies anything, including military intervention – such as the colonial war in Iraq in 1991 – to protect the flow of petroleum from South to North.[33] If it does not secure a cheap source of petroleum through NAFTA, the United States, which imports half the petroleum it consumes, is capable of using force. What remains of Mexican *agrarismo* from the era of Emiliano Zapata, the man who started a revolution to reject the type of capitalist social exchange that history was offering? It seemed that little remains, and even less when President Salinas converted the national *ejidos*, established during the agrarian reform, to private land that could be bought and sold. It seemed that little remains also of the nationalism that defended Mexican petroleum. However, it is possible that popular ecology could revive those old themes of Mexican history. Mexico is *not* really a petroleum producing country; in the market economy what is really extraction is constantly being called 'production'. The opposition to NAFTA in Mexico could combine Mexican oil nationalism with the defence of *milpa* agriculture, by pointing out that the trade agreement means the intensification of ecological dumping. Cheap exports of oil from Mexico to the United States – at prices which certainly do not internalise local and global externalities – will be exchanged for imports of maize at low prices. Such imports will destroy the agriculture of southern Mexico despite the fact that maize production in the United States is more wasteful of fossil fuel energy, and biologicaly more fragile. Hence Víctor Toledo's wonderful wishful expression after the Chiapas uprising, *un neozapatismo ecológico*. There have been traditions of political 'agrarismo' since the times of Zapata, and of petroleum nationalism since President Lazaro Cárdenas in the 1930s, both of which would easily connect with the new ecological awareness. In Mexico, as in the Andean countries and in India, there are prospects for a popular movement in defence of agroecology, linking ecological and nationalist themes.

Chapter 7

The Failure of Ecological Planning in Barcelona

One of the projects for the desurbanization of Moscow makes a proposal for having huts in the forest. Splendid idea! But only for the week-end.[1]

INTRODUCTION

There is at present a reaction not only against modern agriculture (as explained in previous chapters) but also against the architecture and urban planning of the rationalist, modern, international style characterised by the tower blocks of cement, steel and glass; separate zones for working, entertainment, and sleeping; and an endless urban sprawl of little houses. Historically there have been two main lines of town-planning: the modern internationalists who praised industrialisation and progress, and the trend which mourned lost rural landscapes and the destruction of the historical buildings and structures of the medieval city. The first approach, associated with Le Corbusier for example, favoured technological civilisation – and since the 1920s and 1930s, urban development in favour of the car – and it opposed the apparently reactionary, romantic approach of those who fought the city's loss of organic unity with its region due to the pressure of industrialisation: ecological and cultural town-and-country planners such as Patrick Geddes, who had tried to prevent the loss of identity suffered by smaller cities captured and absorbed by the expansion of the conurbations and who also opposed the destruction of historic human environments. There is one clear example of this conflict between the two approaches in India. Patrick Geddes proposed that India, as well as Europe, should conserve its historic areas, but Le Corbusier's influences led to the disastrous development of Chandigarh, the capital of Punjab and Haryana states, a city built taking into account the car but not the poverty of India, and which is now full of abandoned, dirty spaces.[2]

Now, post-modernism is a free-for-all, and such a conflict of ideas looks at first sight outmoded. Post-modernism has relegitimated a variety of styles in architecture, even mixtures of styles, and urban planning, let alone regional planning, is out of fashion. But within post-modernism, there is also an emerging trend towards a revived regional and urban planning, and a new bioclimatic architecture strongly influenced by the ecological criticism of unrestrained industrialisation and of the automobile.[3]

Post-modernism came after the Modern International Style. But when Catalans talk about *modernisme* they do not mean the Modern International Style but, rather, the movement and style of a previous age, between 1880 and 1920, which was inspired by John Ruskin and William Morris, the architecture of Domènech i Montaner and Antoni Gaudí, and many others. Modernisme was the Catalan version of Art Nouveau and Jugendstil. Why was it so strong in Catalonia? Was there an ecological urban planning movement at that time in Barcelona connected to the ideas of Ebenezer Howard (who pioneered the garden city movement of self-contained cities, independent from the conurbation), and of Patrick Geddes? These are the starting points of this chapter,[4] which must be seen as a contribution to the study of ecological town-planning.[5]

In the past 10 years, Patrick Geddes' rooms in Edinburgh's Outlook Tower have been reopened to the public, and his work is once again taken seriously. Geddes, even more than Howard, believed that planning ought to be based on an ecological understanding of regions and on economic and social trends, rather than imposing an arbitrary vision of the world. Perhaps Geddes' intellectual training had something to do with this. He was a biologist turned geographer and sociologist, and not an architect, who by definition thinks in terms of the structures that he wishes to build.[6] Geddes' and Howard's ideas clearly reached Barcelona, but they were defeated with the exile around 1920 of Cebrià de Montoliu (of whom more later), and the crushing of the anarchist movement during and after the Civil War.

The town-planning tradition of Patrick Geddes is anti-industrialist and romantic, but it turns out that the romantics were more ecological and thus scientific because they saw the cities in their *regional* context: Where does the energy and water come from? Where does all the rubbish go? Geddes and his American disciple Lewis Mumford were the first proponents of the ecological history of cities and technologies, distinguishing between *palaeotechnologies* based on iron and coal, which had led to ugly and anti-ecological urban forms, and a new town-planning based on *neotechnologies* that had the potential for more decentralised implantation, for example (they thought) hydro-electricity.[7] More than their specific technological recommendations, what is suggestive about Geddes and Mumford is their historical–ecological perspective on the processes of industrialisation and urbanisation. Hydro-electric power has not fulfilled the expectations of decentralisation that were once placed upon it. Moreover, the predominant source of electricity has been fossil fuels, apart from some countries such as France (and Catalonia) where it is now nuclear power.

A CITY FOR CARS

In Catalonian architecture, after the *modernisme* (in the sense of Art Nouveau or Jugendstil) of 1880–1920, there was a period in which the influence of the Modern International Style was finally dominant both in architecture and urbanism. This was cut short by the Civil War of 1936–39, and Franco's preference for a monumental style, until the 1950s, when through Group R of the young Oriol Bohigas and other architects, links were revived with the rationalist Sert (an exiled architect who had become a professor at Harvard), combining the international style with some vernacular elements. Oriol Bohigas has been the main intellectual force behind the urban developments of Barcelona as an Olympic city in the l980s and l990s. In terms of money spent, the principal Olympic public works have been the ring motorways around and inside Barcelona, which facilitate access by car to the city. Subsequent gigantic public works will be the conversion of the Llobregat Delta, immediately to the south of Barcelona, into an extension of the harbour with a large industrial and transport centre, at the cost of the loss of a large area of agricultural land and marshes. The conurbation of Barcelona keeps growing. This city of architects wishes to become the Rotterdam of the Mediterranean, at a time when Rotterdam would like to be the Barcelona of the North. Most tourists in Barcelona, which is to them certainly a nice place, never witness the impact that the city has on its surroundings.

The problems of Barcelona are minor in a wider world context, particularly in a Third World context. Urban development occurs as a result of emigration from rural areas, due to the reduction of the active population in the agricultural sector as productivity increases (measured by conventional economic criteria, rather than ecological ones). The size of Third World cities also increases due to the internal growth of the urban population. Among the largest cities in the world are Mexico City and São Paulo (together with Tokyo). Mexico and Brazil are not rich countries but their active agricultural population is experiencing a marked relative decrease. It is an anomaly that the largest cities are not in the countries with the largest populations. If China and India follow the path blazed by the 'developed' economies (i.e. if their active agricultural populations fell to 10 or 15 per cent of the total, due to the replacement of human and animal energy in agriculture by fossil fuels), then we would see hitherto unknown urban monsters, such as a city like Beijing or Shanghai with 80 million inhabitants, or cities like Bombay, Delhi, Calcutta, and Madras with 60 million inhabitants each. So humanity really has a lot to learn from planners' dreams of cities organically linked to their rural surroundings (the figure of not more than 100,000 inhabitants was often given) – without doubt, utopian schemes. They were, however, a more agreeable prospect than the nightmare awaiting a large part of the world's population, being cooped up in immense, unpleasant conurbations. While urbanisation in rich countries has lead to environmental disasters such as the loss of agricultural land, air, soil and water pollution, and the increased production of waste that cannot be recycled and is dangerous to treat, these are all relatively minor in comparison with the phenomenon of cities in poor countries trying to follow the same pattern.

Will we see, perhaps, a spontaneous ecological movement of the poor against the car in the world's poor cities? Meanwhile, in Barcelona the tendency is towards almost universal car ownership and the construction of more and more urban motorways, following on a small scale the model of the urban sprawl of Los Angeles. This is an anti-ecological model but at least it is a more equitable model (within the city) than that of Mexico City or Bangkok, as in Barcelona almost everybody has a car (except children, old women, and African immigrants), and the pollution produced thus affects those responsible for its production.

Opposition to cars has scarcely existed in Barcelona. In the working-class districts that have suffered most from the construction of urban motorways for the Olympic Games (such as Nou Barris, to the north of the city) there have been citizens' movements demanding that these motorways be underground, or at least that panelling be installed to mitigate the noise. Often the authorities have covered a stretch, but there has not really been a strong anti-car movement. Only the ecological–anarchist group Amics de la Bicicleta (Friends of the Bicycle), a few local initiatives which would like to pedestrianise some streets, and the environmental umbrella movement under the name of *Barcelona estalvia energia* (Barcelona saves energy), oppose the predominance of the automobile. They argue against the cars not only because of local pollution and congestion, but also because of global issues such as the enhanced greenhouse effect because of carbon dioxide emissions. However, since 1992, motor traffic has increased in the Barcelona area faster than the use of public transport.

THE CONURBATION

The new Olympic Village by the sea housed the participants in the 1992 Olympic Games, and was built on former industrial land in the Poble Nou district. It was given the name of Nova Icària (New Icaria). It has a fine view of the sea, a large, new, clean, beautiful beach, a new port for yachts, and a splendid large McDonald's fast food restaurant. It is all reminiscent of Miami Beach, but it was called Nova Icària, because there were people in 19th-century Barcelona who had identified with Cabet's utopia, full of revolutionary ideas, *Voyage en Icarie*. The fact is that this vast property development is not very utopian. It includes two huge tower blocks that are the typical glass towers, but taller than the tallest ones in Madrid. They were designed by internationally fashionable architects, like so many of the installations for the Olympic Games. It is not yet clear whether these towers are premonitions of the future or leftovers from the Le Corbusier Plan for Barcelona (1932–34). This plan consisted of Le Corbusier's typical ingredients for urban development: immensely tall buildings, overhead motorways, and the destruction of the old town. No attention was paid in the Olympic Village to construction following bioclimatic criteria, taking advantage of the orientation to install solar heaters for water, or collecting organic rubbish for composting in local allotments. The domestic rubbish is in fact all ground up together using a primitive system that was fashionable in the United States in the 1960s. In social terms the construction does not permit any other lifestyle than the small family crammed into an apartment.

Some of the other construction projects for the Olympics are on Montjuïc mountain in Barcelona. The most important developments have been outside the city, behind the Collserola hills, in the Maresme region, and in the Llobregat Delta, if one excludes the Olympic Village and the area at the end of Diagonal Avenue in Barcelona itself. The idea is to achieve the urban *mise-en-valeur* of several thousand hectares all around Barcelona, in a half-circle (because of the sea) of about 30 km radius. A few years ago it was possible to take the train to the Autonomous University of Barcelona, a trip of about half an hour from the centre of Barcelona, and see vineyards and the almonds flowering in February and March. Now, few of them are left; they have been replaced by developments with semi-detached houses.

This lust to build is not a new phenomenon in Barcelona, as there were plans in the 1960s to build on the land now occupied by the Olympic Village, demolishing obsolete factories and enabling the owners to make money when the town-planning status of their land changed. The plan was known as the Pla de la Ribera, and its promoters included Narcís Serra and Miquel Roca, who were then two young lawyers and economists, and who have been leading Catalan politicians in the post-Franco era. Many aspects of contemporary Barcelona have their roots in thé 1950s, when the plans were drawn up for the grand metropolis. But they also go back further, to the urban expansion plan of the 1930s inspired by Le Corbusier's ideas. This planning approach, based on the creeping occupation of the perimeter, was the object of criticism right from the beginning of the century, although this opposition never had a chance, and we can now see the continuity of the current development plans. This is demonstrated not only in the urban motorways, but also in the Collserola tunnels, and the diversion of the river Llobregat (which is the subject of ecological opposition).

The dreadful quality of much of Barcelona's construction work also dates from the 1950s and 1960s. Surprisingly little has been said in Barcelona about asbestosis, but there is much talk of aluminosis. Many of the flats bought by working class families in Barcelona (often immigrants from southern Spain) will not last very long, and some have already started to collapse, because the use of aluminous cement, which has become fragile from humidity and the passing of time. It is undeniable that the cement was produced by the company Cementos Molins, and that a member of this Barcelona bourgeois family was Minister for Public Works in the government of the Generalitat of Catalonia in the 1980s. This brings to mind the famous saying of one of the mayors of Barcelona when he looked down from Tibidabo mountain and said to his guests, 'So much urban property!'.

Barcelona would like to be a city with an industrial and professional bourgeoisie, new technology, and a literary and music culture. Unfortunately, the truth is that the most profitable businesses, and the best jobs, are in building, as they were at the beginning of the century, in the 1960s, and now more than ever. Soon, when one looks away from the sea, from Tibidabo or even more so from the new Collserola communications tower, towards the interior and the Pyrenees, one will see another sea of factories, tower blocks, and detached housing in the Sant Cugat and Cerdanyola areas, which cover an area greater than that of the Eixample, the grid developed after 1859 under Ildefons Cerdà's plan. It was a poet, not property developer like Nuñez (President of Barcelona Football Club), who wrote the famous verse, 'Barcelona, spring over the hills ...'. The current municipal and regional administrations do not intend to reduce the Collserola hills – both socialists and Catalan nationalists agree on this point – from a height of 500 m to one of 100 m or 200 m., but they do intend to drill two or three tunnels through the hills. These tunnels are for *cars* and to improve access to the city from the outside, in keeping with the model of development that is being imposed, not by general plan but as a result of piecemeal planning schemes. Improved car access to Barcelona through urban and peri-urban motorways is turning Barcelona into a city for car traffic and the development of car parks. A week's rent for a flat costs as much as a month's rent for a parking place in the centre of the city, but instead of making the inflow of cars more difficult, the administration makes it easier by building motorways around and into Barcelona, finding it more lucrative to permit more car parks. There is as yet no talk in Barcelona of a 'congestion tax' to be paid by cars. This is a great pity, since the structure of a part of Barcelona, the old medieval town and also the

Eixample district planned by Cerdà, allows people to move easily on foot or by bike. A great mistake has been made by choosing to invest in facilities for car transport which lead to urban sprawl. But what is happening now 'spontaneously' looks similar to what was foreseen in the plans drawn up under the Franco dictatorship, from the first plan in 1953 to the last in 1976. These plans intended to locate at least half a million more people on the other side of the mountain, extending the conurbation to Sabadell, with the Tibidabo city park jutting out. The feature that used to serve as a limit to the city, Tibidabo, should serve the same function as New York's Central Park, according to mayor Maragall, who studied at the New School for Social Research in New York. That is to say, a park to serve as the centre for the entire conurbation as it extends.

Much has been said about Barcelona's effects on its surroundings and on Catalonia as a whole. Although the English term 'regional planning' was used but no one really considered following Lewis Mumford's ideas which are discussed in Chapter 10. There was also talk of Gross Barcelona after Gross Berlin, and of Catalonia-city, which meant a highly urbanised Catalonia with services dispersed among all the regions, not concentrated in Barcelona. A more rural version would combine a not-so-big Barcelona with important local cities: Girona, Lleida, Tarragona, and also Vic, Manresa, Tortosa and Reus. This is a merely theoretical version, because it would have been necessary to maintain a strict *agricultural belt* around Barcelona to avoid urban sprawl like an oil-stain. But that is something the Barcelona authorities could never have considered, either under democracy or under the Franco dictatorship, even though the geography of Catalonia greatly favoured the possibility of maintaining an agricultural belt around Barcelona. The land in the Maresme, Baix Llobregat, Delta del Llobregat, and the Vallès areas is extremely fertile, with undeniably valuable environments and considerable agricultural production. This production could have been maintained in the form of local allotments or larger agricultural areas, as well as woodlands and the large wetland of the Llobregat Delta (which can still be partly saved), all of which, within reason, could be open to the local population. But these areas are being dug up and paved over, obliterated by the logic of differential rent. The actual model adopted has been that of Barcelona as a metropolis, a conurbation with an overall population of four million who use cars for transport. Recent census figures indicate a reduction in the population of Barcelona city, but this is not a symptom of what in other European countries and in America has been called 'counterurbanisation'.[8] This change is simply the effect of the low birth rate in Barcelona and the displacement of some inhabitants towards the outside areas *within* the conurbation, some in search of lower rents, others in search of fresh air and more socially distinguished neighbours.

The population of Catalonia (see Table 7.1) is basically growing within the Barcelona conurbation; there is no division at all between Barcelona city and areas such as L'Hospitalet, Badalona, Santa Coloma de Gramenet and Cornellà, not even a 5 metre-wide strip of greenery. At the same time, the cities in the interior or on the coast which are not within a short distance of Barcelona, have lost demographic weight in relative terms.

There are more inhabitants in Badalona and Santa Coloma (the worst developed area of the entire conurbation, to the north-east) than in the entire Eixample district. Similarly, in L'Hospitalet and Cornellà (to the south of the city, through which one passes *en route* from the airport) there are more inhabitants than in the whole Eixample. But these municipalities are full, and it is necessary to develop other territories along the coast to the north, to connect with Mataró, and on the other side of the Collserola range of hills towards Terrassa and Sabadell.

Table 7.1

Population of the largest towns in Catalonia

1857		1986	
Barcelona	183,787	Barcelona	1,701,812
Reus	28,171	L'Hospitalet	279,779
Tortosa	24,977	Badalona	225,016
Lleida	19,627	Sabadell	186,115
Tarragona	18,023	Terrassa	160,105
Mataró	16,595	Santa Coloma	135,238
Manresa	15,264	Lleida	107,749
Igualada	14,000	Tarragona	106,495
Sabadell	13,945	Mataró	100,021
Vic	13,712	Cornellà	86,928

Source: Lluís Cassassas, Barcelona i l'espai Català, 1977, p. 293, and Spanish National Institute of Statistics, Padrón Municipal de Habitantes, 1 de abril de 1986, Madrid 1986.

THE LLOBREGAT DELTA

For much of the history of humanity, wetlands were considered unhealthy areas; their potential was not exploited and it was thought that the best thing to do was to drain and improve them. This is what has happened in Catalonia with the Ebro Delta since the 18th century, although much of the wetland remains. The Llobregat Delta has suffered not only the incursions of agriculture, but also urban sprawl in the form of industry, warehouses and the airport. The primitive and negative vision of wetlands has changed all over the world, due to the educational work of ecologists. In Catalonia there have been well-known conflicts over wetlands, such as the *aiguamolls* (fresh water marshes) of the Empordà region, which were threatened and have been partially destroyed by tourism and property speculation over the last few years. Part of this area has been saved and is now a much-visited natural park 130 km to the north of Barcelona. (The Ebro Delta is 160 km to the south of Barcelona.) At the same time the pressure exerted by Barcelona on the Llobregat Delta is increasing. Which attitude will prevail?

The Llobregat Delta is immediately south of the city and covers an area approximately the size of the municipality of Barcelona. It has many important ecological functions; it is an area with a high production of biomass; it serves as a staging point for migratory birds; it acts as a flood plain to regulate the water flow in the Llobregat; it prevents the seepage of water from the sea and thus the salinisation of the aquifer on which many people depend; it provides a habitat for the juvenile stages of many fish and other marine species; and, in addition to all of these, it recycles or acts as a sink for nitrogen and phosphorus, as well as heavy metals and other pollutants. It also provides a place where young and old alike can learn a little about nature. Its conservation is compatible, at least in some areas, with non-intensive agricultural use, but not with industrial use. The Llobregat Delta has been greatly damaged by property speculation. The Zona Franca, or Free Trade Zone, ruined the left bank of the Llobregat, and there are also many industrial constructions on the right bank. As some industries go into decline, such as the large SEAT–Volkswagen factory in the Zona Franca that has been replaced by a new factory in Martorell, would it not be possible to change the land use to something greener?

Barcelona's new airport is a genuinely attractive building designed by Ricardo Bofill. The new control tower is in the remaining wetland and there is the threat to build another runway. The ecological value of the delta, and perhaps its economic value – if we knew how to assign a monetary value to its ecological functions – makes its preservation worthwhile, against proposals to extend Barcelona's port into the delta area, divert the river, and expand the airport. What is really needed is a moratorium on new public works in the area between the Llobregat river and the municipality of Gavà beyond the small lagoon of El Remolar, and from the town of El Prat to the sea. In the meantime, the ecological value of the delta should be studied. At the same time the level of environmental education in the area must be improved, as the El Prat Council has done. However, after the 1993 election

The Barcelona Conurbation

Source: Corporacion Metropolitana de Barcelona, 4 Años de Acción, CMB, Barcelona, 1983

this council and the Communist Party of Catalonia have been prepared to accept the diversion of the river, a *volte-face* probably triggered by the large investment promised (equivalent to US$3,000 million), besides the well-known links between public works and the finances of political parties. Ecologists oppose this development, and propose that the Llobregat Delta be included in the Ramsar Wetlands Convention.

THE ECOLOGY OF THE CITY

It is unfortunate that the name *Human Ecology* was taken by the Chicago school of urban sociology in the 1920s. This school used concepts derived from the ecology of plants (succession, climax, etc.) as analogues to describe urban social phenomena, for example the social degradation of some districts, but did not really analyse cities in ecological terms, as consumers and excreters of energy and materials. The concept of 'ecological footprint' has been developed in the past few years in order to account for the space required to provide for the city or metropolitan region (i. e. its consumption of food, raw materials, energy, water) and to dispose of wastes.[9] There are other similar studies, some produced as part of UNESCO's Man and Biosphere programme, for several cities around the world. There is also a study of the ecology of Madrid, one of Naredo's pioneering works, and two on the city of Barcelona.[10] But this is still an almost unexplored field of historical study, one rich in fields of specialisation, such as, for instance, the history of the 'heat island' effect in cities or the social history of the rubbish produced, its composition, trends in per capita production by districts, the extent of recycling, toxic effects, etc. In the absence of written documentation, archaeologists have reconstructed the social norms and lifestyles of the past by means of studying the wastes produced. There is a large quantity of contemporary documentation on wastes yet to be explored, although it is also necessary to insert a little archaeology. Industrial archaeologists therefore should not limit themselves to machinery, but should also analyse air, soil and water pollution.

Catalonia is relatively one of the world's leading producers of energy from nuclear power. The nuclear power stations Ascó 1 and 2 and Vandellòs 2 (sited on a beautiful beach, next to Barcelona–Valencia motorway, 30 km to the south of Tarragona) produce a vast amount of thermal energy, about one-third of which is converted into electricity: almost 3 million kilowatts every hour. This electricity would be enough to allow every inhabitant of the Barcelona conurbation to have an electric heater on day and night, 12 months a year. The radioactive waste is partially reprocessed in France in order to recover the uranium not consumed and the plutonium produced. This waste used to pass right through the heart of Barcelona along the underground railway route following Aragón Street, but it now is transported on a new railway line behind the Collserola hills. The city has banned the transport of radioactive materials and is also moving lorry traffic to new motorways running parallel to the railway line. It has even expelled the dead, hence the construction of the new cemetery in the woodland on the northern side of the Collserola.

Barcelona expels and absorbs. Most of the rubbish is burnt in the incinerator at Sant Adrià de Besòs and then deposited in dumps, such as the one in the Garraf (south-west of the city, towards Sitges). This has been heavily criticised 'because it is in a karstic area, and there is a serious risk of leaching that could affect the neighbouring localities by contaminating subterranean water supplies'.[11] There is a new proposal for a giant new incinerator in the Llobregat Delta. Some districts within the conurbation of Barcelona are now beginning to recycle rubbish, mainly because of the activities of environmental groups such as CEPA, but much rubbish is still produced unecessarily. For instance, many citizens of Barcelona drink water from outside the city, packed in plastic bottles, but the regional authorities so far have declined to impose a refundable deposit on the bottles.

In 1990, arose the most important ecological controversy ever in Catalonia, soon after the controversy following the major fire in 1989 in Vandellòs 1 nuclear power station, which was a total write-off. The regional public works minister, Molins, proposed a plan to 'eliminate' Catalonia's industrial wastes, based on dumps and incinerators located in rural areas, some of which (e.g. Castellbisbal) were close to Barcelona, while others were up to 100 km away. Spontaneous local opposition led to this plan being withdrawn (followed by an electoral defeat in several of these villages, such as Castellbisbal, where a young ecologist became mayor), although this opposition has not yet managed to introduce terms like 'dioxin' into the Catalan political vocabulary.

Have you ever heard of Andorra? Not the Andorra of the playwright Max Fritsch, nor the 'state' of Andorra in the Pyrenees, a VAT-free tax haven for Catalan consumers, but the Andorra in Aragon (200 km to the southwest of Barcelona) where there is a large power station belonging to ENDESA, the national electricity company. (Its director, Feliciano Fuster, likes to present himself through the media, in paid advertisements, as a good ecologist, but there has been a court case for excessive SO_2 emissions.) This power station generating almost 1,000 megawatts burns lignite and supplies other areas, including Barcelona, with electricity. The sulphur dioxide and nitrogen oxides are released into the atmosphere, the wind in turn carrying them to the Els Ports area and the medieval city of Morella, at the junction of Catalonia, Valencia and Aragon. The pinewoods, crop and grazing land have been severely damaged in the process of providing Barcelona with the electricity it needs. Greedy Barcelona! In the past, some electricity was generated in Barcelona, and the three chimneys of the power station can still be seen in the Paralelo, next to the El Molino nightclub, near Montjuïc. This power station became famous in 1917 as a result of the 'Canadiense' general strike, so named for the power company owned by Mister Pearson, a famous man who has been honoured with a pretty avenue in the richest area of Barcelona, Pedralbes. Next to the mouth of the River Besòs, near the Olympic Village, there are three more tall chimneys, part of another power station, which sometimes still operates. Nowadays, nearly all the electricity consumed comes from outside Barcelona, from the Catalonia it has colonised and depopulated, or even from outside Catalonia. Some of it comes from the Pyrenees. Hydro-electric power is exported to Barcelona from its region of origin. Bills are paid in Barcelona, where the electricity companies have their headquarters (they are not yet transnationals), rather than where the power is generated. Market accounting takes precedence over ecological accounting. *Barcelona es poderosa, Barcelona tiene poder* (Barcelona is powerful, Barcelona has all the power), in the words of the Olympic rumba. The high-voltage supply lines that spoil the gentle landscape of rural Catalonia are like a huge spider's web; if one looked at them from the air, one would soon see where the spider is lurking.

Barcelona does not only absorb kilowatts, it absorbs food, oil, Algerian gas (tasting increasingly of blood), and a lot of water. The amount of energy imported in the form of gas, oil and electricity to serve the exosomatic use of Barcelona's citizens is 40 times greater than the amount imported in the form of food. Barcelona is a modern, prosperous city with a car for every three inhabitants. However, this city full of cars is not as proportionately full of dogs as the cities in the north of Europe, although we do have more pigeons (more than fifty thousand) and seagulls, who feed on waste. The sewer rats, *Rattus norvegicus*, are common animals (there are about two million), and without doubt the ecological functions of this urban fauna would repay investigation.

The average consumption of water in Barcelona is about 400 litres per person per day, without distinguishing between different social classes, and including industrial and public urban use. A considerable part of this water is lost before it reaches the consumers. There have been fierce debates over increased water charges. The general consensus is that Barcelona needs more water: in some housing developments with detached housing and gardens, average consumption may reach Californian levels of a 1,000 litres per person per day. Average rainfall per square metre is almost as high as that of London, about 600 l/m^2, but its distribution is quite different, being concentrated in the spring and autumn. It sometimes rains too much. Most of the water Barcelona consumes comes from the River Ter near the border with France. There are now controversial plans to take water from the Ebro, or from the River Segre, a tributary of the Ebro, by means of the new Rialb dam, which has drowned small, beautiful villages with Romanesque ruins. This would reduce the amount of water reaching the Ebro Delta, which is being eaten away by the sea and suffering salinisation. Even without evaporation, and even if all the rain that falls in Barcelona were stored in the city, it would still be necessary to import about five times more in order to maintain current levels of consumption.

The new ecological history now provides some studies of air pollution in some cities.[12] Socio-ecological history knows of many popular struggles against sulphur dioxide produced by industrial installations, for example the copper foundries ranging from Río Tinto in Andalusia to La Oroya in Peru. In Germany, the new ecological historians have studied acid rain, including the controversies over chimney heights and emission standards. The smoke created by industry is no longer considered a mark of progress, but a sign of the different types of pollution the chimneys disguise by spreading it more widely. Many rich countries have recently achieved a reduction in sulphur dioxide pollution both within and outside cities, due to the elimination of lignite and reduction of the use of coal as fuel, as well as the installation of filters in metal smelters. The current tendency in the world's rich cities, including Barcelona, is a reduction in sulphur dioxide and an increase in nitrogen oxides and surface ozone. London smog has been replaced by Los Angeles smog, although the word *smog*, derived from the combination of *smoke* and *fog*, is not linguistically applicable to the air pollution characteristic of Los Angeles. Air pollution produced by cars is diffuse and difficult to localise from a social point of view, and so responsibility is much more dispersed in cities where almost everyone owns or uses cars.

THE PARADOXES OF 'MODERNISM'

Are you aware that Cebrià de Montoliu (1873–1923), the secretary of the Sociedad Cívica Catalana 'La Ciutat-Jardí' (The Catalan Garden City Civic Society), and the editor of its journal *Civitas*, left Barcelona in 1920 in self-exile – disgusted by the property-holding interests – and went to the United States to help establish a 'single tax' (after Henry George) and an 'organic' settlement called Fairhope, dying there in 1923? Cebrià de Montoliu came from a rural aristocratic family but tried to join the popular movements of his time. He unsuccessfully denounced private ownership of the land in Barcelona's area of expansion as an obstacle to development in the form of new garden-cities (not garden-suburbs), separate from the conurbation. Perhaps because he was excessively influenced by the garden-cities movement, he did not attach enough importance to the potential role in Catalonia of the regional cities in the process of decentralisation. As he was a man with practical aspirations, he collaborated with major landowners in Barcelona, although their intention was to develop their properties near the city rather than to create an alternative model of urban development. In the end, however, he wound up a frustrated man, defeated by the property speculators. He considered himself a disciple of Patrick Geddes and

Ebenezer Howard, and an admirer of John Ruskin and William Morris. To use modern terminology, Cebrià de Montoliu was an ecological town–planner, the theoretician of 'organic' town-planning in Catalonia. Chronologically Cebrià de Montoliu belongs to the rationalist period, as a *noucentista*, but although he was born too late to join the initial Arts and Crafts and Art Nouveau movement in Catalonia, his ideas remained quite the opposite of rationalist *noucentisme*. He translated Ruskin and was the author of the introduction to a Catalan translation of *News from Nowhere* by William Morris. Isn't it incredible that a city full of buildings inspired by the Pre-Raphaelite movement should have forced him into exile?

Olympic Barcelona disguises itself as a utopian project and receives Harvard prizes for urban design, but it is the same Barcelona that considers land merely a means to make money. After 1880 and until as late as 1920 the patricians in this city were building themselves houses and even factories in the Art Nouveau style or Jugendstil, of which Catalans are very proud and which they confusingly call *modernisme*. There is a double paradox. First, why did these families of industrialists, such as the Batlló or the Güell (a business and slave-trading family in Cuba who became industrialists), build themselves Art Nouveau houses, and even some factories, influenced by the Pre-Raphaelites? Other cities in Europe – Brussels, Glasgow, Vienna – also adopted this architectural style, with its romantic ideals of protest against the social and aesthetic ugliness of industrialism. (Solvay, the industrialist, had his house in Brussels built by the art nouveaux architect Victor Horta.) This return to the medieval became a national style in Catalonia, the result of simultaneous economic, political and artistic factors, because Catalan patriots liked to remember the Catalan expansion of the Middle Ages, and because the moment was right for investment in property. The first paradox is, how could a style based on anti-industrialist protest in the fields of architecture and domestic art be adopted by Catalan industrialists? This protest against the social and aesthetic disasters of industrialism, a protest originally British and in tune with a line of thought derived from Carlyle and continued by Ruskin and William Morris, leads to a socialist critique, or in the case of Morris, mildly anarchist (as in his booklet *The Policy of Abstention*) or utopian socialist in the best sense of the term (as shown by his famous *News from Nowhere*).

The second paradox is, why did the model of urban development consistent with the social and aesthetic critique of industrialism, represented by Art Nouveau, and the idea of the garden-city separate from the metropolis, fail so completely in Barcelona, one of the capital cities of Art Nouveau? Were the material interests at stake in urban development more important than those at stake in architecture?

There is now a certain respect for Barcelona's *modernist* architectural heritage, but local politicians, even the Socialists, declare that they are the heirs of the rationalist *noucentista* tradition. They support industrialism and urban expansion, now and in retrospect. Thus Barcelona, which used to have an architecturally eccentric bourgeoisie and a rebellious proletariat, hoped that the European Union would locate an agency or two in the city. It did not want something like the European Environment Agency, however, and hoped vainly that the European Bundesbank would be sited here, in one of the glass towers in the 'New Icaria'. What a farce! But nobody laughs.

Modern town-planning began at the turn of the century and involved Patrick Geddes, Ebenezer Howard, Camilo Sitte and Raymond Unwin. This 'science of cities' was a rather late response to industrialisation and the accompanying phenomena of unprecedented urban growth. This was not the first time that cities had been planned, but the profession of town planning, with its congresses, journals and university chairs, was quite new. Now, at the end of the 20th century, when there are already urban conurbations with populations of more than 20 million, and ecology provides a different and critical perspective on the Industrial Revolution, the ecological vision of urban development and town planning advanced by Patrick Geddes and Lewis Mumford is more relevant than ever. However, the position generally held by architects and town planners is still not one of clear adhesion to the proposals of ecological urban development, rather it is closer to a total rejection of the very idea of planning. The idea of overall planning for cities sounds suspiciously modern at a time when being post-modern is all the rage. Nowadays what is favoured are urban schemes and projects limited to specific sites (rehabilitation and gentrification in the centre, chaotic development of peripheral agricultural land through isolated schemes). This is how Barcelona's agricultural belt is being destroyed by the new rings of motorways and projects on the periphery, some of which develop hundreds of hectares at a stroke. Recent projects include the Cerdanyola Technology Park, the development of the campus of the Autonomous University in Bellaterra, the occupation of a large part of the Llobregat Delta, the expansion of Gavà, the development of Montigalà, the threat to develop what remains of Gallecs, and others. The occupation of agricultural land and woodland by leaps and bounds has been made easier by the trend of building golf courses, promoted by property speculation interests. Golf courses need to be watered, and they use water treated with public money, but which still contains much nitrogen and phosphorous. The polluted water used to go straight into the sea or the rivers, and now at least it serves some purpose. Each golf course (what could be greener?) is followed by a new housing development.

The current rejection of the idea of general town planning in favour of limited specific projects makes it possible to hide the fact that in the 'science of cities' there were *two* approaches, not just one. There was an organic, cultural, historic, regional, and anti-metropolitan approach that had a sound basis in Patrick Geddes' and Lewis Mumford's ideas on regional planning, with an explicitly ecological content that perceived the role of the flows of energy and materials in the human economy. This was perfectly compatible with an appreciation of the aesthetic approach of Ruskin and William Morris, but could also have been compatible with a new bioclimatic architecture designed on rational lines. This approach favouring organic urban development includes regional proposals for town- and country-planning, which are of course different from those advanced by the other, metropolitan, line favouring 'progress' and industrialisation.

The so-called rationalist approach had appeared quite early in the Eixample district of Barcelona in the work of Ildefons Cerdà (1859), the author of a *General Theory of Urbanisation*. That grid of square city blocks, of 100 m each side and about five stories high, could have turned out somewhat differently. Those blocks in the Eixample district of Barcelona (easily transformed into pedestrian islands) are more and more inhospitable (now that the pavement have been invaded by cars and motorbikes), and things are getting worse as the interiors of many blocks are converted into car parks. However, this city block structure is potentially more humane than Le Corbusier's isolated tower blocks, ships in an ocean where the car is the only lifeboat.

On one side, then, there is the line expounded by Ruskin, Morris, Howard, and Geddes, and in Barcelona by Cebrià de Montoliu, and perhaps some anarchists. On the other side, there is the industrialising and dehumanising approach (intended to be rationalist) from Cerdà to Le Corbusier and beyond. Now *both* these proposals for overall town planning are being rejected. The holistic side of town-planning, the hint of general rules that must be obeyed, clashes violently with the spirit of post-modernism. But this is no excuse for ignoring ecological and organic town-planning.

It is not correct to say that those of the historicist, culturalist, and organicist tradition preferred to work at the level of architecture – the Art Nouveau or Jugendstil houses in Barcelona's Eixample – rather than at the level of town planning. Among the adjectives used for Geddes' approach is 'organicist' because he himself used it. Although biological reductionism is not an adequate explanation for the phenomena that make up human history, such as cities, we keep the word 'organic' for its natural connotations, for its emphasis on the fact that the 'biology' of the city requires a supply of energy and materials and generates wastes. The city cannot be ecologically separated from its region, and this is meant in a more material sense than in the French school of regional geography. The incoming and outgoing flows of energy and materials will vary in accordance with the form of urbanisation adopted, with the social structure of the city, with its monetary wealth, and it will also depend on the technologies of transport and construction, the extent to which rainwater is collected and used water is recycled, and the rubbish collection and heating systems. The rural land around the city is not considered by ecological town-planning to be a mere reserve for the 'production' of urban land where housing and communication facilities can be built, but as the site where the energy of the sun produces the plant material necessary for food. Furthermore, it is aesthetically pleasing and plays an important climatic role, as do also the surrounding forests and wetlands. This leads to attempts to stop urban sprawl by defending woodland reserves, wetlands and agricultural belts where no building is allowed, and by constructing *new towns* beyond this belt, or, as could be the case for Catalonia, regional cities with good public transport links to, but separated from, the metropolis. Underlying this 'disconnected', ruralist vision of urban development, there was in Geddes' and Howard's (and Mumford's) thought a genuinely ecological attitude.

Such a vision of town-planning was ecological, but this version of ecology had nothing to do with the later anti-urban and anti-industrial rhetoric of the anti-rational European fascisms. The new ecological history views the history of technology, related to the history of industrial development and town-planning, from a position closer to Lewis Mumford's critique than to J. D. Bernal's optimism. The history of scientific discoveries must include their social context, the history of the socio-economic reasons behind specific technological applications, and also the history of the environmental effects of these technologies. Society is never immediately conscious of these environmental effects: ignorance and technological knowledge are both social constructs. It is interesting to study the fear of new technologies, and it is just as interesting to study the lack of social awareness of the effects of DDT and nuclear power, or indeed the motor car, over so many years. A new approach to the history of technology is taking form, one that considers its environmental effects.[13] This is an innovation among economic historians.

It is easy to mock the Luddite attitude of those who have opposed the introduction of new technologies because of irrational fears or, sometimes, because of self-interested concerns. Rural nostalgia has persisted in European popular culture, even within the proletariat, over the last 150 years of industrial society, and this nostalgia acquires a new significance when considered from the perspective of ecological history. In the case of Catalonia there are some extremely interesting fields awaiting study, such as the history of the local radical forms of vegetarianism, birth control, feminism, and cycling, all possibly linked to anarchism. This subject is rather complicated from the political point of view because there have also been right-wing forms of rural nostalgia, which fascists tried to take advantage of using the rhetoric of *Blut und Boden* (blood and soil).

In the 20th century industrialisation and car production have been more or less synonymous. In the late 1970s, there were attempts to identify the greens in Germany with the ruralist tendencies of some Nazis, such as Walther Darré, who advocated a return to the land, because the peasantry was considered the backbone of the German race. Since political ecology is a critique of industrialism (because of its ecological, social, and aesthetic effects) which undeniably sees many virtues in traditional agriculture, the equation 'ecology = blood and soil' is still used by some, such as the French philosopher Luc Ferry, to discredit the Greens. In reality, however, Nazism, like the Italian and Spanish fascisms, favoured industrialisation and demographic growth, not really 'green' causes at all. In the field of architecture, Nazism favoured a rural *Heimatstil* in some constructions (as did Franco's Rural Colonisation Institute with its picturesque villages) and opposed the international style of Mies van de Rohe or Le Corbusier. However, the real favourite architect of the Nazi regime was Albert Speer, who developed a neo-classical monumental style.

Nazism used the rhetoric of *Blut und Boden*, but had a praxis of *Blut und Autobahnen* (blood and motorways). This was true to such an extent that Hitler himself enthusiastically praised the car. 'It makes us bitter to think that millions of working human beings, both virtuous and brave, do not have the means of transport that, especially on Sundays and holidays, would be a hitherto unknown source of joy to them . . . We must finish with the class nature of the car, the sad fact that cars separate society into different social classes; it is necessary for the car to be something that everybody uses, not a luxury'.[14] This pronouncement of Hitler's could have been uttered by Henry Ford 20 years earlier or by some prominent bureaucrat in the former East Germany 30 years later. It effectively dispels the notion that fascism was ruralist and opposed to 'progress'.[15] Leaving aside the origin of Volkswagen but bearing in mind the fact that Volkswagen–SEAT is the largest enterprise in the conurbation of Barcelona, it would be very difficult to launch a successful campaign in Barcelona against cars, not only as consumer goods but as a source of jobs.

CORBUSERIAN MONSTROSITIES

The obvious connection between the architecture of Gaudí and Domènech i Montaner and the aesthetics of Ruskin and William Morris raises the question of why there was no 'organic' school of town-planning in Catalonia, even though there was an 'organic' school of architecture. Cebrià de Montoliu's attempt to create one failed. Later, during the Second

Republic, the 1932–34 Macià Plan for Barcelona was devised, inspired by Le Corbusier. It signalled the Barcelona authorities' support for the 'rationalist' (not rational) approach to town planning, the opposite of the 'organic' approach. In fact, although it was perhaps correct to call Le Corbusier's architecture rationalist, his ideas on town-planning were not at all rational from an ecological point of view. Fortunately, the economic and political circumstances of the 1930s did not allow the reconstruction of the city of Barcelona in accordance with Le Corbusier's town-plan, which was drawn up together with a local group called GATCPAC. Why has this plan been regarded so favourably in Barcelona by both Socialists and Communists? The reasons may have something to do with the period when the plan was proposed, the Second Spanish Republic, and with its official name, the Macià Plan (Macià was a hero of radical Catalan nationalism, and his name was given to this plan even though he did not participate in it at all). Other reasons for their enthusiasm relate to the left's depressing tendency to support progress in the form of cars and the cement industry.

Local experts on the history of town-planning have concealed Cebrià de Montoliu's clear opposition to the expansion of the Barcelona conurbation. The most valuable academic study of the planning of Barcelona during the first third of this century is the doctoral thesis by Torres Capell,[16] under the title *El Planejament Urbà i la Crisi de 1917 a Barcelona* (Town-Planning and the Crisis of 1917 in Barcelona). Torres Capell dedicates a whole chapter to Montoliu and the Garden City Society, but attaches little importance to Montoliu's resignation and departure to the United States after the failure of his plans around 1919–20. The ecological and social significance that the idea of the garden city could have had in Catalonia, connecting Ruskin, Geddes and Morris (and Howard) with the ecological town planning of Montoliu, is not really studied by Torres Capell who hardly mentions Patrick Geddes. But Montoliu specifically described Geddes as his mentor from 1913 onwards, before the publication of Geddes' book *Cities in Evolution* in 1915. From reading Torres Capell nobody would guess that the term *ciencia cívica* (civic science) which Montoliu used came from Geddes, as did the regional survey procedure that Montoliu recommended before drawing up a town-plan. It is due to Geddes' influence that in Great Britain the term of *town-and country-planning* is used rather than town-planning, thus putting the city into its regional and ecological context. The distorted interpretation by Torres Capell attributes to Montoliu responsibility for introducing in Barcelona the idea of 'urban rationality'. In fact, this would be adequate if we took rationality to mean an ecological approach, but it is wrong to use this term if it places Montoliu within the general consensus regarding the plans for expanding the Barcelona conurbation, which range from the Eixample plan by Cerdà in 1859 to the Jaussely 'traffic links plan' dating from the beginning of this century, the working class blocks and garden suburbs of the 1910s and 1920s (quite different from garden cities *separate* from the conurbation) and the Corbuserian Plan in 1932–34. In Catalonia this plan has been considered 'progressive' or 'leftist', as Torres Capell, and Francesc Roca, interpret it. [17]

There is another possible interpretation: there was an organic or ecological approach to town-planning (which came to nothing in practice) ranging from Cebrià de Montoliu to those anarchists who took an interest in town planning problems, especially Alfonso Martínez Rizo, author of the leaflet 'The Town Planning of the Future' (1932). [18] The alternative approach opposed urban sprawl but it ran into several problems. In the field of ideas, it had to confront the illusion of unlimited urban expansion. In practice, it clashed with the interests of the owners of the land that could be built on. Martínez Rizo clearly understood the theory of the garden city and agricultural belts, which he supported. He also clearly summed up the reasons for its failure in practice:

The large cities in order to house the stream of new citizens that causes them to grow continuously, should build city nucleuses *separated* from the city centre by a specific distance that allows good communications *but leaves free the agricultural land* necessary for social health and hygiene ... the truly rational thing to do would be to *disconnect* the large cities ... but these conclusions are limited to laying down principles that cannot be put into practice. The owners of the land that would have to be turned into free areas are, in the capitalist system, a force that is showing itself to be effectively invincible. [19]

The current crisis in general town-planning does not bother Barcelona's planners; on the contrary, they are like children at the post-modernist school taking their recreation break. There is no longer any comprehensive town- and country-planning. However, the triumph of isolated projects, which can consist of hundreds of hectares in the peripheral areas, but which do not conform to a general planning policy, a triumph over regional planning, is in my opinion a short-lived triumph of metropolitan ideology over the ecological critique. The rejection of the general idea of town-planning leads to the conception of the city as something totally alien to its ecology, as literally a metaphysical entity. Urban development occurs in the form of a scheme here, a project there, the 'anything goes' approach that is post-modernism. But should these interventions not be seen in some sort of context? What is this context? Is it the usual conception of urban expansion, or is it the ecological blending of the city into its surroundings? The absence of an general approach to town planning allows this question to be ignored. Its absence has had profoundly anti-ecological implications: at the same time as a beautiful beach is being opened in Barcelona and the old city is gradually being renovated, the neighbouring territory is being destroyed by motorways, the Llobregat Delta is being ruined, the potential agro-forestry green belt is being built over, enormous amounts of energy created by nuclear power are being imported, and water resources are being managed in a colonial style.

The architects of Barcelona have a vision as far-reaching as that of a city pigeon. They do not see the very wide region in which the conurbation is ecologically located, nor even its relation to Catalonia in the narrow sense. Their attitude to technology is that of uncritical users. After the Spanish Civil War (1936–39), these 'rationalist' architects managed in the 1950s to renew the links with the international movement. It is true that a victory was won against fascist architecture, but these architects have never considered an ecologically rational approach to urban planning. Oriol Bohigas, in his writings on 'modernism', does not mention Geddes or Cebrià de Montoliu.[20] It is not necessary to renounce beautiful individual buildings, in any style (no absurd return to Art Nouveau is proposed here). However, architecture should take ecology into account, and specific urban schemes within the conurbation should form part of an ecological interpretation that includes their regional surroundings in the widest sense. In Barcelona, architects have been too powerful over the last few years, and architects are not well prepared for the role of town-planners. Town-planners should be ecologists who come out of their woods and wetlands and get involved in politics.

PART TWO

Chapter 8

Mahatma Gandhi and the Environmental Movement[1]

Gandhi is one of the great thinkers of our time who, without ever intending it to be so, has become the man for all seasons, and all things to all men.

Abu Abraham

The life and work of Mohandas Karamchand 'Mahatma' Gandhi (1869–1948) have had a considerable influence on the environmental movement in India. This movement began with the Chipko Andolan, in April 1973; in one of the first printed accounts of Chipko, a breathless journalist announced that Gandhi's ghost had saved the Himalayan trees. Ever since, Mahatma Gandhi has been the usually acknowledged and occasionally unacknowledged 'patron saint' of the Indian environmental movement. From Chipko to the 'Save the Narmada Movement' (Narmada Bachao Andolan) of the present time, environmental activists have relied heavily on Gandhian techniques of non-violent protest or *satyagraha*, and have drawn abundantly on Gandhi's polemic against heavy industrialisation (cf. Chapter 1). Again, some of the movement's better-known figures, for example Chandi Prasad Bhatt and Sunderlal Bahuguna of Chipko, or Baba Amte and Medha Patkar of Narmada, have often emphasised their own debt to Gandhi.

Of course, one must not deny other influences, for under the broad umbrella of the environmental movement are many groups with little connection to Gandhi; for example, the Kerala Sastra Sahitya Parishad, with a background of Marxism, but whose contribution to Indian environmentalism is second to none. Other groups are variously influenced by socialism, liberation theology, and traditions of charity or self-help. All the same, it is probably fair to say that the life and practice of Gandhi have been the single most important influence on the environmental movement in India.

I myself had the privilege of studying, at close quarters, the work of two extraordinary Gandhian environmentalists of the present day, Chandi

Prasad Bhatt and Sunderlal Bahuguna. My personal acquaintance with Bhatt and Bahuguna is slight, but I was to acquire some intimacy with their life-work through my research on the movement with which they are indissolubly linked, the Chipko Andolan.[2] Of course, it is misleading to think of Chipko itself as only a 'Gandhian' movement, for its roots lie more strongly in a century-old tradition of peasant resistance in defence of forest rights. However, Bhatt and Bahuguna, the movement's best-known leaders, themselves exemplify the highest traditions of Gandhian constructive work.

Urban admirers of Chipko can be usually identified as being supporters of either Chandi Prasad Bhatt or Sunderlal Bahuguna, but there is in fact ample reason to celebrate both men. Bhatt and his organisation, the Dashauli Gram Swarajya Mandal (DGSM), played a seminal role in the origins of Chipko: the tree-hugging technique of protest was itself suggested by Bhatt to the peasants of the upper Alakananda valley. Since co-ordinating those early protests against commercial forestry, the DGSM has focused increasingly on environmental restoration. Here it has taken the lead in organising women for afforestation work in the villages of the Alakananda valley, where its tree-planting and protection progammes have been a good deal more successful than the lavishly funded schemes of the state Forest Department.

Whereas Chandi Prasad Bhatt must be reckoned the pioneer of Chipko – if we were to bestow that accolade on an individual – Sunderlal Bahuguna has a record of social work that goes back even further. He and his wife Vimla were among the first group of Sarvodaya workers trained by Sarla Devi (Catherine Mary Heilman), a remarkable English disciple of Mahatma Gandhi who moved to the hills in the 1940s. In the Bhageerathi valley which is his home base, Bahuguna organised several important Chipko protests between 1977 and 1980. In the years since, where Bhatt and his colleagues have concentrated on ecological restoration within the Himalaya, Bahuguna has chosen to take the message of Chipko beyond the hills. An indefatigable walker and trekker, with the endurance of a man half his age, he has travelled widely in India and abroad. He is a captivating speaker too, and in this capacity has done a great deal to alert the urban intelligentsia to the dangers of unbridled materialism.

These two Chipko leaders are among the greatest living Indians. The example of Gandhi animates the lives of both men, but I like to think that each has taken something distinctive from the life of the master. Bahuguna is a prophet and moralist, who appeals, as Gandhi did, to the conscience of individuals, urging them to abjure consumerism and return to a simpler way of life. In contrast, by working out in practice a sustainable economic alternative to centralized development, Bhatt and his group are more in line with the Gandhi who emphasised constructive work by training activists in

154

his Sabarmati and Wardha *ashrams*. Chandi Prasad's work has helped infuse a new ecological meaning to the Mahatma's ideal of *gram swaraj*, or village self-reliance.

GANDHI'S ENVIRONMENTAL ETHIC

I speak of Chandi Prasad Bhatt and Sunderlal Bahuguna only because my study of the Chipko movement brought me in close contact with their work. Writers and scholars associated with the Narmada Bachao Andolan – which has succeeded Chipko as the most significant environmental initiative in India today – have remarked on the Gandhi-like spirit that also animates the lives and actions of its main leaders, the septugenerian social worker Baba Amte, and Medha Patkar, the 40-year-old woman activist who has sustained the struggle despite relentless repression. The Chipko and Narmada movements are outstanding but by no means isolated examples of the living heritage of Gandhi, as it is embodied in the contemporary environmental movement.

However, the environmentalists of today do not merely claim that they are following the example of Gandhi; they go on to argue that the Mahatma himself foresaw the ecological crisis of modern industrial society. The question whether Gandhi was indeed an 'early environmentalist' is usually answered in the affirmative by his admirers, but rarely with supporting evidence. That is, it is taken for granted that Gandhi anticipated our environmental concerns, but without demonstrating precisely where and in what ways he did so. If his writings are invoked for this purpose at all, it is almost always his work *Hind Swaraj* (published in 1909), which a distinguished Gandhian of the present day has claimed gives us an 'alternate perspective' on development while explaining how 'the current mode of development is exploitative of man by man and of nature by man'.[3] Rereading *Hind Swaraj* recently, I found myself unable to agree with this verdict. Despite the book's eloquent denunciation of modern Western culture, the book has nothing to say about man's relationship with nature, still less does it offer an alternative perspective on development.

But perhaps *Hind Swaraj* is not the place to look. That book was written while Gandhi was living in South Africa, where he spent 21 years as a lawyer and political campaigner. On his return to India in 1914, Gandhi began immediately to acquaint himself with economic and social conditions in the village. Through his travels in the Indian countryside and the organisation, in 1917 and 1918, of peasant struggles in the districts of Champaran and Kheda, Gandhi was to come face to face with colonialism as a system of economic exploitation, not merely – as had been his experience in South Africa – of racial discrimination.

From this deeper understanding of colonialism, Gandhi came to see that it would be impossible for India to emulate Western patterns of industrial development. It must be acknowledged at once that he does not anywhere offer an alternative *model* of development for India. Gandhi was not a systematic thinker; moreover, he was preoccupied with pressing questions of political mobilization and social reform – the struggle for national independence, harmonious relations between India's two major religious groupings, Hindus and Muslims, the emancipation of women and of the lower castes – and could scarcely have had the time, to chart out an economic or environmental programme in detail. All the same, scattered through his writings of the nineteen 1920s, 1930s and 1940s are clues to such an alternative path. It is to these writings that I now turn.[4]

Gandhi's reservations about the wholesale industrialization of India are usually ascribed to moral grounds – the selfishness and competitiveness of modern society – but they also had markedly ecological undertones. Take this remarkable passage, from his journal *Young India*, dated the 20th of December 1928: 'God forbid that India should ever take to industrialisation after the manner of the West. The economic imperialism of a single tiny island kingdom (England) is today keeping the world in chains. If an entire nation of 300 million took to similar economic exploitation, it would strip the world bare like locusts'.

Two years earlier, Gandhi had claimed that to 'make India like England and America is to find some other races and places of the earth for exploitation'. As it appeared that the Western nations had already 'divided all the known races outside Europe for exploitation and there are no new worlds to discover', he pointedly asked: 'What can be the fate of India trying to ape the West?' (*Young India*, 7 October 1926).

The answer to his question is by now painfully obvious, for in the past few decades, we have attempted precisely to 'make India like England and America'. Without the access to resources and markets enjoyed by those two nations when they began to industrialise, India has had perforce to rely on the exploitation of its own peoples and environment. The natural resources of the countryside have increasingly been used to meet the needs of the urban–industrial sector, and this diversion of forest, water, and other resources to the élite has accelerated the process of environmental degradation while at the same time depriving rural and tribal communities of their traditional rights of access and use. Meanwhile, the modern sector has moved aggressively into the remaining resource frontiers of India, the north-eastern states and the Andaman and Nicobar islands.

Perhaps Gandhi would not have been surprised. As he recognised, the bias towards urban–industrial development could result only in a one-sided exploitation of the hinterland. In 1946, he had expressed this with characteristic lucidity: 'The blood of the villages is the cement with which the edifice of the cities is built' (*Harijan*, 23 June 1946). On an earlier occasion, Gandhi had alerted a gathering in Indore to the concentration of resources on which city life has come to rest. 'We are sitting in this fine *pandal* under a blaze of electric lights', he remarked, 'but we do not know we are burning these lights at the expense of the poor' (*Harijan*, 11 May 1935).

From this diagnosis of the ills of industrialism flowed Gandhi's preferred solution, wherein economic development would be centred on the village. He wished, above all, to see that 'the blood that is today inflating the arteries of the cities run once again in the blood vessels of the villages'. Pre-eminent here was the decentralisation of political and economic power, so that villages could resume control over their own affairs. When he was accused of turning his back on the great scientific inventions, including electricity, Gandhi remarked (in words to inspire all proponents of decentralised energy systems): 'If we could have electricity in every village home, I should not mind villagers plying their implements and tools with the help of electricity. But then the village communities or the State would own power houses, just as they have their grazing pastures' (*Harijan*, 22 June 1935).

In 1937, some years after he had moved to Wardha to devote himself to rural reconstruction, Gandhi defined his ideal Indian village as follows:

It will have cottages with sufficient light and ventilation, built of a material obtainable within a radius of five miles of it. The cottages will have courtyards enabling householders to plant vegetables for domestic use and to house their cattle. The village lanes and streets will be free of all avoidable dust. It will have wells according to its needs and accessible to all. It will have houses of worship for all, also a common meeting place, a village common for grazing its cattle, a co-operative dairy, primary and secondary schools in which industrial [i.e. vocational] education will be the central fact, and it will have Panchayats for settling disputes. It will produce its own grains, vegetables and fruit, and its own Khadi. This is roughly my idea of a model village ... (*Harijan*, 9 January 1937).

There are many elements in this picture that would fit nicely into the utopia of the environmentalist: local self-reliance, a clean and hygienic environment, the collective management and use of those gifts of nature so necessary for human life, water and pasture. But Gandhi himself had an uncanny knack of combining a utopian vision with practical means. Notable in this connection is the attention he paid to the crucial problem of soil fertility. Towards the end of his life, he warned the proponents of the rapid mechanisation of agriculture that 'trading in soil fertility for the sake of quick returns would prove to be a disastrous, short-sighted policy. It would result in virtual depletion of the soil' (*Harijan*, 25 August 1946). He was a enthusiastic supporter of organic manure, which enriched the soil, improved village hygiene through the effective disposal of waste, saved foreign exchange, and enhanced crop yields – all this, as we now know (cf. Chapters 3 and 4), without the attendant pollution and resource exhaustion caused by modern chemical techniques. He singled out the work of Albert Howard, who had pioneered methods of organic agriculture at his Institute of Plant Industry in Indore. Gandhi described approvingly and in great detail the methods developed by Howard and his associates to convert a mixture of cowdung, farm wastes, wood ash and urine into invaluable fertiliser (*Harijan*, 17 August and 24 August 1935).

Finally, Gandhi's philosophical critique of modern civilisation also has profound implications for the way we live and relate to the environment today. For him, 'the distinguishing characteristic of modern civilization is an indefinite multiplicity of wants', whereas ancient civilisations were marked by an 'imperative restriction upon, and a strict regulating of, these wants' (*Young India*, 2 June 1927). In uncharacteristically intemperate tones, he spoke of his 'wholeheartedly detest[ing] this mad desire to destroy distance and time, to increase animal appetites, and go to the ends of the earth in search of their satisfaction. If modern civilization stands for all this, and I have understood it to do so, I call it satanic' (*Young India*, 17 March 1927).

At the level of the individual, Gandhi's code of voluntary simplicity offers a sustainable alternative to modern lifestyles. One of his best known aphorisms, that the 'world has enough for everybody's need, but not enough for everybody's greed', is, in effect, an exquisitely phrased one-line environmental ethic. This was an ethic he himself practiced, for resource recycling, and the minimisation of wants, were integral to his life.

His analysis of macro processes of economic development, his prescriptions for rural reconstruction, and his ethics for living: at all levels, then, Gandhi's writings offer sharp insights into the environmental crisis. During his lifetime, this economic philosophy was elaborated and fleshed out by one of the Mahatma's close disciples, J. C. Kumarappa. Kumarappa has strong claims to being considered the first Gandhian environmentalist; as his work is largely unhonoured and forgotten today, a brief assessment is perhaps not out of place here.[5]

Kumarappa, born in 1892, was a Tamil Christian who had been trained as an accountant in London. He had a flourishing practice as an auditor in Bombay, which he left temporarily to take a Master's degree at Columbia University in New York. There he embarked on a study of public finance (under the supervision of the economist E. R. A. Seligman) in the course of which he systematically uncovered the colonial exploitation of the Indian economy. He returned home in 1929, now a nationalist, and soon came into contact with Gandhi. His thesis on public finance was serialised in *Young India*, and Kumarappa himself abandoned his practice to join the Mahatma. He was put in charge of Gandhi's schemes of village reconstruction, and over the next decade conducted surveys of the agrarian economy and helped run two key Gandhian institutions, the All India Spinners Association and the All India Village Industries Association.

In a number of books written in the 1930s and 1940s, Kumarappa attempted to formalise a 'Gandhian economics'. Scattered through Kumarappa's writings, as with Gandhi's, are observations with deep implications for the way we relate to the environment. This remark, for instance, could well serve as a basic condition for ecological responsibility: 'If we produce everything we want from within a limited area, we are in a position to supervise the methods of production; while if we draw our requirements from the ends of the earth it becomes impossible for us to guarantee the conditions of production in such places.'

Like his teacher, Kumarappa strongly denounced industrial civilisation. 'There can be no industrialisation without predation', he wrote, whereas agriculture is, and ought to be, 'the greatest among occupations', in which 'man attempts to control nature and his own environment in such a way as to produce the best results'. He expressed this contrast between agriculture and industry in terms of their impact on the natural world:

In the case of an agricultural civilisation, the system ordained by nature is not interfered with to any great extent. If there is a variation at all, it follows a natural mutation. The agriculturist only aids nature or intensifies in a short time what takes place in nature in a long period ... Under the economic system of [industrial society] ... we find that variations from nature are very violent in that a large supply of goods is produced irrespective of demand, and then a demand is artificially created for goods by means of clever advertisements.

Like other Gandhians of his generation, Kumarappa was interested not so much in theoretical reflection as in ameliorating the lot of the Indian peasant and artisan. A theme that runs through much of his work is the careful husbanding of natural resources in the agrarian economy. He stressed the need to use night soil as manure, asked for subsidies to be given to individuals, as a means of overcoming caste prohibitions, and advocated conversion of human excreta and village waste into organic fertilizer. Kumarappa also dwelled on the importance of maintaining soil quality by checking erosion and water-logging.

Water and forests are, of course, the two resource sectors that have most absorbed the Indian environmental movement in recent years. In this regard, Kumarappa was not slow to criticise the poor maintenance of irrigation tanks under British rule, or to urge the conservation of water to augment the water table and reduce brackishness. And in a pithy comment on actual and preferred models of forest management, he says:

The government will have to radically revise its policy of maintaining forests. Forest management should be guided, not by considerations of revenue but by the needs of the people ... Forest planning must be based on the requirements of the villagers around. Forests should be divided into two main classes: (1) those supplying timber to be planned from the long-range point of view, and (2) those supplying fuel and grasses, to be made available to the public either free of cost or at nominal rates. There are village industries such as palm gur, paper making, pottery, etc. which can flourish only if fuel and grass can be supplied to them at cheap rates.

Equally farsighted are Kumarappa's remarks on potential biomass shortages in the rural economy. He was especially concerned about fodder availability, pointing out that cash crops like jute, tobacco and sugar-cane reduce food availability for man and his domestic animals. He also noted the widespread complaint of peasants that there was not enough grazing land, taking the colonial government to task for its reluctance to allow grazing on waste land without payment of a fee.

Soil maintenance and fertility, water conservation, recycling, village forest rights, biomass budgets – this is an agenda of rural environmental problems that are still very much with us. In setting agriculture so firmly in its natural setting, Kumarappa could be said to have begun the task of building an ecological programme on Gandhian lines. Although they are, for the most part, unaware of his work, the environmentalists of today are only taking up where he left off.

Another Gandhian with environmental ideas in advance of her time was Mira Behn (Madeline Slade), the daughter of an English admiral who joined the Mahatma's Sabarmati ashram in 1925. Mira Behn, like Kumarappa, was part of Gandhi's inner circle, the core group of his followers: and like the Tamil economist, she too spent many years working for rural reconstruction, elaborating in practice the precepts of her teacher. In 1947 she set up an ashram near Rishikesh, at the foot of the Himalayas, moving her base several years later to the Bhilangna valley in the interior hills. In articles written at the time, Mira Behn drew the attention of the public and of policy makers to the intimate links between Himalayan deforestation, soil erosion and floods. Years before the Chipko movement was to give popular force to these criticisms, she identified the lacunae of forest management as being, first, the lack of involvement of villagers, and second, the replacement in many areas of oak with pine, a species with much less capacity to absorb and retain rain water. She sent detailed reports with photographs to the Indian Prime Minister, Jawaharlal Nehru, who passed them on to the forest officials concerned, but (as Mira Behn wryly noted) the 'necessary changes were too fundamental' for the forest department to make.[6]

In her years in rural north India, Mira Behn wrote penetratingly on the environmental problems of Indian agriculture: the large-scale water-logging that appears to be an almost inescapable feature of canal irrigation; the ploughing up of lands more suitable for growing pasture for cattle, adversely affecting the quality of livestock; and rampant soil erosion. For Mira Behn, the rapidity of ecological change and disturbance was a distinguishing feature of modern life. Ancient civilisations in North Africa and the Middle East had collapsed due to their abuse of the natural environment, but, as she wrote in the *Hindustan Times* of 5 June 1950 'in those days it took centuries and centuries to reach complete destruction, but in these days of modern machinery and science, what took a thousand years or more in the past may be accomplished in a paltry hundred years today!'

As with Gandhi and Kumarappa, Mira Behn's primary concern was with the rehabilitation of the village economy. Yet her interest in the natural environment was not merely instrumental: at times she expresses a spiritual affinity with nature of a Wordsworthian kind, straight out of the European romantic tradition. She called herself a 'devotee of the great primeval Mother Earth'. As she wrote in 1949.

The tragedy today is that educated and moneyed classes are altogether out of touch with the vital fundamentals of existence – our Mother Earth, and the animal and vegetable population which she sustains. This world of Nature's planning is ruthlessly plundered, despoiled and disorganized by man whenever he gets the chance. By his science and machinery he may get huge returns for a time, but ultimately will come desolation. We have got to study Nature's balance, and develop our lives within her laws, if we are to survive as a physically healthy and morally decent species.

GANDHI AND NEHRU

I began this chapter by recognising and commenting on the visible influence of Mahatma Gandhi on the Indian environmental movement. I then went back in time to investigate to what extent Gandhi himself had anticipated the ecological problems of the present day. The evidence in this respect does confirm that the ideas of Gandhi, and of his followers Kumarappa and Mira Behn, do constitute an eminently usable past for the environmental movement.

It is time now to turn our attention to one prevalent myth that has its origins in the environmentalist's reclamation of Mahatma Gandhi. It is an unfortunate tendency, present especially among the radical fringe of the movement, to identify good and evil with particular individuals. While celebrating Gandhi as a model to honour and to follow, some environmentalists want simultaneously to demonise Jawaharlal Nehru, the first and long-serving Prime Minister (1947–64), whom they blame for the ecological crisis that confronts Indian society today. Many environmentalists even believe that Gandhi had outlined a detailed, well-worked-out model of ecologically sound development, and that this Gandhian alternative was cast aside by Nehru, who then imposed on independent India his own model of capital-intensive, energy-intensive, environmentally destructive economic development. A tale to illustrate this was recently told by an expatriate Indian environmentalist based in Britain. Let the story be told in the environmentalist's romantically fanciful words:

Mahatma Gandhi was staying with the first Indian Prime Minister, Mr Nehru, in the city of Allahabad. In the morning Gandhi was washing his face and hands. Mr Nehru was pouring water from the jug as they talked about the problems of India. As they were deeply engaged in serious discussion, Gandhi forgot that he was washing; before he had finished washing his face, the jug became empty.

So Mr Nehru said, 'Wait a minute and I will fetch another jug of water for you.' Gandhi said, 'What! You mean I have used all that jugful of water without finishing washing my face? How wasteful of me! I use only one jug of water every morning.'

He stopped talking; tears flowed from his eyes. Mr Nehru was shocked. 'Why are you crying, what has happened, why are you worried about the water? In my city of Allahabad there are three great rivers, the Ganges, the Jumnar [sic] and the Saraswati, you don't need to worry about water here!' Gandhi said, 'Nehru, you are right, you have three great rivers in your town, but my share in those rivers is only one jug of water a morning and no more'.[7]

No source is given for the story, which is certainly a figment of the environmentalist's imagination, its credibility destroyed by, among other things, the portrait of a person of conspicuous balance and moderation as a weeping, repentant Calvinist. Apocryphal or not, the story is meant to exemplify the prudence of Gandhi, and the profligate ways of his host; ways which after 1947 – when India gained independence – are believed to have found expression in the path of destructive development followed by the new nation. The beliefs underlying this tale are in fact widely held by the neo-Gandhian environmentalists of today. Let me give one more example, out of several I could have chosen, to illustrate this. In an essay published some years ago, a prominent Indian environmental writer and activist claimed that Mahatma Gandhi 'tried in vain to persuade Jawaharlal Nehru not to take India down the path of over-consumption'.[8] This statement expresses in succinct fashion the two core elements of the myth:

first, that ecologically speaking Nehru was as wasteful as Gandhi was prudent; and second, that Gandhi had his own, alternative plan of development for India, which Nehru in his arrogance rejected out of hand. It is in this manner that the environmental debates of today have brought Gandhi and Nehru into fierce, if posthumous, public competition, violating in spirit and in letter the intimate relationship that actually existed between the two men.

The environmentalists' opposition of Gandhi and Nehru stems, in part, from the need to explain a puzzle: that the development experience of independent India has been marked by a profound insensitivity to ecological considerations despite the fact, as previously demonstrated, that the 'Father of the Nation' was, in our terms, emphatically an 'early environmentalist'. The puzzle can be most conveniently explained by contrasting the prudent Gandhi with the profligate Nehru, and by putting forth a conspiracy theory whereby the younger man first took over the Congress party in some kind of palace coup, then swiftly rid it of its Gandhian heritage.

I do not dispute, that the puzzle exists; but I do wish to qualify, perhaps even challenge, the way it is usually explained by my friends in the environmental movement. To challenge their black-and-white portraits of Nehru and Gandhi is not, of course, to ignore the profound philosophical differences between the two men. Gandhi's vision of free India centred on village renewal; Nehru's vision, just as firmly, on rapid industrial development. The older man preferred stability to change; the restless Nehru, change to stability. One's value system was based on religion; the other's on science and the scientific temper. Although both men were deeply shaped by Western thought, Nehru followed the statist, modernising tradition of the British Fabians and the Russian Marxists, whereas Gandhi was inspired by the anti-industrial, communitarian tradition associated with (the Briton) John Ruskin and (the Russian) Leo Tolstoy.

These differences are shown most clearly in an exchange of letters between Gandhi and Nehru in October 1945. Following a Congress Working Committee meeting on social and economic objectives after independence, Gandhi wrote to Nehru of his belief that India could 'realise truth and non-violence only in the simplicity of village life'. He went on to liken industrial society to the moth that whirls faster and faster around the light, only to perish in it. Nehru, in reply, disputed that the village, for him a mileu backward both intellectually and culturally, could ever embody the principles of truth and non-violence. He identified, as the chief goal of economic planning, not 'overconsumption' (as the environmentalist quoted earlier would have us believe) but rather, 'a sufficiency of food, clothing, housing, education, sanitation, etc.' for every Indian. To remove poverty was a goal on which both Nehru and Gandhi were agreed, but the younger man, in common with other intellectuals of the time, was convinced that this could be achieved only through rapid industrialisation and the use of modern technology.

These differences notwithstanding, we must also recognise the deep and abiding love between Gandhi and Nehru. 'I cannot think of myself as a rival to Jawaharlal or him to me', wrote Gandhi in July 1936. He continued: 'Or if we are, we are rivals in making love to each other in the pursuit of the common goal. And if, in the joint work for reaching the goal, we at times seem to be taking different routes, I hope the world will find that we had lost sight of each other only for the moment, and only to meet again with greater mutual attraction and affection.'

I do not know how environmentalists reconcile this with the Gandhi/Nehru polarity they so fervently uphold; or indeed how they ignore the Mahatma's public confirmation of Nehru as his heir in the early 1930s, a succession repeatedly confirmed by Gandhi in later years. More substantively, the environmentalists' interpretation of the crucial years before Indian independence fails to recognise that by about 1940, Gandhi's own economic ideas had been decisively rejected by the national movement. There had come about an overwhelming consensus, among politicians and intellectuals, that rapid industrialisation was the only viable economic strategy for reducing poverty and unemployment, thus making for a strong, self-reliant, genuinely independent society. It was believed that in modern science lay the key to unlimited human knowledge; in modern technology the key to unlimited expansion of human welfare. The alliance of science and technology in the development process might be seen, therefore, as the distinguishing characteristic of what is sometimes called the Nehruvian model. Nehru expressed this consensus in a particularly eloquent fashion, but behind him stood a solid phalanx of utterly sincere and deeply patriotic men.

Indeed, if the Gandhian model had been adopted as the basis for economic policy in 1947, this would have been an undemocratic imposition in the face of strong, majority opinion to the contrary. The actual marginalisation of the 'Gandhian alternative', such as it was, is well illustrated by the career of J. C. Kumarappa. In 1937, he was appointed to the National Planning Committee of the Congress as a representative of the All India Village Industries Association, but resigned when his fellow members of the committee did not agree to put the village at the centre of planning. After independence, Kumarappa was deputed by the Sarva Seva Sangh to represent it in the Planning Commission's Advisory Body. Again, the Gandhian economist quickly sensed that he was in a minority of one, and left the committee.

Kumarappa's hostility to the policies of Nehru and his colleagues might be contrasted with the attitude of Vinoba Bhave, commonly regarded as Gandhi's 'spiritual' successor (as Nehru is acknowledged to be the 'political' heir). Where Kumarappa was uncompromising, Bhave recognised that, in the India of the 1950s, Nehru's ideas were very widely shared. It was thus that he did not reject the pattern of economic development followed at the time, but tried rather to spiritualise and soften it, most distinctively through his work for voluntary land reform, or Bhoodan.

From our own vantage point it is of course possible to celebrate Gandhi and Kumarappa as environmentalists before the age of environmentalism. By contrast, India's first Prime Minister represented the majority intellectual opinion within the national movement, namely, that the revitalisation of India could only come about through massive industrialisation. One may justly honour Gandhi and Kumarappa for being ahead of their time; but it is grossly unhistorical, as well as unfair, to condemn Nehru for being, merely, a man of his time.

The great British socialist Edward Carpenter once remarked that the outcast of one age is the hero of another. Perhaps the converse, that the hero of one age is the outcast of another, is equally true. For no man was as greatly adored during his lifetime as Jawaharlal Nehru, yet no man has been more greatly villified since his death. It appears that Nehru was responsible for all that is wrong with India today. And so the right holds Nehru's policies of 'pseudo'-secularism and state planning squarely responsible for religious conflict and economic stagnation, while the left, just as effortlessly, traces the roots of economic inequality and environmental degradation to the same man's practice of 'pseudo'-socialism and ecological arrogance.

This demonisation of Nehru, within and outside the environmental movement, fails to allow for the possibility that times change, and men and ideas with them. Consider, for instance, the controversy around the Sardar Sarovar dam project, which environmentalists have found easy to represent in terms of the Gandhi/Nehru polarity. Thus a critic of the project wrote recently of a historic old temple being submerged by the rising waters of the dam, characterised by him as 'one of Jawaharlal Nehru's temples of modern India'. Here a man who died 30-odd years ago was being held guilty for the construction of a dam today, on account only of a phrase he had used to describe another dam built in the early years of Independence. But how can one be so sure that a man as generous and open-minded as Nehru would have held steadfast to a viewpoint, despite mounting evidence to the contrary? Indeed, in a little-known speech of November 1958, Nehru came down sharply on the propensity of dam-builders to 'think big'. Addressing the Central Board of Irrigation and Power, he deplored a 'dangerous outlook developing in India', the 'disease of giganticism'. The 'idea of having big undertakings or doing big tasks for the sake of showing that we can do big things', remarked Nehru, 'is not a good outlook at all'. For it was 'the small irrigation projects, the small industries and the small plants for electric power which will change the face of the country, far more than half a dozen big projects in half a dozen places'. Nehru reminded the technocrats of all the 'national upsets, upsets of the people moving out and their rehabilitation and many other things, associated with a big project'. In small schemes, in contrast, these upsets were minimal, and one could 'get a good deal of what is called public co-operation', the willing participation with the state and the engineers of the peasants in the locality where the dam was being built.[9]

Four decades later, the democrat and scientist in Nehru would also have acknowledged the enormous environmental costs associated with large dams: deforestation, water-logging, species extinction. Having lost sight of his Master while guiding India's first Five Year Plans, he was moving back towards him in the last years of his life. I have little doubt that were Nehru and Gandhi alive today, on the Sardar Sarovar controversy at least they would have found themselves both on the side of the Narmada Bachao Andolan, the movement to stop the dam.

THE HERITAGE OF GANDHI

The urge to demonise Nehru comes from a 'cowboys and indians' vision of history, in which the world is divided into good and bad guys. These black and white portraits are especially congenial to social activists: they were once characteristic of the Marxist, and they now, sadly, appear to be characteristic of the radical environmentalist. But the ideas and actions of individuals must be set in context : that is the task of the historian, who might find himself qualifying, to lesser or greater degree, the beliefs of the activist. It is in this spirit that I have contested the environmentalists' portrayal of Nehru in uniformly dark colours, and it is in the same spirit that I now wish to qualify their portrayal of Gandhi in uniformly light ones. As I have argued, the historical figure of Gandhi provides a body of ideas, and a vocabulary of protest against unjust laws, that have proved critical to the environmental movement. This much is indisputable, but perhaps it is now time to ask: are there ways in which the heritage of Gandhi might actually limit the movement? Or, put more plainly, does Gandhi provide *all* the answers to those working for environmental and social renewal today? Some environmentalists are emphatic that he does; one recently wrote to me that 'for each and every environmental event or crisis or challenge one can find inspiration and guidance in Gandhi'. This most emphatic statement notwithstanding, I think that Gandhi does not provide all the answers – sometimes, indeed, he does not even ask the right questions.

The heritage of Mahatma Gandhi has, I believe, limited the vision of the environmental movement in two crucial respects. First, it is striking how heavily focused on the countryside the horizons of most environmentalists are. Like Gandhi, his present-day followers appear to have little understanding of the urban context and its distinctive social and environmental problems. In their angry denunciations of the urban–industrial way of life, Indian environmentalists, by and large, have yet to come to terms with the fact that by the turn of the century India will have the largest urban population in the world. The consequences of such rapid, and unregulated, urbanisation are already with us: massive pollution, overcrowding and the diseases associated with it, water shortages, inadequate housing and sanitation, and a system of transportation that is highly inefficient from an energy conservation and environmental point of view. In engaging with these problems, and in trying to make our cities and towns habitable, Indian environmentalists can find little help from Gandhi, who in his own life and work simply turned his back on the city.

Like the city, the wilderness has no attraction for Gandhi. It is true that his practice of vegetarianism and non-violence oriented Gandhi towards a respect for all life, yet by all accounts he was hardly moved by the glories of unspoilt nature. This might perhaps be attributed to his severely practical temperament, for there was nothing of the romantic in Gandhi. Intriguingly, it was Jawaharlal Nehru who was deeply appreciative of the natural beauty of India. There is an almost mystical quality to Nehru's invocation, in his last will and testament, of his affinity with the soil, the mountains, the rivers of India.

An anecdote to illustrate this contrast was told by Edward Thompson, the British educationalist and writer who was a close friend of both Gandhi and Nehru. When the Congress Ministries were formed in different provinces of British India in 1937, Thompson tried hard to interest the nationalist leaders in the cause of saving India's disappearing wildlife, with (as he noted) 'animal after animal ... either extinct or on the danger list'. When he confronted Gandhi with the problem, the Mahatma merely joked, saying, 'we shall always have the British lion'. But then, noting Thompson's disappointment, Gandhi asked him to speak to Jawaharlal, as one who might show more interest. Nehru did, indeed; he went on to speak of the issue to the Prime Ministers (as they were then called) of Congress-ruled states. Later, Nehru was able to report to Thompson, with some pride, that C. Rajagopalachari's last act, as Premier of Madras, was to put through a proposal to establish the Periyar Nature Reserve.[10]

Nature lovers and those with a focus on the urban environment would, therefore, find little direct help from Mahatma Gandhi. But between the wilderness and the city lies a vast terrain, home to the 700,000 villages Gandhi spoke of so often and so eloquently. It is here that his life and message admit of more direct application, in the resistance to environmentally destructive projects or in the restoration of the relationship between the agrarian economy and its natural environment. And all of us, without exception – whether living in the city, the country or the wild – can try and simplify our lifestyles to the extent compatible with individual circumstance, taking our lead from a man who, in his own life, made remarkably few demands on the earth. And so it is that the environmental movement must perennially return to Mahatma Gandhi, and yet go beyond him.

Chapter 9

In Memory of Georgescu-Roegen

A cloak of deadly silence has easily been cast over old dissenters.[1]

A BRIEF PERSONAL ENCOUNTER

Ecological critics of economics have argued for over 100 years that economists should study the flow of energy and materials in the economy. The services nature offers to the human economy cannot be adequately valued in the accounting system of neo-classical environmental and resource economics. Today's ecological economics does not only criticise, it also tries to provide physical indicators in order to judge whether the economy is ecologically sustainable. Beyond its decisive role in strengthening ecological economics, Georgescu-Roegen's work currently still holds sway in two additional fields: consumption theory and agrarian economics. This chapter focuses on the agrarian question, its relation to ecological economics, and to the pro-peasant 'varieties of environmentalism' which this book brings to light.

I met Nicholas Georgescu-Roegen only once, in Barcelona for a few days in 1980, when he spent half a week in the modest accommodation of the Hostal de Sant Pancras in Bellaterra (near the Autonomous University of Barcelona), a small hotel which reminded him of Romania before the war. I had read a letter by him in the *Herald Tribune*, explaining why the industrial applications of solar energy could still not be considered as truly 'Promethean' technologies. I wrote inviting him to come to Barcelona to give one or two lectures. He arrived at the airport in Barcelona one hot afternoon in May after a long trip from Florence, where he had been awarded an honorary doctorate. That same afternoon – he had enviable vitality – he was speaking at the Autonomous University. He began his talk in English. After a student complained, as students sometimes do, he continued in perfect French without interruption. When he had finished, a young professor, who had recently returned to Barcelona after earning his doctorate in economics at the University of Minnesota, asked him an acerbic question. Georgescu-Roegen, who by 1980 was quite deaf and irascible, answered him with, 'Are you an economist?', to the amusement of the students.

Georgescu-Roegen, a diabetic who used to put a small device into his drinks to measure the sugar content, liked his *grappa* chilled and very dry. From Barcelona he returned to Nashville, Tennessee, where he had been living since 1949, as a professor at Vanderbilt University. Nashville is (I believe) the capital of country music, but it is probably not the place to enjoy a great variety of chilled *grappas*.

Georgescu-Roegen was one of the great names of the Romanian diaspora, comparable to Cioran or Ionescu or Mircea Eliade. He was also perhaps an object of discrimination within the university environment, despite the relative openness of US academe compared to that of Europe. Perhaps in part also due to a lack of social graces, Georgescu-Roegen did not directly create a school. Apart from Herman Daly, they are very few well-known ecological economists among his students at Vanderbilt.

Georgescu-Roegen was born in 1906 in Constanza, Romania. He completed his university studies in mathematics in Romania, influenced by a primary school teacher, and earned his doctorate in Paris with a thesis on statistics, *Le problème de la recherche des composantes cycliques d'un phénomène*, published in 1930. Afterwards he spent two years, 1930 to 1932, as a post–doctoral fellow at University College in London, where he worked with Karl Pearson, the well-known philosopher of science, statistician and propagandist of eugenics. He returned to Romania as a professor of statistics at the University of Bucharest and in 1934, at the age of 28, won a Rockefeller fellowship to Harvard, where he stayed until 1937. There he studied economics and began to publish articles on the subject, particularly on consumption theory. He was an intellectual contemporary of Paul Samuelson and Wassily Leontieff (two later Nobel Prize winners), and the Marxist Paul Sweezy. At Harvard he was a protegé of Joseph Schumpeter, of whom he had never heard, but with whom he shared an interest in economic cycles. An anecdote describes how, working as a new research fellow, Georgescu-Roegen was never certain exactly how to respond to the polite North American question 'What can I do for you?' until one day he arrived at the office of Schumpeter, who put to him an easier question: 'What can you do?'.

Georgescu-Roegen himself thought he had made a mistake when he returned to Romania in 1937. He stayed until 1948, first at his chair at Bucharest, later also doing administrative work. He was a member of the Armistice Commission at the end of the war when the Soviet Army arrived. He fled in 1948, first to Turkey and eventually to the United States. In 1949 he became professor of economics at Vanderbilt University, and in 1976, at age 70, professor emeritus. My impression is that Georgescu-Roegen thought that he should have been a professor at Harvard, but Schumpeter died in 1950. The recent history of ecological economics would have been easier with Georgescu-Roegen at Harvard.

Ecological Economics and its Precursors

In 1949, when Georgescu-Roegen arrived in the United States for the second time, he had written on statistics and on consumption theory (in international publications), and on international trade and on agrarian topics (mainly in Romanian), but he had still not contributed to the ecological criticism of economics. Of course, any Romanian economist could easily identify the depletion of a natural resource like oil as an economic problem, as well as the issue of unequal exchange of natural resource exports for manufactured products. In an attempt to ascertain his political ideas during the 1930s, I mentioned to Georgescu-Roegen the name Mainolescu, a theorist of corporatism in that period. Georgescu-Roegen directed me to the earlier work of Mainolescu on international trade in which he defended protectionism in non-industrialised countries. Despite a thorough awareness of the role of natural resources in the economy – not surprising in a person interested in peasant farming – Georgescu-Roegen's *magnum opus* was not published until 1971. Neither, I believe, is there any published text of Georgescu-Roegen regarding the relations between thermodynamics and economics until 1966, when a long introduction to some of his articles collected under the title *Analytical Economics* appeared. Georgescu-Roegen possibly had, since the 1920s, an interest in the relations between the laws of thermodynamics and the regularities of human societies. As a student in Paris he read *Mécanique Statistique* by Emile Borel, his doctoral dissertation advisor; 'Statistical Mechanics' is, since Boltzmann, another name for thermodynamics. To me, this remnant of scientific culture, and, probably, the memory of polemics over the supposed contradiction between the second law of thermodynamics and the theory of evolution, influenced Georgescu-Roegen's *The Entropy Law and the Economic Process*, begun in 1964 and published in 1971. According to Jacques Grinevald, Vernadsky and Lotka inspired the work of Georgescu-Roegen.[2] Surely he read Lotka's 1925 publication *Elements of Physical Biology*. Georgescu-Roegen correctly attributed to Lotka the distinction between endosomatic and exosomatic instruments for the consumption or use of energy, one basic tool for the analysis of human ecology. Humans have genetic instructions with regard to endosomatic consumption, but not with regard to the exosomatic use of energy. In fact, what is discussed in ecological economics is whether the income-elasticity of the exosomatic use of energy (and materials) is greater than zero, and even greater than unity, or whether, on the contrary, it is possible to delink increases in consumption from increases of the energy (and material) throughput in the economy, improving what is today often called 'industrial metabolism'. Vernadsky had published in Paris in 1924 and 1926 two relevant works, *La Géochimie* and *La Biosphère*. However, I have proof of the originality and independence from these works of Georgescu-Roegen's ecological economics. In *La Géochimie*, Vernadsky, in the context of a long discussion of authors who had written on evolution and thermodynamics since the late 19th century, briefly mentioned Sergei Podolinsky (1850–91), a Ukrainian author who between 1880 and 1883 applied the principles of the thermodynamics of biological phenomena to the study of the economy. However, Georgescu-Roegen did not know of Podolinsky until, in 1980 in Barcelona, I showed him an article that Naredo and I had published in 1979, as well as photocopies of Podolinsky's articles and letters to Marx regarding economics and energy. Later Georgescu-Roegen suggested the title for the English version of our article, 'A Marxist Precursor of Energy Economics: Podolinsky' (*Journal of Peasant Studies*, January 1982 – a better title would have been: 'A Marxist–Narodnik Precursor of Ecological Economics'), and provided us with detailed comments on the drafts of the article. For example, Georgescu-Roegen had read carefully Engels's Dialectics of Nature. Whether for reasons of political–professional strategy or because of a profound scientific respect for Marxism, even though Georgescu-Roegen knew *Dialectics of Nature*, he never cared to expound on the unfortunate observations of Engels regarding the Second Law of Thermodynamics. He preferred instead to highlight Engels's anticipation of arguments against an absurd theory of energy-value: Engels wrote in 1875 that 'no-one could convert specialised work into kilogrametres and determine salary differences based on that criteria'.

Georgescu-Roegen was always conscientious in quoting with scientific honesty the precursors of his ideas. But in fact, despite the long history of isolated reflections on economics based on thermodynamics, there had never before been a school of ecological economics. Georgescu-Roegen did not know of Podolinsky, Popper-Lynkeus, Pfaundler or Patrick Geddes. Neither had he read Frederick Soddy. However, he had read, before 1971, Hayek's objections to 'social energetics' and, because of Hayek, he also knew of Max Weber's 1909 article in defence of neo-classical economics against Wilhelm Ostwald.[3]

In my view, in the discussion of the relationship between energy and economics, there have been two erroneous positions and one correct one. Mirowski's book on this question considered only the two erroneous positions and did not take the correct one into account.[4] One erroneous position is the 'theory of energy-value' which some ecologists, such as Howard Odum and his disciples, have proposed. Georgescu-Roegen vigorously contested this 'energetic dogma'. The second erroneous position is based on the isomorphism between the equations of mechanics and those of the economic equilibrium of neoclassical economics after 1870. Over one 100 years ago authors like Winiarski proposed that economics was social physics, in other words that the market exchanges studied by economists were similar not only in form but in content to the natural phenomena studied by physicists. The use of the mathematics of mechanics in economics made this view plausible. However to describe economic phenomena in the language of physics is different from applying the concepts of physics (like the Law of the Conservation of Matter or the Laws of Thermodynamics) to attain an understanding of how the human economy is placed within ecosystems. This would be the third position, that of Georgescu-Roegen and his precursors and of today's ecological economists. This sees the economy not as a circuit or spiral of exchange value, a merry-go-round of producers and consumers, but instead as an entropic flow of energy and materials that runs through the economy. An economic history inspired by orthodox economics would study commercial transactions utilising the categories of economic science, while an economic history inspired by ecological economics would study, for example, the energy systems of humanity.

Mirowski does not think that economics has ignored the study of energy. On the contrary, beyond those who have proposed a theory of energy-value or have seen economics as literally a physical science (with exchanges of social or psychic 'energy'), he believes that orthodox economists have also been obsessed with energy. Mirowski's thesis is that the entire analytic structure of neo-classical or orthodox economics is based upon the 'metaphor of energy'. However, I believe that Mirowski has mixed up formal analogies with substantive ecological study. True, economic science has used the mathematics of mechanics since the first neo-classical economists, such as Jevons and Walras. From this formal point of view, therefore, it cannot be said that economics has been divorced from physics. However, the neoclassical economists (as Geddes had indicated to Walras in their correspondence in 1883), discarded completely the *biophysical* framework in which the human economy was necessarily based. In fact, one can be a competent neoclassical economist and still ignore the Second Law of Thermodynamics. On the other hand, ecological economics (as opposed to neo-classical economics) sees the human economy as embedded within a broader ecosystem. From a reproductive approach, ecological economics studies the social, temporal and spatial conditions under which the economy (which absorbs resources and excretes residues) is encased within the evolving ecosystems. From an allocative approach, ecological economics studies the valuation of services lent by the ecosystem to the economic subsystem, reaching the conclusion that such values cannot be measured on a single scale of (chrematistic) value.[5] Economic incommensurability is thus a foundation stone for ecological economics.

In the context of the analysis of economic valuation, what relationship was there between the two great critics of neo-classical economics, Piero Sraffa and Georgescu-Roegen, who were almost contemporaries? There are recent ideas in this respect, partly stimulated by the unthinking enthusiasm (in my view) with which some ecological economists embraced the notion of 'natural capital'.[6] Georgescu-Roegen was already in his fifties when the Sraffian challenge arose in the 1960s. In retrospect, it is a pity that (apparently) nobody asked Georgescu-Roegen what he thought about the Cambridge controversies on the theory (and on the valuation) of capital.

Georgescu-Roegen considered 'enjoyment of life' as a supreme use value that is derived from consumption. This is different from the Sraffian schemes in which demand is absent. In addition, the Sraffian schemes of economic reproduction see economics, in a sense, as neo-classical economic theory does, as a circular (simple reproduction) or spiral (extended reproduction) process, although without the mediation of the equilibria between supply and demand. Ricardian, Marxist, and Sraffian schemes do not take into account the depletion of resources and other irreversible effects such as the production of waste, and, like neo-classical economics, they lack an entropic vision of the economy.

FREEDOM OF MIGRATION

In 1971 books on economics and ecology were published by Barry Commoner, Howard Odum, and Georgescu-Roegen and also the *Manifesto for Survival*, a collective work organised by Edward Goldsmith, since then editor of *The Ecologist*. In 1972, the Meadows Report to the Club of Rome was published. Georgescu-Roegen's book was one of the great ones on relations between ecology and economics released in 1971, prior to the report of the Club of Rome. But despite Georgescu-Roegen's intellectual pre-eminence, he was not invited by the United Nations to the environmental conference in Stockholm in 1972. Instead he attended a parallel conference by invitation of the pacifist association, Dai Dong, where he drafted the manifesto *Toward a Human Economics*. At this non-governmental, alternative forum, Georgescu-Roegen's proposal to permit the free movement of all peoples to any part of the world, without passport or visa restrictions, was received without enthusiasm and considered too utopian. It would have been worthwhile to resubmit this proposal at the Rio de Janeiro Conference of 1992, since the restrictions on migration become more severe each day as international inequalities increase. We realise that the worldwide territorial distribution of population is a major problem of human ecology, and at the same time a political problem, for which neither economists nor ecologists have a solution. Ecologists are competent to explain the pattern of migration of birds and fish, but they cannot explain the restrictions to migration between South and North America, or between North Africa and Europe. At such borders, there stand a sort of 'unnatural', political Maxwell's Demons, who successfully maintain (at the cost of many human lives each year), the large differences in the per capita use of energy and materials between adjacent territories.

Economic Growth

Frederick Soddy, a precursor of Georgescu-Roegen, had insisted in the 1920s that the exponential growth of the economy was impossible due to the existence of the Law of Entropy. He also pointed out that the substitution of 'capital' for natural resources had limits, because the production and operation of capital required natural resources. This argument was used by Georgescu-Roegen (without credit to Soddy) in his response to an article with which Robert M. Solow, Nobel Prize winner for his metaphysical models of economic growth, attempted to defend the honour of economists after 1973. Solow asserted that the world could sustain the depletion of natural resources by substituting other factors of production, primarily labour and reproducible capital. When Solow received the Nobel Prize, rather than Georgescu-Roegen, the only public protest that I know of came from letters in *Economic and Political Weekly* of Bombay (an excellent publication) from far-away followers of Georgescu-Roegen such as Narindar Singh, the author of a notable work on ecological economics. Commenting on Solow's growth models, Georgescu-Roegen asserted that Solow clung to the idea of exponential growth in order to avoid the difficult question of the destiny of the poor of today and of posterity. Growth theory supported, and was in turn supported by, the idea that the situation of the poor could only improve if the rich became richer. Certainly, we could forget about the poor, but then economics would be open to the fulminations which Thomas Carlyle and John Ruskin directed towards economists in the 19th century. And, if we care about distribution issues today, how could we then forget about intergenerational equity?[7]

Ecological economists are not necessarily pessimists. Seeing the economy entropically does not imply ignoring anti-entropic properties of life or of systems open to the entry of energy. In Georgescu-Roegen's book

The Entropy Law and the Economic Process (1971), we observe that the author considered systems that receive energy from the exterior (such as the earth) in terms of a constant development of organisation and complexity. Georgescu-Roegen often quoted Schrödinger's *What is Life* (1944) but he was an enemy of those who profess a faith in economic growth and technological progress that allows them to ignore from consideration the issues of current distribution of goods among rich and poor, and of the intergenerational allocation of scarce resources and pollutants – and also, although this was not explicitly included in his analysis, the destructive impact of humans on other species. Georgescu-Roegen's radicalism was perhaps already evident in his article on neo-classical consumption theory, 'Marginal Utility of Money and Elasticities of Demand'[8] in which a hierarchy of needs, or 'lexicographic ordering', was established that was not based just on inscrutable consumer preferences.[9]

EXTERNALITIES AND THE DISCOUNT RATE

Neither A. J. Coase, with his well known article of 1960 on attributing 'rights of property' over the environment and instituting a market of externalities, nor A. C. Pigou, who in the 1920s proposed taxing polluters, were sources of inspiration for Georgescu-Roegen. He was not an 'environmental and resource economist', but rather something new, an 'ecological economist' or, as he called himself, a 'bioeconomist'. His 1971 book has a structure that is very different from the texts on what is known as 'environmental and resource economics', such as, for example, that co-authored by David Pearce and Kerry Turner, and countless other texts since the surge of interest in environmental issues after the mid-1970s. Those economists place externalities in a synchronic framework and discuss the different ways by which the internalisation of externalities (the reduction to their chrematistic value) can be achieved. Later in their texts, the economics of natural resources, renewable or not, is discussed and at this point discussion of the discount rate and Gray-Hotelling's criterion on the 'optimum' intertemporal allocation of exhaustible resources is introduced. Georgescu-Roegen's book rarely mentions externalities, much less tries to convince the reader that they can be internalised, for example, by estimating the cost of neutralizing them, or by asking those suffering them how much they would pay to eliminate them or how much money they would accept to withstand them. These methods of internalisation of externalities are incapable of confronting the matter of intergenerational allocation. It is easy to draw curves in which the private marginal profit to a polluting firm intersects the 'marginal external cost' (expressed in monetary values) in order to determine an optimum level of pollution, to be sought through a market of externalities (like the one proposed by Coase), through a Pigovian tax, through mandatory physical norms and a system of fines, or through the sale of polluting permits. It is easy to draw such curves, but the majority of externalities have future uncertain, irreversible effects, not only immediate effects. The 'marginal external cost' curve depends on the discount rate to be applied; therefore, the discount rate would need to be discussed first, in evaluating externalities. In Georgescu-Roegen's 1971 book, the approach of which is more 'reproductive' than 'allocative', there is no explicit discussion of the discount rate, but in the next few years he spoke of it in many colloquia. Thus, on one occasion, he gave the following example. Let us assume three men are on an island or in a boat. They know that one of them will die each day, and they have six rations of food. Which is the rational allocation? It is 3, 2, 1, rather than 2, 2, 2. However the morality of *carpe diem* makes sense, in general, for individuals, but not for humanity on the whole, nor even for a single nation. If we give equal weight to future utilities, Hotelling's elegant solution is worthless. The analytical solution is to allocate exhaustible resources equally over time. An infinite time horizon would imply an infinitessimal amount of the exhaustible resource for each generation. In such cases we should abandon the principle of maximising utility, and resort instead to the reasonable principle of minimising future regrets.[10] Other ecologically inclined economists, such as Ciriacy-Wantrup, also proposed such a 'principle of caution' against future uncertainty, an uncertainty which cannot be dealt with by actuarial calculation. In the literature of economic this type of uncertainty is associated with Knight, Shackle and Georgescu-Roegen.

AGRARIAN ECONOMICS

Years before Georgescu-Roegen became well-known because of his ecological economics, and at a time when he was known to professional economists mainly for his work on consumption theory, he published an article presenting economic models in agreement with the ideas of pro-peasant populists in eastern Europe.[11] This article still did not unite ecological-economic criticism with *narodnik* praise of peasant economics. It cited the pre-World War II German translation of A. V. Chayanov's work, which until that time was known in Anglo-Saxon academic circles only for a few minor extracts in Pitirim Sorokin's anthology, *Rural Sociology*. Chayanov was new to the West when the English translation of his work appeared in 1966, but he was well known in pro-peasant circles in eastern

Europe between the two World Wars. And behind Chayanov, there was a long *narodnik* lineage. As Georgescu-Roegen himself wrote in 1965, German academic circles, keen on historical and institutional studies, provided an effective channel for the diffusion of *narodnik* ideas in central and eastern Europe, where powerful agrarian political parties emerged after World War I. In Romania, the school of sociology founded by D. Gusti accumulated a wealth of information on peasant life through extensive field work, in the manner preached by the Narodniki.[12]

Contrary to the anti-peasant attacks of liberal and Marxist economics, *narodnik* praise of peasant economic rationality, in the case of high population density, contains arguments based as much in economic efficiency as in equity. Georgescu-Roegen was above all an economic theorist, but with a *narodnik* political background. A Romanian contemporary, David Mitrany, wrote a well-known diatribe against Stalinist collectivisation called *Marx against the Peasant* (English edition published in 1951, based on a work first written in the late 1920s). Georgescu-Roegen shared this pro-peasant political line, rather unusual among economists in industrialised Europe or the United States, but he was not a dogmatic anti-Marxist. He wrote one or two articles containing mathematical models of Marxist economics. Georgescu-Roegen was aware of Marx's doubtful hopes (in the last years of his life) on the viability of a *narodnik* road to socialism in Russia. Thus, in his 1960 article on agrarian economics, Georgescu-Roegen included citations from Marx's letter of 1881 to Vera Zasulich and its drafts, in order to demonstrate that Marx himself was not as anti-peasant as were his Bolshevik followers. Marx had indeed briefly considered paths to socialism based on peasant communes.

In the 1970s, research in peasant economics that had been initiated many decades earlier in eastern Europe flowered in other regions of the South. Through the contributions of economic anthropology and other disciplines, it was established theoretically and empirically that peasant households' production was a specific form of economic organisation with a logic or rationality of its own that challenged the economic rationality of capitalist enterprise. Chayanov's ideas of the 1920s were given a warm reception in the 1970s, despite a double-edged opposition: from Marxists who were opposed to such 'populist' doctrines, and from liberal theorists of modernisation who saw peasants as a thing of the past. Without yet embracing detailed ecological aspects such as the flow of energy, biodiversity and multi-cropping, nutrient cycles, and pollution from agrochemicals, in his work on peasant economic rationality Georgescu-Roegen was necessarily led to question the capitalist logic of the market. There is an obvious continuity between Georgescu-Roegen's studies of peasant economics and the new ecological economics to which he would contribute decisively from 1966 onwards.

Forty years ago there was a consensus on the superiority of large-scale mechanised farming, whether in the United States or in the Soviet Union, and on the inevitable decrease in the number of peasants. The explanation for the disappearance of the peasantry is that, as agricultural productivity increases, and because of a relatively low income-elasticity of demand for agricultural production as a whole, the agricultural sector must make part of its active population redundant. This has indeed been the case in many countries. However, as Boserup explained, up to a point peasants adapt to high population densities by intensifying production. In each farming system there are decreasing returns to the labour input, but the pressure of population leads to a change in the farming system.[13] Smallholders adapt ecologically, and also adapt socially, using household labour in a way that a capitalist economy would be unable to do. Nevertheless, such intensive use of labour may lead to what Geertz described as 'agricultural involution' in Java, and Elvin as a 'high-equilibrium trap' in China, and therefore the question arises of smallholding as an obstacle to economic growth.[14] But, in a static context, Chayanov's peasant economics, showing correlations between household size (or workers/consumers ratios) and farm size, is a convincing application of marginalist economics to non-capitalist institutions – family labour, and customary needs satisfied by self-provisioning and by the market.

Although Chayanov himself had no theory of sharecropping, Chayanovian economics also explains why landowners, instead of employing wage labour, often prefer tenancy contracts since incentives to work hard, and to use household labour, are provided by crop sharing, or some other types of tenancy contracts. In wage employment, work of very low marginal productivity value will not be employed; moreover, by linking effort to remuneration, sharecropping will have an incentive effect compared to wage labour paid by the hour. The theory of 'sharecropping as piece-work' was proposed in the 1960s by several authors, including myself. It fits exactly into the notion of the 'self-exploiting' peasant family. In that sense, the theory is already implicitly in Chayanov, and also in Georgescu-Roegen's article on agrarian economics of 1960. It is an improvement on previous views of sharecropping, seen as inefficient (e. g. by the economist Alfred Marshall), or as 'semifeudal' (by many Marxists until the 1960s). What from one point of view looks like increased efficiency –getting more work out of the labour force – from another point of view looks like increased 'self-exploitation' turned to the landowners' advantage by means of tenancy contracts.

Georgescu-Roegen's work on the economics of peasant farming was received coldly not only by mainstream economists, who were in favour of capitalist farming, but also by young Marxist scholars, alienated by his praise of peasant farming. He was explicitly and dismissively described as a *narodnik* populist by the agrarian economist Utsa Patnaik in the *Journal of Peasant Studies*, i.e. as somebody who had no feeling for the process of social differentiation of the peasantry and for the rural proletariat. Patnaik herself is well known for her studies of rural classes in northern India. For reasons I never understood, in his rather tame reply, Georgescu-Roegen chose not to mention the ecological question.[15] This would have been an opportunity to introduce new political ecology material in a periodical such as the *Journal of Peasant Studies*, which started in the early 1970s, at the same time as the UN Stockholm conference on Development and the Environment (1972, where Indira Gandhi made her ill-advised speech on the environment as a luxury good or 'too poor to be green'), at the same time as the Chipko movement (1973), and at the same time as Pimentel's work (1973) on energy flows in maize growing (comparing efficient *milpa* agriculture in Mexico and inefficient corn cultivation in the mid-West). Despite efforts by Paul Richards, Victor Toledo, and a few other 'ecological neo-Narodniki', the intellectual community waited for more than 20 years to combine political economy and political ecology in the study of the peasantry.

Pimentel's (1973) and Leach's (1975) work on energy flows (cited in Chapter 6) had shown the greater energy efficiency of traditional small-scale farming. The ecological perspective throws doubts on the economic measurement of agricultural productivity, i.e.

$$\frac{\text{value of output minus value of inputs}}{\text{quantity of input whose productivity is measured}}$$

because some value should be taken from output value on account of the externalities from modern agriculture (pesticides, nitrites in the water, loss of biodiversity, etc.), and the monetary values of inputs are perhaps too low because oil and other inputs (which explain the increase in productivity and the decrease in energy efficiency in modern agriculture), are undervalued because future demand is much discounted. Is agricultural productivity *really* increasing? As suggested in Chapter 6, there are no 'ecologically correct' prices that would allow us to give an unambiguous answer, because there are no known or convincing methods to internalise future, uncertain, unknown externalities into the price system, but there might be 'ecologically *corrected* prices', which would give quite a different picture, historically and at present, of the evolution of agricultural productivity.

Therefore, some would argue that because traditional smallholding agriculture is more energy-efficient than modern agriculture, and because energy prices will rise (driven by increasing scarcity of fossil fuels and by internalisation of externalities into the price system), peasants will be needed as savers of fossil fuels because they use the energy of the sun.[16] This is naive. Ecological economics shows that prices are not good indicators of the economic impacts on the environment.[17] Indeed, physical and biological indicators often move in an opposite direction to economic indicators. The prices of the economy are embedded in the social perception and valuation of externalities and opportunity costs for future generations.

Since modern agriculture, although wasteful of energy, is not an important consumer of fossil fuels (compared to industry, transport, and the domestic sector), and since energy is cheap, a decrease in the active agricultural population not only in relative but in absolute terms might also occur in China and India, although the scale of environmental problems in urbanisation and industrialisation would be much larger than in the countries which have already followed that road. Smallholding families, even if they are as ecological as Chinese peasants used to be, would make a small contribution to energy saving if they stayed ecological, in comparison to the expenditure of energy in the rest of their countries' economies and in the rich economies of the world. Ecological sustainability would be helped by agroecological farming, but the existence in the world of one billion ecological smallholders (including family members), assuming they still exist, does not save a large amount of fossil fuels, compared to that used elsewhere. If ecologically-corrected prices would be introduced – this would be a political process and not a market-led process – then small-scale agroecology, *together* with alternative industries and transport and with a different sort of architecture and urban planning, might come to dominate the scene.

Another, more convincing argument could be made for the traditional peasantry as a repository of in-situ biodiversity (cf. Chapter 6). Losses of biodiversity, because of the modernisation of farming, are rarely discussed in the conventional economic history literature. Mainstream economics, by its praise of technical change, implicitly praises the disappearence of agricultural biodiversity. Georgescu-Roegen did not introduce into his analysis of the peasant economy the role of the peasantry in the coevolution of agricultural biodiversity; it did not fit well either in his discussion of the links between the economy and the use of energy.

There is another point. Agroecological practices are not necessarily linked to farm size. The 'ecological rationality of peasant production' (in Victor Toledo's phrase) is conditioned by the extent to which the peasant family is involved in the market. If the peasant family relies on the market for inputs and outputs, ecological rationality is inapplicable because market prices take no account of the environment. If, in the peasant family's outlook, the direct exchanges with nature still predominate over market exchanges, then it is likely that there will be careful management practices, provided that extreme inequality and poverty, or overpopulation, do not force peasants to damage the land. If the market predominates, and unless peasants become involved in specific agroecological markets, there is no reason to expect that smallholders will be more friendly to the environment than large landowners.

Anti-ecological practices arise sometimes from the substitution of capital for labour. In that case, smallholders, because of their lower implicit cost of labour, would be at the same time more ecological. But modern agricultural techniques (e.g. pump irrigation, new seeds) often increase yields without decreasing labour intensity. Smallholders are often keen to adopt commercial seeds, giving up in-situ agricultural biodiversity, and they are also prone to lowering the water table by individually extracting water, unless communal institutions prevent this. The point is that traditional agriculture, large and small, was ecological, and modern agriculture is not. In many areas, the change in techniques came earlier in commercial farms than in smallholdings, with peasants then displaced by modernising large farms.

In my view, the theoretical connection between smallholding and ecology must come through a theory of 'peasant resistance' and 'moral economy', i.e. how peasants are to some extent able to resist outside exploitation or outside competition which drives them out of the market, by making use of their own land (including the commons), of rain water and perhaps also of irrigation facilities, of sun energy, and of their own seeds, becoming more or less involved in markets according to circumstances. They have to fight for survival. For instance, the Chipko movement retained the use of the forest against external commercial interests, not because (or not only because) they were well adapted to the environment, but because they found a useful idiom of resistance, and successful forms of action.[18] Georgescu-Roegen would have liked, perhaps, our notion of the 'environmentalism of the poor', i.e. the discussion and research on the ecological contents of social conflicts involving the rural poor. Peasants engage in social struggles in order to keep access to land, forests, sun energy, water, and seeds, when confronted by commercial interests, by the state or by enclosing landowners.

PROMETHEAN TECHNOLOGIES

In a conference paper written in 1965 on peasant communal institutions,[19] Georgescu-Roegen brought together his main topics of interest: utility theory (explaining that the utility derived from consumption depended on social institutions), agrarian economics, and the thermodynamic analysis of the economy. He wrote

We tap low entropy by two essentially distinct procedures. We mine – or we shovel, as it were – the low entropy existing in the form of a *stock* in the earth's crust. We also catch the low entropy which surrounds us in the form of a *flow*, the most vital of all being the flow of solar radiation. The first activity corresponds to mining, the second to husbandry. A third activity, manufacturing, merely transforms further the flow of low entropy fed by the first two sectors. Finally, consumption transforms the low entropy flow of consumer goods into high entropy. In this struggle, man has always striven to discover new sources of low entropy....

Following this line of thought on the technical differences between economic sectors, Georgescu-Roegen later introduced the idea of a difference between feasible and viable technologies. He also utilised the notion of 'Promethean' technologies. These are different from the usual classifications of economists, for example according to whether the technologies are labour- or capital-saving. Technologies must be studied (as Geddes and Mumford also proposed) from an ecological, rather than economic, point of view. As Georgescu-Roegen explained, the history of human technology is one of innumerable feasible 'recipes', for instance, the technologies for bread-making, logging, vaccination against viruses, space travel, heating a house or moving a car using solar energy. However there are many other technologies still not feasible, for example vaccination against cancer or a fusion-energy motor. For a technology to be *viable*, and be able to make the economy grow in real, ecological terms, it is not enough that it be feasible. It must also include a 'prescription' for the harnessing of 'low entropy' in the environment, of energy and materials that we can put at our disposal. This harnessing must fulfil a very special condition, a 'Promethean' condition. Prometheus gave fire to the Greeks, fire which converted cold materials into heat and permitted not only cooking and heating but also metallurgy and ceramics. But energy from wood and forests is not sufficient, and coal, oil or natural gas are inadequate not only because they are exhaustible, but because of the pollution they produce, a factor which is included in the input–output tables of Georgescu-Roegen. We are therefore waiting for a new Promethean technology. In my view, the general awareness of this situation explains the enthusiasm with which some scientists, journalists and politicians greeted the grotesque spectacle of 'cold fusion' in the spring of 1989. The normally sober publication *The Economist* trumpeted the arrival of 'cold fusion' on its covers.

We go back here, as a final point, to Georgescu-Roegen's encounter with Schumpeter in the 1930s, and discuss briefly the points of agreement and disagreement between Schumpeterian evolutionist economics and what has come to be called ecological economics. The role of technology is one of the main issues.

There is one central point of agreement; both Schumpeterian evolutionist economics and ecological economics study economic systems out of the equilibrium. Both are interested in irreversible changes, instead of trying to establish allocative optima under restrictions. Both emphasize changes in technologies and institutions. Such points of agreement should be enough for fruitful dialogue, and eventually perhaps for a marriage. However, there are considerable differences between both approaches.

Schumpeterian evolutionist economics uses biological analogies to explain the 'evolution' of firms or other economic institutions. It is anthropocentric in that it only studies social and economic phenomena. It sees the technological innovations as the main cause of economic growth. Growth is its main subject of study. It emphasizes the existence of increasing returns (against the equilibrium perspective) and the positive external and internal economies (cf. the use of the concept of 'industrial district'). It attributes the competitive success of firms to high throughput, that is, to the speed in processing the input in order to get more production in less time.[20]

Ecological economics studies, at the same time, the physical–biological system and human systems. It is less anthropocentric in that it uses the idea of co-evolution. It researches decreasing returns in physical terms (e.g. the increasing energy cost of obtaining energy), hidden by the price system, which does not value future environmental damages. It emphasizes future, uncertain, accumulative and irreversible negative externalities, and it incorporates the study of social protests against externalities, which are seen as 'cost-shifting' or 'ecological distribution conflicts'. It puts emphasis on technological risks more than on the advantage of innovations. It studies uncertainty and 'surprises', applying instruments such as the 'precautionary principle'. It emphasises equity with other species. It does not take economic growth as its main topic. On the contrary, it studies the ecological sustainability of the economy, paying attention to the different biochemical and economic rhythms, and it considers the need to reduce the throughput of energy and material inputs into the economy.[21]

Chapter 10

The Forgotten American Environmentalist

There is a certain advantage in writing about the intellectual and ideal development of the modern world from America; for here one is brought face to face with a more naked reality, here the bottom has dropped more completely out of the old traditions; and one gets a fuller sense of what is missing for a complete life.

(Lewis Mumford to Patrick Geddes, 11 December 1925[1])

When the Western environmental movement started in the early 1970s, a young British journalist wrote a book profiling scientists whose work had a direct bearing on the ecological predicament. Not surprisingly, her roster was dominated by university dons with impeccable scholarly credentials, including René Dubos, Raymond Dasmann, Estella Leopold, and Kenneth Boulding. Yet she chose to begin her book with a man without any formal training in ecology – indeed, without any formal training whatsoever. (The man's only university, he was to recall in his autobiography, was the city of New York.) However, for Anne Chisholm, this man had the most visible influence on contemporary environmental thought – as she wrote, 'of all the wise men whose thinking and writing over the years has prepared the ground for the environmental revolution, Lewis Mumford, the American philosopher and writer, must be preeminent'.[2]

Anne Chisholm's judgement would have found strong support within the scientific community; they chose Lewis Mumford to sum up the deliberations of two seminal symposia on ecological change.[3] Yet in the two decades since Anne Chisholm wrote her book, Mumford's reputation as an ecological thinker has suffered an extraordinary eclipse. Meanwhile, the environmental movement has grown enormously and, in the manner of any mature and self confident social movement, begun to construct its own genealogy and pantheon of heroes. This prehistory, as it were, of environmentalism has been documented most abundantly for Mumford's own country, the United States, yet nowhere else is the ignorance of Mumford's environmental writings more acute. That is the conclusion which must follow from a reading of the authoritative histories of American environmentalism; for example, those written by Roderick Nash, Stephen Fox, and Samuel Hays.[4]

The commonly acknowledged 'patron saints' of American environmentalism, this reading further tells us, are the naturalist and nature lover John Muir, and the forester and biologist Aldo Leopold. Why American environmentalists can make Muir and Leopold into cultural icons while neglecting Mumford is a fascinating question that we will return to towards the end of this chapter. Although American environmentalists have failed to recognise one of their own most authentic voices, I find Mumford's ecological thought as congenial as apparently did Anne Chisholm, likewise an outsider to North America. In his writing, as I shall show, lies some of the earliest and finest thinking on bioregionalism, anti-nuclearism, biodiversity, alternate energy paths, ecological urban planning and appropriate technology – all this combined with the deeply humane sensibilities of a democratic socialist.

THE INFLUENCE OF PATRICK GEDDES

Mumford's own appreciation of nature began with boyhood summers spent in Vermont. Towards the end of his life, he remembered those early encounters in the wild with skunks, woodchucks, deer and river trout as having 'deepened my sense of my native American roots'.[5] Mumford's experience was in tune with a long line of American environmentalists – from Henry Thoreau to Edward Abbey, via Muir, Leopold and Joseph Wood Krutch – whose love of nature followed directly from their engagement with the diversity and beauty of the North American wilderness.

However, had Mumford's ecological horizons remained confined to the wild, he would merit no more than a footnote in the history of environmental ideas. What distinguishes Mumford from the galaxy of American wilderness thinkers – and the reason I am writing about him in the first place – is his fundamentally ecological understanding of the ebb and flow of human history. For the origins of his ecological approach, we must turn briefly to the only man Mumford acknowledged as his teacher, the Scotsman, Patrick Geddes. A polymath who ranged widely over the humanities and life sciences Geddes, unlike his disciple, was a maddeningly obscure writer. As a Professor of Botany and activist town-planner in Scotland, he inspired students primarily through the spoken word and by force of example. For those with patience, however, there are veritable nuggets to be found in his writings.

The centrality of nature to Geddes's theory of town-planning is evident in the one general treatise he wrote on the subject, as well as in the several dozen town plans he wrote on assignment in India between 1915 and 1919, all of which reveal a subtle understanding of the ecological processes in the formation, functioning, rise and decline of cities.[6] But apart from his groundbreaking work in the theory and practice of town planning, Geddes also made a more general contribution to ecological thinking. No less a person than A.G. Tansley, one of the premier ecologists of this century, noted Geddes's influence on early ecological studies of the Scottish Highlands, while the American biologist Paul Sears hailed his impact on the geographer Dudley Stamp, the ecologist C.C. Adams, and our own subject, Lewis Mumford.[7] In a 1950 essay, Mumford wrote that by 'both training and general habit of mind Geddes was an ecologist long before that branch of biology had obtained the status of a special discipline ... And it is not as a bold innovator in urban planning, but as an ecologist, the patient investigator of historic filiations and dynamic biological and social relationships that Geddes's most important work in cities was done'.[8] At a more philosophical level, Geddes was an early harbinger of that 'general revolution in science now in rapid progress, the change from a *mechanocentric* view and treatment of nature and her processes to a more and more fully *biocentric* one'.[9]

'Biocentric' is, of course, a term much favoured by radical environmentalists of the present time. But where self-styled 'deep ecologists' use the term only as a standard by which to judge the alleged moral failings of those they call shallow ecologists, Geddes (and in time, Mumford) used a biocentric approach to a more constructive end – the patient investigation and understanding of 'historic filiations and dynamic biological and social relationships'. Mumford inherited from Geddes both a fundamentally ecological approach and a repertoire of neologisms – palaeotechnic/neotechnic, conurbation, megalopolis, etc. – that he put to innovative use, especially in his authoritative histories of technology and the city. Mumford also owed to Geddes his respect for pre-modern technologies and patterns of resource use. Notably, it was Geddes who drew his disciple's attention to the work of that forgotten American conservationist, George Perkins Marsh. As Mumford noted in an early appreciation, it was Marsh who first treated man as an 'active geological agent', who could 'upbuild or degrade', but who was, one way or another, a 'disturbing agent, who upset the harmonies of nature and overthrew the stability of existing arrangements and accomodations, extirpating indigenous vegetables and animal species, introducing foreign varieties, restricting spontaneous growth, and covering the earth with "new and reluctant vegetable forms and with alien tribes of animal life"'.[10]

Marsh focused on the destruction of forest cover, an example of the many ways in which Americans, in 'the very act of seizing all the habitable parts of the earth', had 'systematically misused and neglected our possessions'.[11] The wider ecological implications of early American economic development were fleshed out by Mumford in a remarkable and unjustly forgotten series of essays on regionalism, published in *The Sociological Review*, a journal edited by Patrick Geddes's associate Victor Branford. These essays constitute Mumford's first systematic attempt to apply the Geddesian ecological framework to historical phenomena.[12] This regional approach to social analysis, which the Indian sociologist Radhakamal Mukerjee was also developing at this time,[13] was a development of Geddes's conceptual trinity of Folk/Work/Place (itself borrowed from the work of the French sociologist Frederick Le Play).

In his *Sociological Review* essays, Mumford used the regional framework to analyse the ecological crimes of American pioneer civilisation (the epitome of 'irregionalism'), and to outline the prospects for a more sustainable economy and culture (what he termed 'regionalism').[14] The refusal to base industry and institutions on regional ecological endowments had led on the one side to enormous ecological devastation, and on the other to a parasitical relationship between the city and the hinterland. 'In America during the last century', wrote Mumford, 'we mined soils, gutted forests, misplaced industry, wasted vast sums in needless transportation, congested population and lowered the physical vitality of the community without immediately feeling the consequences of our actions.' During that period, it 'suited us to ignore the basic realities of the land: its contours and landscape, its vegetation areas, its power [and] mineral resources, its industry, its types of community ...'. This was a 'miner's kind of civilisation', exalting the miner's cut-and-run attitude to nature, as exemplified by timber mining and the relentless skimming of the soils. American cities were likewise unmindful of ecological realities: bloated in their proportions, they became 'prime offenders in their misuse of regional resources'. Mumford did not fail to notice, either, the proliferation of slums and slag heaps *within* city boundaries.

Mumford characterised the processes of what he (following Geddes) called the palaeotechnic age as 'doubly ruinous: they impoverish the earth by hastily removing, for the benefit of a few generations, the common resources which, once expended and dissipated, can never be restored; and second, in its technique, its habits, its processes, the palaeotechnic period is equally inimical to the earth considered as a human habitat, by its destruction of the beauty of the landscape, its ruining of streams, its pollution of drinking water, its filling the air with a finely divided carboniferous deposit, which chokes both life and vegetation'.[15]

Mumford warned that the day of the pioneer had passed; no longer could American economic development afford to neglect regional realities.

For if one thought not discretely of products and resources, but of the region as a whole, it would be clear 'that in each geographic area a certain balance of natural resources and human institutions is possible, for the finest development of the land and the people'. In America, the movement of 'regionalism' (as with the Regional Planning Association which Mumford helped initiate) emphasised the conservation of natural resources, but only in a more inclusive framework. Regionalism 'must not merely, through conservation, prevent waste: it must also provide the economic foundations for a continuous and flourishing life'. Regionalism sought in particular to harmonise urban living with the countryside, making the city an integral part of the region. Here Mumford drew attention to Ebenezer Howard's Garden City movement (also influenced by Geddes) – the creation of cities, limited in size, surrounded by farmland, with easy access to natural areas, and in other ways too in organic unity with their hinterland.[16]

These early and penetrating essays illustrate Mumford's deepening interest in the ecological infrastructure of human life. (Shortly afterwards, he wrote that the three main threats to civilisation were the continuing destruction of forest cover and soil erosion, the depletion of irreplaceable mineral resources, and the destructive potential of modern warfare.[17]) The *Sociological Review* series acted as a trailer, as it were, of his masterly histories, *Technics and Civilization* (1934) and *The Culture of Cities* (1938). These, Mumford's most celebrated books, and written at the height of his powers, need to be read as essentially *ecological* histories of the rise of modern Western civilisation. Both works outline a three-stage interpretation of the development of industrial civilisation. These successive, but overlapping and interpenetrating, phases Mumford termed 'eotechnic', 'palaeotechnic' and 'neotechnic,' respectively. The last two terms he owed to Geddes, while he added the first to designate the preparatory stage in which, he argued, most of the technical and social innovations of the modern world had been anticipated.[18]

Most, if not all, treatments of Mumford's histories neglect their ecological underpinnings. But in fact, his three-stage model is based on an ecological understanding of human history. Thus each of the three phases of machine civilization has left its deposits in society. Each has changed the landscape, altered the physical layout of cities, used certain resources and spurned others, favored certain types of commodity and certain paths of activity and modified the common technical heritage. Viewed from the point of view of characteristic inputs of energy and materials, 'the eotechnic is a water-and-wood complex, the palaeotechnic phase is a coal-and-iron complex, and the neotechnic phase is an electricity-and-iron complex'.[19]

In a strictly ecological sense, the eotechnic phase was benign. The resources it most heavily relied on – wood, water, and wind – were all renewable, it created exquisite landscapes, and it did not lead to pollution.

The 'energy of the eotechnic phase did not vanish in smoke nor were its products thrown quickly on junk-heaps: by the 17th century it had transformed the woods and swamps of northern Europe into a continuous vista of wood and field, village and garden ...' Its ecological impact would be regarded even more favorably when set against the record of its succeeding phase, the palaeotechnic era of 'carboniferous capitalism'.[20]

After about 1750, industrial development had 'passed into a new phase, with a different source of power, different materials, different social objectives'. The new source of energy was coal; the dominant new material, iron; the overriding social objectives, power, profit and efficiency. The widespread dependence on coal and iron meant that for the first time in human history, societies were living not on the current income from nature but on nature's capital. The characteristic byproducts of carboniferous capitalism were polluted air, water, and homes, and abominable living conditions made worse by the concentration and congestion brought about by factory production and modern urban living. The newer chemical industries also introduced dangerous substances into rivers and the atmosphere. As for that handmaiden of industrial capitalism, the railroad, it 'distributed smut and dirt' all over the world. Indeed, the 'reek of coal was the very incense of the new industrialism', and the rare sight of a 'clear sky in an industrial district was the sign of a strike or a lock-out or an industrial depression'. These varied and often deadly forms of environmental degradation were a consequence of the values of the money economy, in which the environment was treated as an abstraction, while air and sunlight, 'because of their deplorable lack of value in exchange, had no reality at all'.[21]

Despite all this, Mumford was hopeful that the palaeotechnic phase was but 'a period of transition, a busy, congested, rubbish-strewn avenue between the eotechnic and neotechnic economies'.[22] The neotechnic phase which Mumford saw emerging, would rely on a new and non-polluting source of energy – hydroelectricity – and devise long-lasting alloys and chemical compounds. (Mumford was also hoping, in the 1930s, for a push towards solar energy.) As water was readily available in Africa, South America and Asia, the arrival of hydro-electricity would also tend to displace Europe and North America from their position of industrial dominance. So far as pollution was concerned, the 'smoke pall of paleotechnic industry begins to lift: with electricity the clear sky and the clean waters of the eotechnic phase comes back again'. Meanwhile, the renewed utilisation of human excrement and the development of nitrogen-fixing fertilisers would arrest the soil erosion caused by the miner's civilisation of the earlier phase.[23] The neotechnic phase, as and when it came fully into its own, would restore three vital equilibria: that between man and nature; that between industry and agriculture; and that in population, through the balancing of birth and death rates.[24]

Mumford's magisterial history of the city also follows a three-stage interpretation: of environmental use, abuse and renewal. He begins with the medieval city (corresponding to the eotechnic phase) against which he claimed modern writers had developed a violent but largely unfounded prejudice. In his reconstruction, the pre-modern city blended in easily with its rural surroundings, while the extent of usable open space within its boundaries contrasted sharply with the 'notorious fact of *post*-medieval overcrowding'. Again, the waste materials of city life were largely organic, hence decomposable. All in all, the medieval city was more than adequate 'on the biological side', with its sights, smells and sounds infinitely more pleasurable than those of its modern successor. And architecturally speaking, 'the town itself was an omnipresent work of art'.[25]

Once again, Mumford's evocation of a harmonious and organic past was preparatory to his condemnation of the living present, the 'insensate industrial town' of the palaeotechnic era. For the factory and the slum were the two main elements of the urban complex which superseded the medieval city. Whereas the effluents of a single factory often could be absorbed by the surrounding landscape, the characteristic massing of industries in the palaeotechnic city polluted 'the air and water beyond remedy'. Meanwhile, in the congested living quarters of the slum, 'a pitch of foulness and filth was reached that the lowest serf's cottage scarcely achieved in medieval Europe'. Sanitation and waste disposal also fell far short of minimal human standards. As 'night spread over the coal-town', Mumford wrote dramatically, 'its prevailing colour was black. Black clouds of smoke rolled out of the factory chimneys, and the railroad yards, which often cut clean into the town, mangling the very organism, spread soot and cinders everywhere'. To this historian of the palaeotechnic city, it was 'plain that never before in recorded history had such vast masses of people lived in such a savagely deteriorated environment'.[26]

The way out lay in the growing movement for regionalism. As the epoch of land colonisation came to a close, Mumford thought he discerned a change in attitudes towards the earth, with the parasitic and predatory attitudes of the pioneer being supplanted by the more caring values of the emerging biotechnic regime. In European countries, the regionalist movement had fought against excessive centralisation, reclaimed the folk heritage, and fostered the growth of co-operatives. In the United States, the conservation movement, under the romantic impulse, had helped set aside large areas of wilderness; now, under a more scientific guise, it was actively promoting the conservation of raw materials. Meanwhile, the Garden City movement, which stressed the creation of balanced urban communities within balanced regions, was growing in influence.[27]

The analytical framework of Mumford's two great ecological histories has a markedly Hegelian ring: the eotechnic, palaeotechnic and neotechnic stages being analogous to the dialectic of thesis, antithesis and synthesis.[28] While his philosophical frame may have been inherited, his ecological sophistication is, for its time and place, quite remarkable. The major organising principles of his histories are truly ecological in nature: the use of energy and materials as indices of technical and environmental change; the mapping of resource flows, within and between regions, characteristic of different stages; the forms of environmental degradation and movements of environmental redressal typical of different epochs; and the role of values in creating the 'money economy' of destruction and the (future) 'life economy' of renewal.[29] Underlying it all is a commitment to environmental conservation as a positive force, in contrast to the negativism with which American environmentalism, then as now, was beset. In a passage which is strikingly contemporary, he wrote in 1938 that

originating in the spectacle of waste and defilement, the conservation movement has tended to have a negative influence: it has sought to isolate wilderness areas from encroachment and it has endeavoured to diminish waste and prevent damage. The present task of regional planning is a more positive one: it seeks to bring the earth as a whole up to the highest pitch of perfection and appropriate use – not merely preserving the primeval, but extending the range of the garden, and introducing the deliberate culture of the landscape into every part of the open country.[30]

MUMFORD ON MODERN TECHNOLOGY

The optimism of Mumford's ecological histories of the 1930s would surprise those acquainted only with his later writings. At the time, he was hopeful that the emerging values of the neotechnic economy would humanise and domesticate the machine. From the standpoint of democracy, too, neotechnic technology – in particular, hydro-electricity – worked in favor of decentralisation and the human scale, in direct contrast to the giantism and concentration of the palaeotechnic epoch. Mumford even had something positive to say about the automobile. Although he deplored its reliance on petrol, he believed that its growing displacement of the railways meant that humans would no longer crowd around railheads, pitheads and ports.[31]

Mumford's early ecological philosophy was, therefore, deeply *historicist* in nature. He believed that the forces of history were themselves moving in the direction of a cleaner environment, a more benign technology, and a more democratic social order. Meanwhile, his own association with the regionalist movement – about the only time in his long career that he participated in collective action – also favoured a more optimistic outlook on social change.

All this sits oddly with Mumford's more common reputation, based on his later writings, as a prophet of doom. Locating this transition in time, it appears that the aftermath of the World War II fundamentally altered Mumford's faith in the forward march of history. The carpet bombing of German cities, the dropping of atom bombs on Japan, and the paranoia of the Cold War, all deeply affected Mumford. No longer could history be relied upon to usher in the neotechnic age, for technology, and the 'gentlemen' who controlled its development, had gone mad.

This change in outlook is captured in a preface Mumford wrote in 1973 for the reprint of a book first published nearly 30 years earlier. He defended the book's support of John Stuart Mill's theory of the 'steady state', in opposition to the Victorian belief in progress and the expansionary thrust of modern Western civilisation, thus continuing the call in *Technics and Civilization* for a dynamic equilibrium between man and nature, and industry and agriculture. But, he noted significantly, 'the chief effect of the regressive transformations that have taken place in the last quarter of a century [i.e. since the end of World War II] has been to change my conclusions from the indicative to the imperative mood; not "we shall" achieve a dynamic equilibrium but *"we must"* – if we are not to destroy the delicate ecological balance upon which all life depends.'[32]

In this more sombre, reflective phase, Mumford's fundamental values remained steadfast, but he was considerably less sanguine about their wider acceptance. None the less, scattered through his writings are the elements of an ecological philosophy that is both analytic and programmatic. No doubt it is difficult to find a compact or authorised statement of his views in the post-war period; no canonical text exists comparable to *Technics and Civilization* or *The Culture of Cities*. Rather, his perspective on ecology, culture and politics must be reconstructed from his diverse writings, particularly his neglected periodical essays and articles.

Let us first consider Mumford's reconsideration of modern technology, beginnning with his criticisms of nuclear energy and culminating in the full scale attack contained in *The Pentagon of Power* (1970). Abandoning the hope that modern technology would develop in a benign direction, he was now convinced that modern science and technology bore the impress of 'the capitalist's interest in quantity', his belief that there 'are no natural limits to acquisition' being 'supplemented in technology, by the notion that quantitative production had no natural limits either'.[33] Where 'the machine takes precedence of the man', he remarked, 'and where all activities and values that sustain the human spirit are subordinated to making money and privately devouring only such goods as money will buy, even the physical environment tends to become degraded and inefficient'.[34] Mumford reserved his sharpest strictures for atomic energy, which to him exemplified the one-sided, life-denying development of modern technics. He wanted it to be put on 'strict probation', refusing to accept the 'sedative explanations' of the Atomic Energy Commission that pollution would be negligible and easy to control. Such reassurances gave no confidence, for the history of industrial pollution was one where 'our childish shortsightedness under the excitement of novelty, our contempt for health when profits are at stake, our lack of reverence for life, even our own life, continue to poison the atmosphere in every industrial area, and to make the streams and rivers, as well as the air we breathe, unfit for organic life.'[35]

Mumford's faith in science and technology was also shaken by their role in World War II and the arms race which followed. He was an early and percipient critic of the nuclear bomb, urging America to share its nuclear knowledge with the Soviet Union rather than embark on a meaningless and costly competition. Both the development of nuclear energy and the perfection of weapons of mass destruction, he thought, undermined democracy by their fostering of secrecy by and within the state.[36] But the military–industrial complex was itself only part of a wider denial of democracy, wherein large areas of central government had passed out 'of all popular surveillance and control, operating in secret, defiantly withholding or adulterating the information needed by democracy in order to pass judgement on the work of its officers'.[37] He unfavorably compared the state of American democracy to that of a century earlier, when there had existed a great diffusion of property, wealth and political power. (In calling for a renewal of democracy, Mumford was putting forward a cyclical theory of political structures curiously similar to his – by now modified – cyclical theory of technical development: a harmonious but largely irretrievable past, an abominable present, and a future that had yet to be claimed.[38])

Two elements of Mumford's democratic vision bear highlighting. First, he stressed that citizens must have control over public programmes that vitally affect their lives. For Mumford, high among Geddes's revolutionary contributions to planning – that which set him apart from the archetypal administrator, bureaucrat, or businessman – was his 'willingness to leave an essential part of the process to those who are most intimately connected with it – the ultimate users, consumers, or citizens'.[39] Mumford also inherited Geddes's high regard for folk or pre-modern knowledge. In the early days of the most savage war in human history, he hoped for a time when the 'mechanically more primitive cultures ... may influence and civilise their European conquerors; may restore to them some of that deep organic sense of unity with the environment, some of that sensuous enrichment and playful enjoyment that Western man has so often forfeited in his aggressive conquest of the environment ...'[40]

These sentiments were consistent with Mumford's larger plea for what we would now call 'biological diversity'. The machine world, he complained, 'has insulated its occupants from every form of reality except the machine process itself: heat and cold, day and night, the earth and the stars, woodland, crop land, vine land, garden land – all forms of organic partnership between the millions of species that add to the vitality and wealth of the earth – are either suppressed entirely from the mind or homogenised into a uniform mixture which can be fed into the machine'. Against this deadly uniformity, Mumford called for us to cherish our own history, by 'promoting character and variety and beauty wherever we find it, whether in landscapes or in people'.[41]

We have shown in Chapter 4 that the three generic environmental philosophies of our time are wilderness thinking (or primitivism), agrarianism, and scientific industrialism. Mumford is rare, and possibly unique, among environmental thinkers in his ability to synthesise and transcend partisan stances on behalf of the wilderness, countryside or city. As his colleague Benton Mckaye pointed out, the primeval, the rural and the urban were all environments necessary for man's full development. Consequently, a regionalist programme had to incorporate all three elements: the preservation of the primeval wilderness, the restoration of the stable rural landscape, and the salvaging of the true urban environment.[42]

The humanising of technology and the protection of diversity were both contingent on a fundamental change in values. Mumford's biographer suggests that while other radicals 'expected such a value change to occur after the revolution, for Mumford this value change *was* the revolution'.[43] In the machine age, the disintegration of the human personality had reached an advanced stage, as the pathologies of the civilised world bore witness. So, as Mumford told a gathering of international scientists in 1955, 'if we are to achive some degree of ecological balance, ... we must aim at human balance too.'[44] In an address delivered at the centenary meeting of the American Association for the Advancement of Science, and published (coincidentally, but appositely) on Mahatma Gandhi's birthday, he called for a dethroning of technics from its superior place in modern society. In this larger task of cultural renewal,

Not the Power Man, not the Profit Man, not the Mechanical man, but the Whole Man, must be the central actor in the new drama of civilization. This means that we must reverse the order of development which first produced the machine; we must now explore the world of history, culture, organic life, human development, as we once explored the non-living world of nature. We must understand the organics of personality as we first understood the statics and mechanics of physical processes; we must centre attention on quality, value, pattern, and purpose, as we once centred attention on quantity, on physical relationships, on mass and motion.[45]

More than values, individuals and societies need viable myths.

Mumford hoped for the overthrow of the myth of the machine, which had for such an extended period held Western man in its thrall. For sanity, stability and survival, the myth of the machine had to be replaced with 'a new myth of life, a myth based upon a richer understanding of all organic processes, a sharper insight into man's positive "role in changing the face of the earth"..., and [on] a deeply religious faith in man's own capacity to transform and perfect his own self and his own institutions in cooperative relation with all the forces of nature, and above all, with his fellow men'.[46]

With this last citation, it is not difficult to sustain the claim that Mumford's philosophy can fairly be characterised, in contemporary terms, as 'ecological socialist'. But unlike radical socialists and radical environmentalists, Mumford did not put his faith on a chosen agent of history (proletarian or Deep Ecologist). In one sense, the refusal to project one's aspirations on an agent is wholly laudable.[47] But looked at another way, it exemplifies a curious silence in his work – regarding the role and place of purposive social action. Mumford frequently invokes paradigmatic individuals, values, and ways of life, but never social movements. He puts forward a charter of social reform which does not, alas, carry the means of its implementation.[48]

THE NINETEENTH-CENTURY HEROES

I now explore, more tentatively, the outlines of how Mumford might have chosen to be remembered as a social and ecological thinker. I use here three appreciations Mumford wrote of other people – his son, an ecological pioneer, and a 19th century polymath he greatly admired. None of these essays are well known, but it is in these, apparently ephemeral works that we glimpse hints of Mumford's self-image, his uncertainties regarding his place in history[49]

Mumford's only son, named Geddes after Patrick Geddes, died at the age of nineteen in action in World War II. The loss shattered Mumford, contributing significantly to his deepening pessimism about the direction of Western civilisation. Yet in a memoir he wrote after Geddes Mumford's death, the father was able to celebrate in his son the attitudes to land and people he had himself so long cherished.

In a strongly pastoral chapter, 'The Land and the Seasons', Mumford called his son a 'true countryman'. Through his deep feelings for the countryside, Geddes Mumford 'was renewing the spirit Thoreau had brought to the American landscape ... Geddes responded in every fiber to Thoreau's question : "who would not rise to meet the expectations of the land"'. In a later chapter, 'Country Ways and Country Neighbours', written likewise in a pastoral vein, Mumford remembered his son liking to work with his hands and notably, as having an intense dislike for the machine. An illustration of his 'antipathy toward the machine' was Geddes's preference, expressed to his mother when he was a child, for a horse to plough the fields. When his mother suggested a tractor could do the job just as well, Geddes replied in amazement: 'But, Mommie, you'd never use a tractor on the *ground* would you? Have you ever seen the fields after a tractor has gone over them? A tractor doesn't care what it does: it digs right into the earth and hacks it up. A horse goes gently. I'd never use a tractor.'

Moreover, 'Geddes's feeling for the country included country people'. Mumford wrote evocatively of a neighbour of theirs, Sam Honour, a smallholder of English stock who was 'full of country lore ... and nearer to the peasant than any other American I have ever met'. In his person, Sam was 'a living specimen of an older and homelier America, which was closer to Geddes's ideal than the one he was part of'.[50]

If Mumford's own love of the land, like his son's, was derived from an early exposure to the country, his mature ecological consciousness is owed to the work of Patrick Geddes and the great American geographer the latter had introduced him to, George Perkins Marsh. In *The Brown Decades* (1931), Mumford had alerted the American public to the significance of this forgotten writer, so when a comprehensive biography was published a quarter of a century later, Mumford was well placed to write a further appreciation. He remarked of Marsh's *Man and Nature* (first published in 1864) that is was unquestionably a 'comprehensive ecological study before the very word ecology had been invented'. Mumford was also quite justified in claiming that Marsh would have opposed 'the vast programme of pollution and extermination that has been engineered in our country in the name of scientific progress', and in particular, that he would have spoken out, were he alive, against the generation of nuclear energy with its potential for 'permanently crippling' the human race and making the planet unfit for habitation.

It is in setting Marsh's thought in perspective that Mumford truly reveals himself. It was not that 'Marsh undervalued science or the products of science', he wrote, but that 'he valued the integrity of life even more ...'. For Marsh's 'unique contribution was his combination of the naturalist's approach with that of the moralist and the humanist; he supplied both the intellectual tools and the moral direction necessary'. Here, his 'type of mind was the exact opposite of the German-trained specialists who began to dominate America in the 1880s, when Marsh died, for the latter narrowed their life experience and segregated their specialised interests'. Ironically, it was Marsh's very ability to transcend narrow spheres of thought which 'made his work suspect to the following generation, who dodged the task of evaluating his genius by ignoring it'.[51]

This uncharacteristically defensive tone also crept into Mumford's appreciation of William Morris, a 19th century genius whose achievements were more wide-ranging still. Morris, wrote Mumford, was not merely a 'dreamer of dreams' but also a 'resolute realist, who refused to take the sordid Victorian triumphs of mechanical progress as the ultimate achievements of the human spirit'. He was not, as commonly supposed, a revivalist but rather what Henry Russel Hitchcock had called a 'New Traditionalist, seeking not to revive the past but to nourish and develop what was still alive in it'. Morris devoted time and energy to the recovery of traditional techniques that were being rendered superfluous in the machine age – indeed 'a whole generation before the anthropologists began their belated work of salvage with surviving stone age and tribal communities, [Morris] performed a similar task for the arts and crafts of the Old World past'. But 'if he had been more sympathetic with the peculiar triumphs of his own age, he might not have had the copious, concentrated energies to perform this necessary salvage operation'.

Nor did Morris want to abolish all machines: he thought they could do the necessary work and leave other, more joyous tasks to be done by human beings themselves. Morris was in effect an early appropriate technologist who, instead 'of accepting either megatechnics or monotechnics as inevitable ... sought to keep alive or if necessary to restore those forms of art and craft whose continued existence would enrich human life and even keep the way open for fresh technical achievements.'

In challenging the stereotype of Morris as an impractical dreamer, Mumford pointed to his engagement with socialism. Although it came rather late, Morris's lifework was strengthened immeasurably by the socialist vision, which 'bestowed a fuller social content and a larger human purpose on all his private achievements as an artist, and gave him the confidence to work for a future in which all men might know the joys of creative labor that he himself had experienced'.[52]

Written nearly 10 years apart, and on two very different 19th-century giants, there are none the less remarkable similarities in Mumford's tributes to George Perkins Marsh and William Morris. In either case, he appears to have projected himself, and more notably, *society's preferred evaluation of himself*, on to a kinsman in ideas and action, albeit of an earlier generation. He anticipates and contests the criticism that Marsh was against science, and attributes his neglect (by the present generation) to his refusal to be trapped within narrow specialisms. Mumford had faced the first criticism himself, and was coming to terms with a neglect of his counsel in the intellectual and political forums where he might most expect a hearing. His defense of Morris can also be understood as a product of a close personal identification. Morris, Mumford suggests, was not blindly against technology; knew how to use the past without being a revivalist; was as much a 'realist' as a 'dreamer'; and was guided to a deeper social vision by his engagement with socialism. In writing his tribute, Mumford may, or may not, have been conscious of how his defence of Morris was at the same time a defence of his own life and work. He was 73 at the time, almost at the end of his active career, and profoundly unsure of how history would judge him.

CONCLUSION

We return to where we began – the reception, or more accurately, the non-reception of Mumford's environmental thought in the country of his origin and residence. Illustrative in this regard is a major round-table on environmental history recently organised by the prestigous *Journal of American History*. In his keynote essay, Donald Worster recalls Aldo Leopold's call, in *The Sand County Almanac* (1949) for an 'ecological interpretation of history', commenting that it has 'taken a while for historians to heed Leopold's advice', but at long last the field of environmental history 'has begun to take shape and its practitioners are trying to build on [Leopold's] initiative'.[53]

I have nothing against Aldo Leopold, and considerable admiration for Donald Worster, whom I hold to be the most brilliant and imaginative of American environmental historians. What is more, Worster once seriously contemplated writing a doctoral dissertation on the subject of this essay. Why then would he invoke Leopold's call for an ecological history, made in passing and in a wholly different context, rather than the work of the man who may justly be regarded as having founded the field in America? For Mumford was using the term 'ecological history' as early as 1917,[54] outlining an ecological theory of history in his brilliant essays of the 1920s on regionalism, and writing two ecological histories in the next decade. Moreover, he continued to write on environmental themes until the end of his life.

Worster's preference might perhaps be explained positively rather than negatively: that is, through a positive identification with Aldo Leopold in which Mumford's more weighty contributions are obscured. It is none the less emblematic of a far wider neglect of Mumford by American environmental historians, environmental philosophers and environmental activists. Aldo Leopold and John Muir appear to be far more congenial to the mind and heart of the American environmentalist. True, both were remarkable human beings, acute observers of the natural world and powerful moralists. Neither had Mumford's historical sweep, sociological sensibilities or philosophical depth.

This neglect needs to be explained, and the following paragraphs offer a preliminary explanation. A primary influence has been the dominance of wilderness thinking in the American environmental movement. Like Muir and Leopold, Mumford valued primeval nature and biological diversity, but unlike them, he focused simultaneously on cultural diversity and relations of power *within* human society, refusing to divorce individual attitudes to nature from their social, cultural and historical contexts. Indeed, the range and richness of Mumford's thought mark him out as the pioneer American social ecologist and environmental historian. But his subtle and historically rooted philosophy cannot be reduced to the Manichean oppositions of black and white, good and evil, to which environmentalism has so often succumbed. Wrenching Muir and Leopold's thought out of context, radical environmentalists can reduce it to the polar opposition of biocentric/anthropocentric, an option not admissible in this case. There is little hint in Mumford's work of a scapegoat 'out there' (whether capitalist or shallow ecologist); rather, the burden of his work is towards internal social reform, of recognising that the enemy is 'us'.

Secondly, Mumford is not a narrow nationalist. We have earlier in this book commented upon the interpenetration of environmentalism and nationalism in the United States. The wilderness movement itself began as a nationalist crusade to preserve 'monuments' of nature not found in Europe; it has since been identified with the need to challenge the world's identification of American culture with a crass materialism.[55] Politically, Mumford had always opposed American nationalism and its most egregious expression, isolationism;[56] intellectually, he drew as much on European as on North American models and exemplars. Deploring the 'false tribal god of nationalism', he was clear that 'cultural advances usually work by cross-fertilisation', a credo to which his own thought bore such eloquent testimony.[57]

Third, Mumford was indeed too much the polymath. He made fundamental contributions in so many fields that it is easy to overlook the ecological side of his work. Thus two recent books on Mumford – Donald Miller's authorised biography and the collection of essays edited by Thomas and Agatha Hughes – are models of sympathetic and solid scholarship. They carefully appraise Mumford's contributions to architecture, technology, urban history, regional planning and literature, but contain little awareness of his ecologically oriented writings.[58]

And finally, Mumford's political beliefs must also have worked against the wider cultural acceptance of his thought in the United States. An early critic of Stalinism, he was none the less a lifelong socialist, in a culture that has always been deeply hostile to socialists and socialism. Mumford deplored the tyranny and continuing worship of technology in Soviet Russia, but recognised that the promise of equality underlying communism, though perverted in practice, was wholly in keeping with the spirit of the age. The task of democracy, he pointed out, was to show that there were better ways of promoting economic and political equality than tyranny and thought control.[59]

The noted green writer (and former German Green) Rudolf Bahro came upon Mumford's thought rather late, but immediately recognized that his work *'has* the same significance for the ecological movement as the achievement of Marx once *had* for the labour movement'.[60] Once again, Bahro's nationality is perhaps not accidental to his appreciation of a thinker so completely forgotten in his own land. And yet, the treatment of Mumford by American environmentalists is of a piece with the fate of some other thinkers honoured in this book: Cebrià de Montoliu, forced to flee from his native Barcelona; Nicholas Georgescu-Roegen, exiled from Romania into a provincial American university, always peripheral to the 'mainstream' of his profession; and Mahatma Gandhi, quietly forgotten after Indian Independence, his ideas cremated with his body by his closest associates in the anti-colonial movement. Out of tune and out of time in their own lives, they await reclamation by us, now, and for the next century.

NOTES TO INTRODUCTION

1 Thus is not cited or acknowledged, in Jonathan Bate's provocative book *Romantic Ecology: Wordsworth and the Environmental Tradition* (London: Routledge, 1991).

2 Aldous Huxley, 'Wordsworth in the tropics', pp. 113–29 in *Do What You Will* (1929; reprinted London: Chatto and Windus, 1956).

3 It goes unmentioned by his recent, and otherwise eagle-eyed, biographer. See David Cannadine, *G. M. Trevelyan: A Life in History* (London: Harper Collins, 1993).

4 G. M. Trevelyan, 'The Calls and Claims of Natural Beauty' (the Rickman Godlee Lecture for 1931), pp. 92–106 in *An Autobiography and Other Essays* (London: Longman, Green & Co., 1949).

5 Arthur Ekirch, Jr., *Man and Nature in America* (New York: Columbia University Press, 1963), p. 189.

6 James Frykman and Orvar Lofgren, *Cultural Builders: A Historical Anthropology of Middle-Class Life*, translated by Alan Crozier (New Brunswick, NJ: Rutgers University Press, 1987), pp. 561, 83.

7 Ronald Inglehart, *The Silent Revolution: Changing Values and Political Styles Among Western Publics* (Princeton: Princeton University Press, 1977); Inglehart, *Culture Shift in Advanced Industrial Societies* (Princeton: Princeton University Press, 1990); Inglehart and Jaques Rene-Rabier, 'Political Realignment in Advanced Industrial Society: From Class-based Politics to Quality-of-Life Politics', *Government and Opposition*, volume 21, number 4, 1986.

8 Charles Moore, 'Foreword', in Phillip Marsden-Smedley, ed., *Britain in the Eighties: The Spectator's View of the Thatcher Decade* (London: Grafton Books, 1989).

9 Advertisement of *World Development* in the *Economic and Political Weekly* of Bombay, 21 May 1988.

10 Jolyon Jenkins, 'Animal Wrongs', New Statesman, February 1986.

11 *New York Times*, 29 August 1986.

12 Michael McCloskey, 'World Parks', *Sierra*, volume 69, number 6, 1984, p. 36.

13 John Marson, 'Korea Wakes Up to the Environment', *New Scientist*, 8 June 1991.

14 Lester Thurow, *The Zero-Sum Society: Distribution and the Possibilities for Change* (New York: Basic Books, 1980), pp. 104–5 (emphasis added).

15 Eric Hobsbawm, *Age of Extremes: The Short Twentieth Century, 1914–1991* (London: Michael Joseph, 1994), p.570.

16 C. von Furer Haimendorf, *The Chenchus* (London: Macmillan, 1943).

17 K. Balagopal, 'A Little More of the Same', *Seminar* (New Delhi), issue 412, December 1993.

18 Carey Scott Ternei, 'Why Save Tigers – What About Us, Say Russians', *The Sunday Times* (London), 11 December 1994.

19 Tim Johnson, 'Galapagos Islands: Darwin's Lab Evolves Into Tourist Hot Spot', *The Seattle Times*, 29 May 1994; *Action Alert*, dated 6 January 1995, issued by the Charles Darwin Foundation, Falls Church, Virginia. Dr Nathan Stolzfus of Harvard University directed us to the Galapagos case.

20 Quoted in Johnson, op. cit.

21 Abu Abraham, 'These Environmental Fundamentalists', *Mainstream* (New Delhi), 8 November 1986. The 'Gandhism' referred to derives from the anti-colonialist and spiritualist Mahatma, not the politician Indira.

22 We are grateful to Dr Michael Dove of the East-West centre, Honolulu, for providing us with copies of this exchange.

23 Jim Taylor, 'Social Activism and Resistance on the Thai Frontier: The Case of Phra Prajak Khuttajitto', *Bulletin of Concerned Asian Scholars*, volume 25, number 2, 1993. Cf. also Larry Lohmann,

'Peasants, Plantations and Pulp: The Politics of Eucalyptus in Thailand', *Bulletin of Concerned Asian Scholars*, volume 23, number 4, 1991.

24 Based on Ken Saro-Wiwa, *A Month and a Day: A Detention Diary* (London: Penguin, 1995), supplemented by reports in *The Observer*, 5 November 1995 and *The Guardian Weekly*, 12 November 1995.

25 Mercio Gomes, Chandra Kirana, Sami Soganbele and Rajiv Vora, *A Vision from the South: How Wealth Degrades the Environment: Sustainability in the Netherlands* (Utrecht: International Books, 1992). It says something for the Dutch that the invitation was extended in the first place. One cannot easily imagine the Sierra Club, for instance, initiating such an examination.

26 Taylor, op. cit, pp 11, 5.

27 Saro-Wiwa, op. cit., p. 149; Gomes et al, op. cit., pp. 119, 123, 125.

28 A trend illustrated not merely by Inglehart and company, but also by some studies of Third World environmentalism. In a celebrated essay of 1967, Lynn White saw a way out of the ecological crisis only in an eventual victory of Eastern spirituality over Western materialism. Twenty years later, White's hopes found a curious echo in claims that Indian environmentalism in essence reflected the innate ecological wisdom of Hindu women against the destructive development model imposed on them by (Christian?) men. Cf. Vandana Shiva, *Staying Alive: Women, Ecology and Development* (London: Zed Books, 1988), a well-known but in our opinion utterly misguided work.

NOTES TO CHAPTER 1

1 This chapter is based on a paper first presented at a conference on 'Dissent and Direct Action in the Late Twentieth Century', organised by the Harry and Frank Guggenheim Foundation at Otavalo, Ecuador, in June 1994.

2 J. Bandyopadhyay, 'Political Economy of Drought and Water Scarcity', *Economic and Political Weekly*, 12 December 1987.

3 Most authoritatively, perhaps, in the first two Citizens Reports on the Indian environment, brought out by New Delhi's Centre for Science and Environment in 1982 and 1985.

4 The development of the Chipko movement is discussed in Ramachandra Guha, *The Unquiet Woods: Ecological Change and Peasant Resistance in the Himalaya* (New Delhi: Oxford University Press and Berkeley: University of California Press, 1989).

5 See Mary Douglas and Aaron Wildavsky, *Risk and Culture: An Essay on the Selection of Technical and Environmental Dangers* (Berkeley: University of California Press, 1982).

6 Aside from specific sources cited later, this discussion of the KPL case also draws on numerous unpublished and locally printed documents, as well as on my own fieldwork and interviews in the region.

7 See, among other works, Anon, *Undeclared Civil War: A Critique of the Forest Policy* (New Delhi: Peoples Union for Democratic Rights, 1982); Walter Fernandes and Sharad Kulkarni, eds., *Towards a New Forest Policy* (New Delhi: Indian Social Institute, 1983); Ramachandra Guha, 'Forestry in British and Post–British India: A Historical Analysis', *Economic and Political Weekly*, in two parts, 29 October and 5–12 November 1983.

8 Madhav Gadgil and Madhulika Sinha, 'The Biomass Budget of Karnataka', in Cecil J. Saldanha, ed., *The State of Karnataka's Environment* (Bangalore: Centre for Taxonomic Studies, 1985).

9 See Anil Agarwal and Sunita Narain, eds., *The State of India's Environment: A Citizens' Report 1984–85* (New Delhi: Centre for Science and Environment, 1985); J. Bandyopadhyay and Vandana Shiva, *Ecological Audit of Eucalyptus Cultivation* (Dehradun: Natraj Publishers, 1984).

10 *Jagruta Vani* (quarterly newsletter of the Samaj Parivartan Samudaya, Dharwad), volume 2, number 4, December 1986.

11 Writ Petition number 19483 in the High Court of Karnataka, Bangalore (SPS and others versus Karnataka State Pollution Control Board and others). On the anti-pollution movement, see also S. R.

Hiremath, 'How to Fight a Corporate Giant', in Anil Agarwal, Darryl D'Monte and Ujjwala Samarth, eds., *The Fight for Survival* (New Delhi: Centre for Science and Environment, 1987).

12 Sadanand Kanvalli, *Quest for Justice* (Dharwad: SPS and others, 1990), p 7.

13 Writ Petition (Civil) number 35 of 1987 in the Supreme Court of India, New Delhi (Dr K. Shivram Karanth, SPS et. al. versus the State of Karnataka, KPL et. al.)

14 Cf Ramachandra Guha and Madhav Gadgil, 'State Forestry and Social Conflict in British India', *Past and Present*, number 123, May 1989.

15 Ajit Bhattacharjea, 'Satyagraha in Kusnur', in two parts, *Deccan Herald* (Bangalore), 19 and 20 November 1987. Coined by Mahatma Gandhi, the term 'satyagraha' (literally, 'truth-force') is used generically in India to denote any form of non-violent direct action.

16 S. R. Hiremath, 'The Karnataka Pulpwoods Limited Case', paper presented at the training workshop on Environment, People and the Law, Centre for Science and Environment, New Delhi, 12–15 October 1992.

17 Ajit Bhattacharjea, 'KPL Strikes Back' and 'Kusnur: Significant Success', in *Deccan Herald*, issues of 5 May and 15 June 1988 respectively.

18 See, for instance, Madhav Gadgil, S. Narendra Prasad and Rauf Ali, 'Forest Policy and Forest Management in India: A Critical Review', *Social Action*, volume 27, number 1, 1983.

19 *The Hindu* (Bangalore), 20 August 1990.

20 For a fuller definition and application of these categories, see Madhav Gadgil and Ramachandra Guha, *Ecology and Equity: the Use and Abuse of Nature in Contemporary India* (London: Routledge, 1995).

21 The interested reader is referred to, among other works, Bradford Morse, et. al. *The Sardar Sarovar Project: The Report of the Independent Review* (Washington: The World Bank, 1993); Amita Baviskar, *In the Belly of the River: Adivasi Battles over Nature in the Narmada Valley* (New Delhi: Oxford University, 1995); Gadgil and Guha, *Ecology and Equity*, Chapter 3.

22 Tilly's works include *From Mobilization to Revolution* (Reading, MA: Addison–Wesley, 1978) and *The Contentious French* (Cambridge, MA: Harvard University Press, 1986). Cf. also the Tilly-inspired two-part special section entitled 'Historical Perspectives on Social Movements', *Social Science History*, volume 17, numbers 2 and 3, Summer and Fall 1993.

23 In contemporary India these 'Gandhian' techniques are by no means the sole preserve of the environmental movement. They are used in all sorts of ways by all sorts of social struggles: by farmers wanting higher fertiliser subsidies, hospital workers wanting greater security of tenure, or ethnic minorities fighting for a separate province.

24 Kanvalli, op. cit., p1.

25 Important studies of American environmentalism include, to select from a vast and ever proliferating literature, W. R. Burch, Jr, *Daydreams and Nightmares: A Sociological Essay on the American Environment* (New York: Harper & Row, 1971); Donald Fleming, 'Roots of the New Conservation Movement', in Fleming and Bernard Bailyn, eds., *Perspectives in American History, Volume VI* (Cambridge, MA: Charles Warren Center for Studies in American History, 1972); Linda Graber, *Wilderness as Sacred Space* (Washington, DC: Association of American Geographers, 1976); Roderick Nash, *Wilderness and the American Mind*, (3rd edn., New Haven, CT: Yale University Press, 1983); Alfred Runte, *National Parks: the American Experience* (Lincoln: University of Nebraska Press, 1984); Stephen Fox, *The American Conservation Movement: John Muir and His Legacy* (Madison: University of Wisconsin Press, 1985); Samuel P. Hays, *Beauty, Health and Permanence: Environmental Politics in the United States, 1955–1985* (New York: Cambridge University Press, 1987); and, most recently, Philip Shabecoff, *A Fierce Green Fire: the American Environmental Movement* (New York: Hill & Wang, 1993). We cite some only influential books , without taking notice of a huge outcrop of journal and magazine articles.There is nothing like this profusion of work with regard to the environmental movement in India. Useful overviews are provided in Anil Agarwal, 'Human–Nature Interactions in a Third World Country', *The Environmentalist*, volume 6, number 3, 1987 and in Bina Agarwal, 'The Gender and Environment Debate: Lessons from India', *Feminist Studies*, volume 18, number 1, 1992. Other relevant writings include Guha, *The Unquiet Woods*; Vandana Shiva, with J. Bandyopadhyay, P. Hegde, B. V. Krishnamurthy, J. Kurien, G. Narendranath, V. Ramprasad and S.

T. S. Reddy, *Ecology and the Politics of Survival* (New Delhi: Sage, 1991); Madhav Gadgil and Ramachandra Guha, 'Ecological Conflicts and the Environmental Movement in India', *Development and Change*, volume 25, number 1, 1994; *Baviskar, In the Belly of the River* (New Delhi: Oxford University Press, 1995).

26 Wolfgang Sachs, *For Love of the Automobile: Looking Back into the History of our Desires* (Berkeley: University of California Press, 1992), pp 150–1.

27 A point first made by the British sociologist Stephen Cotgrove in his book *Catastrophe or Cornucopia?* (Chichester: Wiley, 1982).

28 This silence is more fully explored in Chapter 5.

29 Cf Roderick Nash, *The Rights of Nature: A History of Environmental Ethics* (Madison: University of Wisconsin Press, 1989).

30 Ruth Rosen, 'Who Gets Polluted: The Movement for Environmental Justice', *Dissent* (New York), Spring 1994, p. 229. Cf also Andrew Szasz, *Ecopopulism: Toxic Waste and the Movement for Environmental Justice* (Minneapolis: University of Minnesota Press, 1994); Bunyan Bryant, ed., *Environmental Justice: Issues, Policies and Solutions* (Washington D.C.: Island Press, 1995). The environmental justice movement is analysed in more detail in the Chapter 2.

31 Cf Chapter 5, and Patrick C. West and Steven R. Brechin, eds., *Resident Peoples and National Parks: Social Dilemmas and Strategies in International Conservation* (Tucson: The University of Arizona Press, 1991).

32 Tim Palmer, *Stanislaus: The Struggle for a River* (Berkeley: University of California Press, 1982), Chapter 8.

33 Mark Dubois to Colonel Donald O'Shei, reproduced in Palmer, op. cit., pp. 163–64 (author's italics).

34 Anon., *The Narmada Valley Project: A Critique* (New Delhi: Kalpavriksh, 1988).

35 Circular letter from Medha Patkar and others, dated 30 January 1990.

36 Habermas, 'New Social Movements', *Telos*, number 49, 1981. Habermas further observes: 'This new type of (environmental) conflict is an expression of the "silent revolution" in values and attitudes that R. Inglehart has ascertained for entire populations.' This endorsement of the post-materialist thesis seemingly denies (as does Inglehart) the very material roots of environmental conflict in industrialised societies, a point elaborated in Chapter 2.

37 Smitu Kothari and Pramod Parajuli, 'No Nature without Social Justice: a Plea for Ecological and Cultural Pluralism in India', in Wolfgang Sachs, ed., *Global Ecology: a New Arena of Political Conflict* (London: Zed Books, 1993).

NOTES TO CHAPTER 2

1 Executive Order 12898, February 11 1994, signed b y President William Clinton.

2 'Political ecology' also refers to the use of ecological ideas in politics, for instance by Green parties, but this should perhaps rather be called 'environmental politics', except that the politics of environmentalists goes far beyond a monographic interest in the environment.

3 For a more technical discussion of these issues, which also explains the ecological orientation (or lack thereof) of different schools of economic thought, see J. Martinez-Alier and Martin O'Connor, 'Economic and Ecological Distribution Conflicts', in R. Costanza, O. Segura, and J. Martinez-Alier, eds., *Getting Down to Earth: Applications of Ecological Economics* (Washington DC: Island Press, 1996).

4 Cf. Hans Magnus Enzensberger, 'A Critique of Political Ecology', *New Left Review*, number 84, 1974.

5 Article in the newspaper *La República*, Lima, 6 April 1991.

6 J. Martinez-Alier, J. and J. M. Naredo, 'La Cuestión de la Energía y la Noción de Fuerzas Productivas', *Cuadernos de Ruedo Ibérico*, Paris, numbers 65–67, 1979; Martinez-Alier and Naredo, 'A Marxist Precursor of Energy Economics: Podolinsky', *Journal of Peasant Studies*, January 1982;

Martinez-Alier and Klaus Schluepmann, *Ecological Economics: Energy, Environment and Society*, (Oxford: Blackwell, 1987, paperback with new introduction, 1990).

7   Vladimir Vernadsky, *La Géochimie* (Paris: Alcan, 1925).

8   Harvey, 'The Nature of Environment and the Dialectics of Social and Environmental Change', in Ralph Miliband and Leo Panitch, eds., *The Socialist Register* (London: Merlin Press, 1993), p. 39, emphasis added.

9   J. P. Deléage, *Une histoire de l'Ecologie* (Paris:La Decouverte, 1991); J. P. Deleage et al., *Les Servitudes de la Puissance* (Paris: Flammarion, 1986).

10   The idea was dismissed in a footnote by Karl Popper in *The Poverty of Historicism*, certainly not because Henry Adams (a Boston aristocrat) was left-wing, which he was not, and not because his law was empirically wrong (Karl Popper did not even mention the word 'energy'), but simply because it was a historical 'law'.

11   This distinction between endosomatic and exosomatic energy use was first proposed, in 1910's, by the biologist Alfred Lotka.

12   It depends, for instance, on women's freedom, as was clearly stated by the ecological feminists of the early 20th century, such as the Brazilian Maria Lacerda de Moura, who wrote the book *Love One Another, and Do Not Multiply*. These were feminists in favour of 'reproductive rights' (to use today's language), against the church and the state, and they thought such reproductive rights should be exercised in an ecological context of increasing pressure of population on resources. The southern European movement for *la grève des ventres* was promoted by anarchist writers such as Sebastian Faure. In Barcelona they published the journal *Salud y Fuerza*, which in some issues carried the subtitle *Revista neomalthusiana*. Other anarchists, such as Kropotkin, were on the contrary strong technological optimists. Cf. articles by Eduard Masjuan in *Ecología Política*, Barcelona, numbers 5 and 6, 1993 and 1994.

13   David Pearce and Giles Atkinson, 'Capital Theory and the Measurement of Sustainable Development: An Indicator of "Weak" Sustainability', *Ecological Economics*, volume 8, 1993, reviewed in Peter A. Victor, 'Indicators of Sustainable Development: Some Lessons from Capital Theory', *Ecological Economics*, volume 4, number 3, 1991; idem, 'How Strong is Weak Sustainability', *Économie Appliquée*, volume 48, number 2, 1995. Also Juan Martinez-Alier, 'The Environment as a Luxury Good or Too Poor to be Green', *Ecological Economics*, volume 13, number 1, 1995.

'Weak sustainability' refers to the maintenance of the sum of manufactured capital and 'natural capital', whereas, 'strong sustainability' refers to the maintenance of critical 'natural capital'. The main critique is that the difficulties in measuring 'natural capital' are not merely technical, but conceptual, and this leads to a general discussion of economic incommensurability as the foundation stone of ecological economics.

14   As discussed in William Rees and Mathias Wackernagel, 'Ecological Footprints and Appropriated Carrying Capacity', in A.M.Jansson et al., eds., *Investing in Natural Capital: the Ecological Economics Approach to Sustainability* (Covelo, CA.:Island Press, 1994); Maria Buitenkamp, Henk Venner and Theo Wamp, eds., *Sustainable Netherlands* (Amsterdam: Dutch Friends of the Earth, 1993).

15   Cf Peter M. Vitousek et al., 'Human Appropriation of the Products of Photosynthesis', *Bioscience*, volume 34, number 6, 1986.

16   John O'Neill, *Ecology, Policy and Politics* (London: Routledge, 1993).

17   Cf. Stephen Thomas, Gordon MacKerron and John Surrey, 'Sustainability and Nuclear Plant Decommissioning', *Paris Symposium on Models of Sustainable Development*, 16–18 March 1994.

18   John O'Neill, op. cit., 1993, chapters 4–7.

19   Otto Neurath (1919), *Empiricism and Sociology* (Dordrecht: Reidel, 1973), p. 263.

20   K. William Kapp, *Social Costs, Economic Development, and Environmental Disruption*, edited and introduced by John E. Ullmann (Lanham, MD:University Press of America, 1983).

21   Cf. Martin O'Connor, 'Value System Contests and the Appropriation of Ecological Capital', *The Manchester School*, number 61, December 1993; Frank Beckenbach, ed., *Die Ökologische Herausforderung an die Ökonomische Theorie* (Marburg: Metropolis, 1991); A. Schnaiberg,et al., eds., *Distributional Conflicts in Environmental Resource Policy* (Aldershot: Edward Elgar, 1986)

22 There is much work by anthropologists and rural sociologists on such lines. To them belongs the credit of introducing the term 'political ecology' for the study of conflicts over access to resources such as land and water. Cf. Eric Wolf, 'Ownership and Political Ecology', *Anthropological Quarterly*, volume 45, number 3, 1972; P. Blaikie and H. Brookfield, eds., *Land Degradation and Society* (London: Methuen, 1987); Susan Stonich, *'I'm Destroying the Land!' The Political Ecology of Poverty and Environmental Destruction in Honduras* (Boulder; CD: Westview, 1993; Michael Painter and William H. Durham, eds.,*The Social Causes of Environmental Destruction in Latin America* (Ann Arbor: University of Michigan Press, 1995). This is not an exhaustive list.

23 Robert D. Bullard, ed., *Confronting Environmental Racism* (Boston, MA: South End Press, 1993), pp 43, 55, etc.

24 It is encouraging to find that the excellent book by Jim Schwab, *Deeper Shades of Green. The Rise of Blue-Collar and Minority Environmentalism in America,* with a foreword by Lois Gibbs, was published by Sierra Club Books, San Francisco, 1994. The Sierra Club, founded by John Muir in 1882, has been devoted to the protection of scenic resources, mountains, wetlands, woodlands, wild shores and rivers, deserts, but not particularly of people.

25 In many poor countries of the world, even those heavily populated and with lack of landfill sites, incineration of waste would be considered an impracticable luxury because of its financial costs.

26 See Martinez-Alier, 'Distributional Conflicts and International Environmental Policy on Carbon Dioxide Emissions and Agricultural Biodiversity', in J.C. van den Bergh and J. van der Straaten, *Toward Sustainable Development: Concepts, Methods, and Policy* (Covelo, CA: Island Press, 1994).

27 Cesar Fonseca and Enrique Mayer, *Comunidad y Producción en el Perú* (Lima: Fomciencias, 1988), p. 187.

28 Bina Agarwal, 'The Gender and Environment Debate: Lessons from India', *Feminist Studies,* volume 18, number 1, 1992.

29 Steven R. Brechin & Willett Kempton, 'Global Environmentalism: a Challenge to the Postmaterialism Thesis?', *Social Science Quarterly*, volume 75, number 2, 1994.

30 An example is Vandana Shiva, *Staying Alive* (London: Zed Books, 1988). For excellent attempts at overcoming the social/essentialist tension in ecofeminism, see B. Holland-Cunz's interview in *Capitalism, Nature, Socialism,* 1991, and Ariel Salleh's chapter in Martin O'Connor, ed., *Is Sustainable Capitalism Possible?* (New York: Guilford, 1994).

31 These Brazilian conflicts have been reported in, among other works, Rosa Acevedo and Edna Castro, *Negros do Trombetas: Guardaes de Matos e Rios* (Belem: UFPA, 1993); D. McGrath, et al., 'Fisheries and the Evolution of Resource Management in the Lower Amazon Floodplain', *Human Ecology,* volume 21, number 2, 1993; Alfredo Wagner Almeida, *Carajas: a Guerra dos Mapas* (Belem: Supercores, 1995); Anthony B. Anderson, Peter H. May and Michael J. Balick, *The Subsidy from Nature: Palm Forests, Peasantry and Development on an Amazon Frontier* (New York: Columbia University Press, 1991); Sonia Barbosa Magalhaes, 'As Grandes Hidroeléctricas e as Populacoes Camponesas', in Maria Angela d'Incao and Isolda Maliel da Silveira, eds., *A Amazonia e a Crisi da Modernizacao* (Belem: Museo Emilio Goeldi, 1994); Claudia Jobb Schmitt, 'A Luta dos Atingidos pelas Barragens do Rio Uruguai', in Isabel Carvalho and Gabriela Scotto, ed., *Conflitos Socio-Ambientas no Brasil, Volume I* (Rio de Janeiro: IBASE, 1995); Mauricio Waldman, *Ecologia e Lutas Sociais no Brasil* (São Paulo: Contexto, 1992).

32 One lawyer involved is Judith Kemerling, the author of the report *Amazon Crude,* Spanish edition *Crudo Amazónico* (Quito: Abya Yala, 1993).

33 'Let Them Eat Pollution', *The Economist*, 8 February 1992. At the time that Lawrence Summers' internal memo was leaked to the press, he was chief economist at the World Bank.

34 See Jussi Raumolin, 'L'Homme et la Destruction des Ressources Naturelles: la Raubwirtschaft au Tournant du Siécle', *Annales E. S. C.*, volume 39, number 4, 1984.

35 Cf M. H. Watkins, 'A Staple Theory of Economic Growth', *Canadian Journal of Economic and Political Science*, volume 29, 1963; C. B. Schedvin, 'Staples and Regions of Pax Brittanica', *Economic History Review,* volume 43, number 4, 1990.

36 Cf Stephen Bunker, 'Staples, Links and Poles in the Construction of Regional Development Theories', *Sociological Forum*, volume 4, number 4, 1989.

37 Elisabeth Dore has published an introduction to the ecological history of mineral extraction in Latin America in *Ecología Política*, number 7, 1994. The human and environmental exploitation of America in the colonial era, with slave or forced labour and without free trade, remains outside the discussion of the staple theory of growth, which is pertinent rather to the era of 'the imperialism of free trade'.

38 In Arthur McEvoy, *The Fisherman's Problem : Ecology and Law in the California Fisheries, 1850–1980* (New York: Cambridge University Press, 1987).

39 In respect to Latin America there is a beginning of this type of ecological history in the excellent though little known volume titled *Desarrollo y Medio Ambiente en América Latina y el Caribe* (Development and Environment in Latin America and the Caribbean), by Fernando Tudela et al., published in 1990 by the Spanish Ministry of Transport and Public Works and by UNEP (Mexico). It follows Alfred Crosby's line (in his *Ecological Imperialism*) for the period of the European conquest and criticises Latin America's desire to export minerals and agricultural produce after achieving independence. It is not a day–by–day account, but a collection of noteworthy episodes with the relevant bibliography spanning the period from before the European invasion and the population crash 500 years ago to the present day. Perhaps the book is lacking in historical research into the social agents of popular social ecology. More is needed than a token discussion of Chico Mendes, because the ecology of survival has been historically significant in Latin America.

40 See Elmar Altvater, *The Future of the Market* (London: Verso, 1993).

41 The habitual perversion of economic language can be seen, for example, when the name 'extractive reserves' is used for still-unprivatised areas of the Amazon, the exploitation of whose products does not imply environmental deterioration. To this 'extractivism' we contrast a 'productive' use that in Amazonia squeezes the land dry, and for that reason should be seen as a destructive rather than a productive use.

42 James O'Connor, 'Introduction', *Capitalism, Nature, Socialism*, number 1, 1988; Enriqué Leff, *Ecología y Capital* (Mexico City: UNAM, 1986).

43 Cf Marilyn Waring, *Counting for Nothing* (Sydney: Unwin, 1989).

44 Anil Agarwal and Sunita Narain, *Global Warming in an Unequal World: A Case of Environmental Colonialism* (New Delhi: Centre for Science and Environment, 1991).

45 FACE, *Annual Report* (Arnhem: FACE, 1995), p18. The Chairman of the Board of FACE is E.H.T.M. Nijpels, a former Minister for the Environment; of the seven members of the Board, four represent government ministers.

46 From a 1995 leaflet distributed by Oilwatch. Contact them at <tegantai@oilwatch.ecx.ec>.

NOTES TO CHAPTER 3

1 The first version of this chapter was written in the autumn of 1988 on a consultancy for the World Bank (Latin American Environment Section). Help from Herman Daly, Shelton Davis, Marc Dourojeanni and Robert Goodland is gratefully acknowledged.

2 K Arrow et al, 'Economic growth, carrying capacity and the environment', *Science*, Volume 268, pp520–521, 1995.

3 The Brundtland Report was published as *Our Common Future* (Oxford: Oxford University Press, 1987).

4 E.g. Ronald Inglehart, *The Silent Revolution* (Princeton, NJ: Princeton University Press, 1977}; idem, 'Public Support for Environmental Protection: Objective Problems and Subjective Values in 43 Societies', *PS: Political Science and Politics*, March 1995.

5 As shown, for instance, by Christian Leipert, *Die heimlichen Kosten des Fortschritts* (Frankfurt: Fischer, 1989).

6 At least since the works of H.J. Barnett and Chandler Morse, *Scarcity and Growth: The Economics of Natural Resource Availability* (Baltimore: Johns Hopkins Press, 1963), and John Krutilla,

'Conservation Reconsidered', *American Economic Review*, volume 57, number 4, 1967.

7   See R. B. Norgaard, 'Economic Indicators of Resource Scarcity: A Critical Essay', *Journal of Environmental Economics and Management*, volume 19, number 1, 1990. Recent contributions to debates on 'de-materialisation' and the energy intensity of the economy include C. J. Cleveland, 'Natural Resource Scarcity and Economic Growth Revisited: Economic and Biophysical Perspectives' in R. Costanza, ed., *Ecological Economics* (New York: Columbia University Press, 1991); S. M. De Bruyn and J.B. Opschoor, *Is the Economy Ecologising?*, Tinbergen Discussion Papers, TI 94-65, Tinbergen Institute Amsterdam, 1994; and Schmidt–Bleek, *Wieviel Umwelt braucht der Mensch: MIPS-Das Mass für Ökologische Wirtschaften* (Birkhäuser: Berlin, 1994).

8   'Public Support for Environmental Protection', op. cit.

9   Manmohan Singh, *Economics and the Environment*, Foundation Day Address, Society for Promotion of Wastelands Development, New Delhi, 1991.

10 Jeffrey A. McNeely, *Economics and Biological Diversity: Developing and Using Economic Incentives to Conserve Biological Resources* (Gland: IUCN, 1988), p. 2.

11 Cf P. Blaikie and H. Brookfield, eds., *Land Degradation and Society* (London: Methuen, 1987).

12 Figures from H. J. Leonard, *Divesting Nature's Capital: The Political Economy of Environmental Abuse in the Third World* (New York: Holmes and Meier, 1985).

13 Rayen Quiroga et al, *El Tigre sin Selva* (Santiago de Chile: Instituto de Ecologia Politica, 1994).

14 Michael Redclift, *Sustainable Development: Exploring the Contradictions* (London: Methuen, 1987), p. 12.

15 *Perfil Ambiental de Guatemala* (Guatemala: Universidad Rafael Landivar—USAID, 1984), p. 217.

16 Eduardo Grillo, 'Peru: Agricultura, Utopia Popular y Proyecto Nacional', *Revista Andina*, volume 3, number 1, 1985; A. Schejtman, 'Analisis Integral del Problema Alimentario y Nutricional en America Latina', *Estudios Rurales Latinoamericanos*, volume 6, numbers 2 & 3, 1983; idem, 'Campesinado y Seguridad Alimentaria', *Estudios Rurales Latinoamericanos*, volume 10, number 3, 1987.

17 Cf Marc Dourojeanni, *Gran Geografía del Perú. IV. Recursos Naturales, Desarrollo y Conservación en el Perú*, (Barcelona–Lima: Manfer–Mejia Baca, 1986), p. 115.

18 Paul Harrison, *Land, Food and People* (Rome: Food and Agricultural Organization, 1984).

19 J. W. Kirschner, G. Ledec, R. Goodland and J.M. Drake, 'Carrying Capacity, Population Growth, and Sustainable Development', in *Rapid Population Growth and Human Carrying Capacity: Two Perspectives*, World Bank Staff Working Papers number 690, 1985, p. 45.

20 F. Tudela, 'El Encuentro Entre dos Mundos: el Impacto Ambental de la Conquista' (The Meeting of Two Worlds: The Environmental Impact of the Conquest of America), *Ecología Política*, number 2, 1991.

21 Philip M. Fearnside, 'A Stochastic Model for Estimating Human Carrying Capacity in Brazil's Transamazon Highway Colonization Area', *Human Ecology*, volume 13, number 3, 1985.

22 Ester Boserup, *The Conditions of Agricultural Growth* (Chicago: Chicago University Press, 1965).

23 D. Pimentel et. al., 'Food Production and the Energy Crisis', *Science*, volume 182, 1973; David and Marcia Pimentel, *Food, Energy and Society* (London: Edward Arnold, 1979); Gerald Leach, *Energy and Food Production* (Guildford, Surrey: IPC Science and Technology Press, 1975).

24 As defined by Clifford Geertz, *Agricultural Involution* (Berkeley: University of California Press, 1963).

25 D. and S. Pimentel, 'Energy and Other Natural Resources Used by Agriculture and Society', in Kenneth Dahlberg, ed., *New Directions for Agriculture and Agricultural Research* (Totowa, N J: Rowman & Allanheld, 1986), p. 278.

26 Cf L. Pfaundler, 'Die Weltwirtschaft im Lichte der Physic', in two parts, *Deutsche Revue*, April and June 1902.

27 Harrison, op. cit. (1984).

28 Georgescu-Roegen's ideas are the subject of Chapter 9.

29 This paragraph draws on Stephen Brush, 'Diversity and Change in Andean Agriculture', in P. Little and M. Horowitz. eds., *Lands at Risk in the Third World* (Boulder, Co: Westview Press, 1987); Ricardo Godoy, 'Ecological Degradation and Agricultural Intensification in the Andean Highlands', *Human Ecology*, volume 12, number 4, 1984; and Benjamin Orlove and Ricardo Godoy, 'Sectoral Fallowing Systems in the Central Andes', *Journal of Ethnobiology*, volume 6, 1986.

30 As predicted in J. Martinez- Alier, *Haciendas, Plantations and Collective Farms* (London: Frank Cass, 1977).

31 Luis Masson, 'La Ocupación de Andenes en el Perú', *Pensamiento Iberoamericano: Revists de Economia Politica*, volume 12, 1988; Jane Collins, 'Land Scarcity and Ecological Change', in Little and Horowitz, eds., *Lands at Risk*; Carlos de la Torre and Manuel Burga, eds., *Andenes y Camellones en el Peru Antiguo* (Boulder, Co: Westview Press, 1987) (Lima: Concytec, 1986).

32 Cases of export pressure on forests, and sometimes of local resistance, are reported in Nancy Peluso, *Rich Forests, Poor People* (Berkeley: University of California Press, 1992) for Java; Robin Broad and John Cavanagh, *Plundering Paradise* (Berkeley: University of California Press, 1993) for the Philippines; and Thomas Rudel, *Tropical Deforestation* (New York: Columbia University Press, 1993), for Ecuador.

33 Marc Dourojeanni, *Recursos Naturales y Desarrollo en América Latina* (Lima:Universidad de Lima,1982).

34 Cf Godoy, 'Ecological degradation', op cit. (1984).

35 Gerald Foley, 'Wood Fuel and Conventional Fuel in the Developing World', *Ambio*, volume 14, numbers 4&5, 1985; *Perfil Ambiental de Guatemala*, volume II, pp. 99, 171f., Leonard, *Divesting Nature's Capital*,(New York: Holmes and Meier, 1985), p. 62.

36 Foley, op, cit (1985).

37 From Olman Segura, and James K. Boyce, 'Investment in Natural and Human Capital in Developing Countries', paper presented at the Second Conference of the International Society for Ecological Economics in Stockholm, August 1992, pp. 7–8, quoting Solon Barraclough and Krishna Ghimere, *The Social Dynamics of Deforestation in Developing Countries* (Geneva: UNRISD, 1991).

38 As explained in the *Hoja Informativa* (Information Bulletin) of the Coordinating Committee for Andean Technology, number 71, October 1991 (Lima).

39 See Sandra J. Cointreau, *Environmental Management of Urban Solid Wastes in Developing Countries* (Washington, DC: World Bank, 1986).

40 J. S. Tulchin, ed., *Habitat, Health and Development* (Boulder, Co: Lynne Rienner, 1985).

41 Anil Agarwal and Sunita Narain, eds., *The State of India's Environment 1984–85: the Second Citizens' Report* (New Delhi: Centre for Science and Environment, 1985), p. 289.

42 Cf. Charles Perrings, 'Debt and Resource Degradation in Low-Income Countries: the Adjustment Process and the Perverse Effects of Poverty in Sub-Saharan Africa', in H. Singer and S. Sharma eds., *Economic Development and the World Debt* (London: Macmillan,1988).

43 Elmar Alvater, *Sachzwang Weltmarkt. Verschuldungskrise, blockierte Industrialisierung, ökologische Gefährdung – der Fall Brasilien*, (Hamburg: VSA, 1987).

44 Cf Andrew Hurrell and Benedict Kingsbury, eds., *The International Politics of the Environment* (Oxford: Clarendon Press, 1992).

45 K. William Kapp, *Social Costs, Economic Development, and Environmental Disruption*, edited and introduced by John E. Ullmann (Lanham, MD: University Press of America, 1983), p. 47.

46 Richard Feachem, et al., *Appropriate Technology for Water Supply and Sanitation. Health Aspects of Excreta and Sullage Management A State of the Art Review* (Washington DC: World Bank, 1981).T. Harpham, T. Lusty and P. Vaughan, eds., *In the Shadow of the City: Community Health and the Urban Poor* (Oxford: Oxford University Press, 1988).

47 Vinod Thomas, *Pollution Controls in Sao Paulo, Brazil: Costs, Benefits, and Effects on Industrial Location*, World Bank Staff Working Paper number 501, Washington DC, 1981.

48 Charles Hall, Cutler Cleveland, and Robert Kaufman, *Energy and Resources Quality: the Ecology of the Economic Process* (New York: Wiley, 1986).

49 Jose Goldenberg, Thomas Johansson, Amulya K. N. Reddy and Robert Williams, *Energy for a Sustainable World* (New York: Wiley, 1988).

50 Harvard University Press, 1976.

51 F. Hirsch, *The Social Limits to Growth* (Cambridge, Mass: Harvard University Press, 1976), p. 20.

52 See Juan Martinez-Alier, 'The Environment as a Luxury Good or Too Poor to be Green', *Ecological Economics*, volume 13, number 1, 1995.

53 Cf F. Aguilera Klink,'Some Notes on the Misuse of Classic Writings in Economics on the Subject of Common Property', *Ecological Economics*, volume 9, number 3, 1994.

54 Cambridge University Press, 1992.

55 This is explored in the research of Manuel González de Molina and his collaborators at the University of Granada, which is due to be published.

56 Ramachandra Guha and Madhav Gadgil, 'State Forestry and Social Conflict in British India', *Past and Present*, number 123, May 1989; Guha, *The Unquiet Woods: Ecological Change and Peasant Resistance in the Himalaya* (New Delhi: Oxford University Press, 1989).

57 John Kurien, 'Ruining the Commons and the Commoners: Overfishing and Fishworkers' Actions in Kerala, South India', in Dharam Ghai and Jessica Vivian, eds., *Grassroots Environmental Action* (London: Routledge, 1992).

NOTES TO CHAPTER 4

1 Lynn White, 'The Historical Roots of our Ecologic Crisis', *Science*, volume 155, number 3767, 1967, reprinted in Robin Clarke, *Notes for the Future* (London: Thames and Hudson, 1975); also John Passmore, *Man's Responsibility for Nature,* 2nd edn. (London: Duckworth, 1980).

2 Robert Underwood Johnson, 'John Muir' (commemorative tribute, dated 6 January 1916), in *Academy Notes and Monographs* (New York: The American Academy of Arts and Letters, 1922), pp. 21–22.

3 Frederick Turner, 'So Necessarily Elite', in *Parks in the West and American Culture* (Sun Valley, ID: Institute of the American West, 1984).

4 Donald Worster, *Nature's Economy: The Roots of Ecology* (San Francisco, CA: Sierra Club Books, 1977); Roderick Nash, *Wilderness and the American Mind* (3rd edn.; New Haven, CT: Yale University Press, 1982); Stephen Fox, *The American Conservation Movement: John Muir and His Legacy* (Madison: University of Wisconsin Press, 1985); Bill Devall and George Sessions, *Deep Ecology: Living as if Nature Mattered* (Salt Lake City, UT: Peregrine Books, 1985).

5 A revised and expanded version of the Ninth Steven Manley Memorial Lecture, delivered at the University of California, Santa Barbara, on 16 May 1989.

6 Williams, 'Ideas of Nature' (1972), reprinted in his *Problems in Materialism and Culture* (London: Verson, 1984), pp. 70, 84. Another gentle but timely reminder not to divorce environmental from social concerns comes from a long-time observer of the environmental movement. 'Our interest in natural resources', writes the sociologist W. R. Burch, Jr., 'must be as much a concern about human value and social justice as about aesthetic visions of vernal woods and the sustained yield of water resources'. Burch, 'In Praise of Humility: The Human Nature of Nature', *Appalachia*, summer 1984, p. 66.

7 Cf. Leo Marx, 'American Literary Culture and the Fatalistic View of Technology', in his *The Pilot and the Passenger: Essays on Literature, Technology and Culture in the United States* (New York: Oxford University Press, 1988).

8 Barrington Moore, Jr., *Social Origins of Dictatorship and Democracy: Lord and Peasant in the Making of the Modern World* (Harmondsworth: Penguin, 1966), p. 505.

9 Williams, *The Country and the City* (New York: Oxford University Press, 1973).

10 Tagore, 'City and Village' (1928), reprinted in *Rabindranath Tagore on Rural Reconstruction* (New

Delhi: Ministry of Community Development and Co-operation, 1962), pp 22–38.

11 Marshall, 'The Problem of the Wilderness' (1930), reprinted in *Sierra Club Bulletin*, volume 32, number 5, 1947, p. 44.

12 The views of deep ecologists are more fully treated in the next chapter.

13 Quoted in George Feaver, 'Vine Deloria', *Encounter* (London), April 1975, p. 39.

14 Shepard, *Nature and Madness* (San Francisco, CA: Sierra Club Books, 1982), pp. 3–7, 28–39.

15 John Wesley Powell, 'From Barbarism to Civilization', *American Anthropologist*, volume 1, number 2, 1888, pp 121, 123.

16 Fernow, 'The Battle of the Forest', *The National Geographic Magazine*, June 1894.

17 George C. M. Birdwood, *Sva* (London: Philip Lee Warner, 1915), pp 157–58.

18 William Adams, 'Natural Virtue: Symbol and Imagination in the Farm Crisis', *Georgia Review*, volume 39, number 4, 1985.

19 J.C. Ransom, 'Land! An Answer to the Unemployment Problem', *Harper's Magazine*, July 1932, p. 218. Cf also Virginia Rock, *The Making and Meaning of 'I'll Take my Stand': A Study in Utopian Conservatism*, unpublished Ph D thesis, University of Minnesota, 1961.

20 W. Berry, *The Unsettling of America* (San Francisco, CA: Sierra Club Books, 1977).

21 Further south, in countries such as Mexico and Peru, an 'agrarian environmentalism' has had more potential, as suggested in Chapter 6 below. This might plausibly be related to the wholesale extermination of pre-conquest agriculture in the United States compared to the more integrative mix of indigenous and modern farming systems characteristic of most parts of Latin America.

22 Raymond Dasmann, 'The Country In Between', in the *Sierra Club Wilderness Calendar*, 1982.

23 Muir used the term often and in numerous writings, one example is his 'Address on the Sierra Forest Reservation', *Sierra Club Bulletin*, volume 1, number 7, 1896.

24 Linda Graber, *Wilderness as Sacred Space* (Washington, DC: Association of American Geographers, 1976), pp. 21–2.

25 Donald Mitchell, quoted in Peter J. Schmitt, *Back to Nature: the Arcadian Myth in Urban America* (New York: Oxford University Press, 1969), pp. 6–7.

26 quoted in Daniel B. Weber, *John Muir: the Function of Wilderness in an Industrial Society*, unpublished Ph D thesis, University of Minnesota, pp 159–60.

27 Lee Merriam Talbot, 'Wilderness Overseas', *Sierra Club Bulletin*, volume 42, number 6, 1957.

28 Hugh Iltis, 'Whose Fight is the Fight for Nature?', *Sierra Club Bulletin*, volume 52, number 9, 1967.

29 Centre for Science and Environment, *India: The State of the Environment 1982: A Citizens' Report* (New Delhi: CSE, 1982), chapter 9; R. Sukumar, *The Asian Elephant: Ecology and Management* (Cambridge: Cambridge University Press, 1989). The next chapter returns to this theme of human–wildlife conflicts.

30 The universal (or 'universalist') claims of scientific conservation are dealt with in my essay 'The Two Phases of American Environmentalism: A Critical History', in F. Appfel-Marglin and S. Marglin, eds., *Decolonizing Knowledge: From Development to Dialogue* (Oxford: Clarendon Press, 1996).

31 According to one historian, 'In spite of its complexity, in spite of its ambiguity, the [scientific] conservationist policy contained an inner vitality that could not be obscured and destroyed. Here was an effort to implement democracy for twentieth-century America, to stop the stealing and exploitation, to inspire high standards of government, to preserve the beauty of mountain and stream, to distribute more equally the profits of the economy.' J. Leonard Bates, 'Fulfilling American Democracy: The Conservation Movement, 1907 to 1921', *The Mississippi Valley Historical Review*, volume 44, number 1, 1957, pp. 36–7.

NOTES TO CHAPTER 5

1   Kirkpatrick Sale, 'The Forest for the Trees: Can Today's Environmentalists Tell the Difference', *Mother Jones*, volume 11, number 8, November 1986, p. 26.

2   One of the major criticisms I make in this chapter concerns deep ecology's lack of concern with inequalities within human society. In the article in which he coined the term deep ecology, Naess himself expresses concerns about inequalities between and within nations. However, his concern with social cleavages and their impact on resource utilisation patterns and ecological destruction is not very visible in the later writings of deep ecologists. See Arne Naess, 'The Shadow and the Deep, Long-Range Ecology Movement: A Summary', *Inquiry*, volume 6, 1973, p. 96 (I am grateful to Tom Birch for this reference).

3   Gary Snyder, quoted in Sale, 'The Forest for the Trees', op.cit., p.32. See also Dave Foreman, 'A Modest Proposal for a Wilderness System', *Whole Earth Review*, number 53 (Winter 1986–87), pp. 42–45.

4   See, for example, Donald Worster, *Nature's Economy: The Roots of Ecology* (San Francisco; CA: Sierra Club Books, 1977).

5   See Centre for Science and Environment, *India: The State of the Environment 1982: A Citizen's Report* (New Delhi: Centre for Science and Environment, 1982); R. Sukumar, 'Elephant–Man Conflict in Karnataka', in Cecil Saldanha, ed., *The State of Karnataka's Environment* (Bangalore: Centre for Taxonomic Studies, 1985). For Africa, see the brilliant analysis by Helge Kjekshus, *Ecology Control and Economic Development in East Afrikan History* (Berkeley: University of California Press, 1977).

6   Daniel Janzen, 'The Future of Tropical Ecology', *Annual Review of Ecology and Systematics*, volume 17, 1986, pp 305–6.

7   Robert Aitkien Roshi, 'Gandhi, Dogen, and Deep Ecology', reprinted as Appendix C in Bill Devall and George Sessions, *Deep Ecology: Living as if Nature Mattered* (Salt Lake City; UT: Peregrine Smith Books, 1985). For Gandhi's own views on social reconstruction, see the three volume collection edited by Raghavan Iyer, *The Moral and Political Writings of Mahatma Gandhi* (Oxford: Clarendon Press, 1986–87).

8   Michael Cohen, *The Pathless Way* (Madison: University of Wisconsin Press, 1984), p. 120.

9   Ronald Inden, 'Orientalist Constructions of India', *Modern Asian Studies*, volume 20, 1986, p. 442. Inden draws inspiration from Edward Said's forceful polemic, *Orientalism* (New York: Basic Books, 1980). It must be noted, however, that there is a salient difference between Western perceptions of Middle Eastern and Far Eastern cultures respectively. Due perhaps to the long history of Christian conflict with Islam, Middle Eastern cultures (as Said documents) are consistently presented in pejorative terms. The juxtaposition of hostile and worshipping attitudes that Inden talks of applies only to Western attitudes toward Buddhist and Hindu societies.

10   Joseph Sax, *Mountains Without Handrails: Reflections on the National Parks* (Ann Arbor: University of Michigan Press, 1980), p. 42. Cf. also Peter Schmitt, *Back to Nature: The Arcadian Myth in Urban America* (New York: Oxford University Press, 1969), and Alfred Runte, *National Parks: The American Experience* (Lincoln: University of Nebraska Press, 1979).

11   Samuel Hays, 'From Conservation to Environment: Environmental Politics in the United States since World War Two', *Environmental Review*, volume 6, 1982, p. 21. See also the same author's book *Beauty, Health and Permanence: Environmental Politics in the United States, 1955–85* (New York: Cambridge University Press, 1987).

12   Roderick Nash, *Wilderness and the American Mind*, 3rd edn. (New Haven, CT: Yale University Press, 1982).

13   Rudolf Bahro, *From Red to Green* (London: Verso Books, 1984).

14   From time to time, American scholars have themselves criticised these imbalances in consumption patterns. In the 1950s, William Vogt made the charge that the United States, with one-sixteenth of the world's population, was utilizing one-third of the globe's resources. (Vogt, cited

in E.F. Murphy, *Nature, Bureaucracy and the Rule of Property* [Amsterdam: North Holland, 1977, p. 29]). More recently, Zero Population Growth has estimated that each American consumes thirty-nine times as many resources as an Indian. See *Christian Science Monitor*, 2 March 1987.

15 For an excellent review, see Anil Agarwal and Sunita Narain, eds., *India: The State of the Environment 1984–85: A Citizen's Report* (New Delhi: Centre for Science and Environment, 1985). Also Chapter I above.

16 Anil Agarwal, 'Human–Nature Interactions in a Third World Country'. *The Environmentalist*, volume 6, number 3, 1986, p. 167.

17 One strand in radical American environmentalism, the bioregional movement, by emphasising a greater involvement with the bioregion people inhabit, does indirectly challenge consumerism. However, as yet bioregionalism has hardly raised the questions of equity and social justice (international, intranational, and intergenerational) which I argue must be a central plank of radical environmentalism. Moreover, its stress on (individual) experience as the key to involvement with nature is also somewhat at odds with the integration of nature with livelihood and work that I discuss in this chapter. Cf. Kirkpatrick Sale, *Dwellers in the Land: The Bioregional Vision* (San Francisco: Sierra Club Books, 1985).

18 John Kenneth Galbraith, 'How Much Should a Country Consume?' in Henry Jarett, ed., *Perspectives on Conservation* (Baltimore, MD: Johns Hopkins Press, 1958), pp. 91–92.

19 Devall and Sessions, *Deep Ecology*, (op. cit, note 7) p. 122. For Wendell Berry's own assessment of deep ecology, see his 'Preserving Wildness', *Wilderness*, Spring 1987, pp 39–40, 50–54.

20 See the interesting contribution by one of the most influential spokesmen of appropriate technology, Barry Commoner, 'A Reporter at Large: The Environment', *New Yorker*, 15 June 1987. While Commoner makes a forceful plea for the convergence of the environmental movement (viewed by him primarily as the opposition to air and water pollution and to the institutions that generate such pollution) and the peace movement, he significantly does not mention consumption patterns, implying that 'limits to growth' do not exist.

21 In this sense, my critique of deep ecology, although that of an outsider, may facilitate the reassertion of those elements in the American environmental tradition for which there is a profound sympathy in other parts of the globe. A global perspective may also lead to a critical reassessment of figures such as Aldo Leopold and John Muir, the two patron saints of deep ecology. As Donald Worster has pointed out, the message of Muir (and, I would argue, of Leopold as well) makes sense only in an American context; he has very little to say to other cultures. See Worster's review of Stephen Fox's *John Muir and His Legacy*, in *Environmental Ethics* , volume 5, 1983, pp. 277–81.

22 I speak here of private communications: published responses to my essay include David M. Johns, 'The Relevance of Deep Ecology to the Third World: Some Preliminary Comments', *Environmental Ethics*, volume 12, number 2, 1990; J. Baird Callicott, 'The Wilderness Idea Revisited: the Sustainable Development Alternative', *The Environmental Professional*, volume 13, number 2, 1991.

23 These anthologies include Thomas A, Mappes and Jane S. Zembaty, eds., *Social Ethics: Morality and Public Policy* (4th edn. (New York: McGraw-Hill, 1992); Carolyn Merchant, ed., *Key Concepts in Critical Theory: Ecology* (New Jersey: Humanities Press, 1994); Louis P. Pojman, ed., *Environmental Ethics: Readings in Theory and Application* (Boston: Jones and Bartlett, 1994); Lori Gruen and Dale Jamieson, eds., *Reflecting on Nature: Readings in Environmental Philosophy* (New York: Oxford University Press, 1994); Larry May and Shari Collins Sharriat, eds., *Applied Ethics: A Multicultural Approach* (Englewood Cliffs, NJ: Prentice-Hall, 1994); Andrew Brennan, ed., *The Ethics of the Environment* (Brookfield, VT: Dartmouth Publishers, 1995).

24 Michael Soulé, *The Tigress and the Little Girl* (manuscript of forthcoming book), Chapter 6, 'International Conservation Politics and Programs'.

25 Daniel H. Janzen, *Guanacaste National Park: Tropical Ecological and Cultural Restoration* (San José: Editorial Universidad Estatal a Distancia, 1986). Also David Rains Wallace, 'Communing in Costa Rica', *Wilderness*, number 181, summer 1988, which quotes Janzen as wishing to plan 'protected areas in a way that will permanently accomodate solitude seeking humans as well as jaguars, tapirs, and sea turtles ..'. These solitude-seeking humans might include biologists, backpackers, deep ecologists, but not, one supposes, indigenous farmers, hunters or fishermen. Daniel Janzen has since been one of the architects of the controversial INBio–Merck deal, which is discussed in the next chapter.

26   Raymond Bonner, *At the Hand of Man: Peril and Hope for Africa's Wildlife* (New York: Alfred A. Knopf, 1993), pp. 35, 65, 70, 85, 221.

27 Arne Kalland, 'Seals, Whales and Elephants: Totem Animals and the Anti-Use Campaigns', in *Proceeedings of the Conference on Responsible Wildlife Management* (Brussels: European Bureau for Conservation and Development, 1994). Also Arne Kalland, 'Management by Totemization: Whale Symbolism and the Anti-Whaling Campaign', *Arctic*, volume 46, number 2, 1993.

28   *The Deccan Herald*, Bangalore, 5 November 1995.

29 A useful countrywide overview is provided in Ashish Kothari, Saloni Suri and Neena Singh, 'Conservation in India: A New Direction', *Economic and Political Weekly*, 28 October 1995.

30 Arne Naess, 'Comments on the Article "Radical American Environmentalism and Wilderness Preservation: A Third World Critique' by Ramachandra Guha", typescript (1989), p. 23.

31 Recent writings by Indian scholars strongly dispute that conservation can succeed through the punitive guns-and-guards approach favoured by most wildlife conservationists, domestic or foreign. For thoughtful suggestions as to how the interests of wild species and the interests of poor humans might be made more compatible, see Kothari et. al. op. cit.; M. Gadgil and P. R. S. Rao, 'A System of Positive Incentives to Conserve Biodiversity', *Economic and Political Weekly*, 6 August 1994; R. Sukumar, 'Wildlife–Human Conflict in India: An Ecological and Social Perspective', in R. Guha, ed., *Social Ecology* (New Delhi: Oxford University Press, 1994).

32 Arne Naess, *Ecology, Community and Lifestyle*, translated by David Rothenberg (Cambridge: Cambridge University Press, 1990), p. 45.

NOTES TO CHAPTER 6

1   I am grateful to Cristina Marco and Trevor Foskett for comments.

2   Viki Reyes, 'The Value of Sangre de Drago', *Seedling* (the quarterly newsletter of GRAIN), volume 13, number 1, March 1996, p.20.

3   This is the case even in Europe, where besides a programme for animal breeds, there are now also proposals for *in situ* conservation of plant genetic resources.

4   On recent developments, cf. Commission on Plant Genetic Resources, First Extraordinary Session, Rome 7–11 November 1994, Revision of the International Undertaking on Farmers' Rights (CPGR. Ex1/94/5 Supp. September 1994).

5   Carson, *Silent Spring* (Boston, MA: Houghton Mifflin, 1962).

6   Pimentel, et al., 'Food Production and the Energy Crisis', *Science*, volume 182, 1973; G. Leach, *Energy and Food Production* (Guildford, Surrey: IPC Science and Technology Press, 1975); J. M. Naredo and Pablo Campos, 'La Energía en los Sistemas Agrarios' and 'Los Balances Energéticos de la Agricultura Española", *Agricultura y Sociedad* (Madrid), volume 15, 1980.

7   Two chapters in Martinez-Alier (with Klaus Schlupmann) *Ecological Economics* (Oxford: Blackwell, 1990) discuss the history of human ecological energetics and the study of the flow of energy in agriculture.

8   J. G. Hawkes, *The Diversity of Crop Plants* (Cambridge, MA: Harvard University Press, 1983); R. S. Paroda and A. K. Arora, *Plant Genetic Resources: Conservation and Management* (New Delhi: Lahotra Publications, 1991)

9   Vellvé, *Saving the Seed: Genetic Diversity and European Agriculture* (London: Earthscan, 1992).

10 FAO, *La Diversidad de la Naturaleza: un Patrimonio Valioso* (Rome: Food and Agricultural Organization, 1993).

11 D. Cooper, R. Vellvé and Henk Hobbelink, eds., *Growing Diversity: Genetic Resources and Local Food Security* (London: Intermediate Technology Publications, 1992); Daniel Querol, *Recursos Genéticos, Nuestro Tesoro Olvidado* (Lima: Industrial Gráfica, 1987); trans., *Genetic Resources: Our Forgotten Treasure* (Penang: Third World Network, 1992).

12 French acronym for the Union for the Protection of New Plant Varieties.

13 A well-known Andean example: in 1638, the Countess of Chinchon, the Viceroy's wife, became ill in Lima with malaria and recovered by taking a medicine made from the quinine tree by indigenous servants whose names are not recorded – the quinine tree is called *Chinchona officinalis*. For further stories on quinine, cf. Lucile Brockway, 'Plant Science and Colonial Expansion: The Botanical Chess Game', in Jack Kloppenburg, ed., *Seeds and Sovereignty: the Use and Control of Plant Genetic Resources* (Durham, NC: Duke University Press, 1988).

14 CLADES is the Latin American consortium for agroecology, based in Santiago de Chile, led by activist–agronomists such as Miguel Altieri and Camila Montecinos. GRAIN, Genetic Resources Action International, is based in Barcelona. There are many other such groups in the world, e.g. in India, the group around Anil Gupta in Ahmedabad, who publishes the newsletter *Honey-Bee*.

15 Cf. Vandana Shiva, 'Farmers' Rights, Biodiversity, and International Treaties', *Economic and Political Weekly*, 3 April 1993; also the item 'Karnataka farmers target Cargill again' in *Down to Earth*, 31 August, 1993. On the *neem* tree, there is an informative article by Miguel Abreu, 'Obtención de una Insecticida Natural para Consumo Propio y Como Fuente de Ingresos para Pequeños Agricultores' (Production by small farmers of a natural insecticide for their own use and for sale), in Olman Segura, ed., *Desarrollo Sostenible y Politicas Economicas en America Latina* (San José, Costa Rica: DEI, 1992), on its use in Santo Domingo as a result of German technical co-operation.

16 Cf. M.D. Nanjundaswamy, 'Farmers and Dunkel Draft', letter to the editor in *Economic and Political Weekly*, 26 June, 1993; Suman Sahai, 'Dunkel Draft is bad for agriculture', in *Economic and Political Weekly*, 19 June 1993. For Latin America, refer to Camila Montecinos (of CLADES), 'Las Negociaciones Internacionales sobre Recursos Geneticos', *Ecología Política*, number 5, 1993; M. Tapia, 'Gestion de la Biodiversidad Andina', in B. Marticorena ed., *Recursos Naturales. Tecnologia y Desarrollo* (Cusco: Centro 'Bartolome de Las Casas', 1993); and to several contributions on Mexico in Enrique Leff and Josefina Carabias, eds., *Cultura y Manejo Sustentable de los Recursos Naturales* (Mexico City: M. A. Porrua and UNAM, 1993).

17 Cf., among other works, Paul Richards, *Indigenous Agricultural Revolution* (London: Hutchinson, 1985); Madhav Gadgil and Ramachandra Guha, *This Fissured Land: An Ecological History of India* (Berkeley: University of California Press, 1992); Victor Toledo,'The Ecological Rationality of Peasant Production', in M. Altieri and S. Hecht, eds., *Agroecology and Small Farm Development* (Boca Ratón, FL: CRC Press, 1989); Darryl Posey, 'Indigenous Management of Tropical Forest Ecosystems: the Case of the Kayapo Indians of the Brazillian Amazon', *Agroforestry Systems*, volume 3, number 2, 1985; Ph. Descola, *La Selva Culta: Simbolismo y Praxis en la Ecologia de los Achuar* (Quito: Abya Yala, 1988); Diane Rocheleau, 'Gender, Ecology and the Science of Survival: Stories and Lessons from Kenya', *Agriculture and Human Values*, winter–spring 1991/2.

18 Henk Hobbelink, *Biotechnology and the Future of World Agriculture* (London: Zed, 1991).

19 Jeffrey A. McNeely, Kenton R. Miller, Walter V. Reid, Russell A. Mittermeir and Timothy B. Werner, *Conserving the World's Biological Diversity* (Gland, Switzerland: IUCN and others, 1990).

20 Herman Daly's classification system includes Natural Capital, Human-made Capital, and, as a special case, Cultivated Natural Capital. See Daly, 'Operationalizing Sustainable Development by Investing in Natural Capital', in Ann Mari Jansson et al., *Investing in Natural Capital: The Ecological Economics Approach to Sustainability* (Covelo, CA: Island Press, 1994). Daly asks whether these categories of capital substitute for each other or are complementary. For two reasons ecological economics has insisted on calling natural resources by the name 'natural capital'. First, this change in name suggests the problematic nature of the substitution of capital for natural resources, contrary to orthodox functions of production. Furthermore, this new name reveals the absence of depreciation or amortisation of natural resources – this becomes obvious when they are called natural capital (or cultivated natural capital).

21 For instance, Dr. Patarroyo of Colombia has given to the World Health Organization, without royalties, the rights over the malaria vaccine he has seemingly obtained. He will be awarded many honours and prizes for his successful work, which he has refused to patent for his own benefit.

22 Walter V. Reid et al., *Biodiversity Prospecting: Using Genetic Resources for Sustainable Development* (Washington DC: World Resources Institute, 1993); Ernst A. Brugger and Eduardo Lizano, eds., *Eco-*

eficiencia. La Visión Empresarial para el Desarrollo Sostenible en América Latina (Eco-efficiency, the business perspective for sustainable development in Latin America) (Bogotá: Oveja Negra, Business Council for Sustainable Development, 1992).

23 *World Resources 1992–93* (Washington DC: WRI, 1992), p. 10.

24 'Regresemos al Agro' (Let's Go back to Farming), *Cuadernos Verdes* del Colegio Verde de Villa de Leyva, number 5, 1992.

25 Personal communication from Daniel Querol.

26 Zvi Grilliches, 'Research Cost and Social Returns: Hybrid Corn and Related Innovations', *Journal of Political Economy*, volume 66, number 3, 1958.

27 Where 'populist' is used in the eastern European pro-peasant sense. Cf. J. Aricó, *Mariátegui y los Orígenes del Marxismo Latinoamericano*, Siglo XXI (Mexico City: Cuadernos de Pasado y Presente, 1980).

28 An exception of sorts would be Gandhi and his associates in colonial India (cf. Chapter 8), who promoted organic manure and careful management of natural resources – water, forests – in the rural economy without, of course, yet considering the inherent genetic diversity of peasant agriculture.

29 Cf Juan D. Quintero, 'Modernización de la Agriculture y Riesgos de Deterioro Ecológico en América Latina y el Caribe' (The Modernization of Agriculture and the Risk of Ecological Deterioration in Latin America and the Caribbean), in Olman Segura, ed., op. cit.

30 Cf. Santiago Levy and Sweder van Wijnbergen, 'El Maíz y el Acuerdo de Libre Comercio entre México y los Estados Unidos' (Maize and the free trade agreement between Mexico and the US), *El Trimestre Económico*, number 131, 1991.

31 For example, *New York Times*, 15 August 1992, p. 34.

32 Ricardo, the theorist of comparative advantage, actually did not use money but labour value as a common measure. Our argument is based on the existence of *different* scales of value.

33 Cf Daniel Yergin, 'Energy Security in the 1990s', *Foreign Affairs*, volume 67, number 1, 1988. It was the left-wing British newspaper *The Guardian* which pointed out that the Gulf War was undertaken to 'protect the American way of driving'.

NOTES TO CHAPTER 7

1 Letter from Le Corbusier to Moïse Ginzburg in *Sovremennaia Arhitektura*, numbers 1 and 2, 1930, in P. Cellarelli, *La costruzione de la citta sovietica* (Barcelona: Gustavo Gili, 1972).

2 New Delhi is quite unlike Chandigarh. New Delhi was planned by Edwin Lutyens in the colonial period and has wide avenues and beautiful parks housing ruins dating from before the Mughal empire. New Delhi is a planning success with gardens and monuments, but this is because it is the capital of the Indian state and thus the centre of official life and the big hotels. New Delhi can absorb sufficient resources to care for its parks and to fill its avenues with traffic; meanwhile many poor cyclists get run over and killed. The inhabitants of Delhi live in the old town or in much poorer suburbs, more and more of which are on the other side of the River Jamuna, where cholera strikes every other year.

3 R. R. White, 'Convergent trends in architecture and urban environmental planning', *Environment and Planning (Society and Space)*, volume 11, 1993.

4 Based on the chapter on Patrick Geddes (the Scottish town-and-country-planner who invented the derogatory word 'conurbation'), in J. Martinez-Alier, *Ecological Economics* (Oxford: Blackwell, 1987, 1990). The present version was intended for the Global Forum on Cities, Manchester, June–July 1994. My gratitude to Eduard Masjuan for information.

5 Cf. Walter L. Creese, *The Search for Environment: The Garden City Before and After*, rev. edn. (Baltimore, MD: Johns Hopkins University Press, 1992).

6   Peter Hall, *Urban and Regional Planning* 2nd edn. (London: Allen and Unwin,), pp. 80–81.

7   See Ramachandra Guha's essay on Mumford, Chapter 10.

8   I.e. the faster growth of population in the municipalities *outside* the area of the metropolitan labour market – A. G. Champion, ed., *Contraurbanization: the Changing Pace and Nature of Population Deconcentration* (London: Edward Arnold, 1989), pp. 21–23.

9   William Rees and Mathis Wackernagel, 'Ecological Footprints and Appropriated Carrying Capacity', in A.M.Jansson et al., eds., *Investing in Natural Capital: the Ecological Economics Approach to Sustainability* (Covelo, Ca.: Island Press, 1994).

10   J. M.Naredo, *Los flujos de energia y materiales en la Comunidad de Madrid*: M. Pares, G. Pou and J. Terradas, *Ecología d'una Ciutat* (Barcelona: Barcelona Council, 1985); Salvador Rueda, *Ecologia Urbana: Barcelona* (Barcelona: Beta, 1996).

11   Pares, Pou and Terradas, *Ecología d'una Ciutat*, (1985) p. 118.

12   Notably Peter Brimblecombe's study of London, *The Big Smoke* (London: Methuen, 1987); also the essays in Brimblecomble and C. Pfister, eds., *The Silent Countdown: Essays in European Environmental History* (Berlin: Springer, 1990).

13   Cf Joachim Radkau, *Technik in Deutschland* (Frankfurt: Suhrkamp, 1989).

14   *Völkischer Beobachter*, 9 March 1934, cited in Wolfgang Sachs, 'Die Automobil Gesellschaft: Vom Aufstieg und Niedergang einer Utopie', in Brüggemeier and Rommelspacher, eds., *Besiegte Natur. Geschichte der Umwelt im 19. und 20. Jahrhundert* (Munich: C. H. Beck, 1987), p. 116.

15   This point is also made by Raymond Dominick, who remarks that at the peak of road construction in Germany, almost one million workers were employed, that between 1932 and 1937 the number of vehicles produced quintupled, and that there was one Defender of Nature, Alwin Seifert, officially in charge of blending the superhighways into the countryside, to cause as little damage to the environment and its beauty as possible. Dominick, *The Environmental Movement in Germany: Prophets and Pioneers* (Bloomington: Indiana University Press, 1992).

16   Presented at the Barcelona School of Architecture in 1978, before a tribunal consisting of Oriol Bohigas, Manuel Solà-Morales, Ernest Lluch, Manuel Ribas Piera and Enric Argullol, and published by the Universitat Politécuica de Catalunya in 1987.

17   Francesc Roca is the current manager of the magazine *Nous Horitzons* (*New Horizons*, the magazine of the Communist Party of Catalonia), and he has written works on town-planning policies in Catalonia. These works do not clearly distinguish between Cebrià de Montoliu's approach and that of the rationalist school of urban development, but rather throw everything together into a progressive mish-mash. Roca misunderstands the British Pre-Raphaelite movement. The Barcelona Council published in 1993 a collective book on Cebrià de Montoliu. In this book, Francesc Roca actually states (though it is difficult to believe) that Ruskin was an admirer of the Renaissance (p.27), and also states that William Morris was a Marxist (p.164 – this mistake is perhaps due to the first edition of E.P. Thompson's biography of Morris, written while Thompson was still a member of the British Communist Party). This is quite ridiculous, and shows how Cebrià de Montoliu has been misunderstood in his home city. Roca presents Montoliu as the introducer and supporter of the idea of the garden city, but at the same time as the introducer of the opposite idea, urban expansion following the model of GrossBerlin. In addition Roca argues that *all* his proposals (p. 129) have been followed in Catalonia. He does not investigate Montoliu's obvious failure. In the same book, a thoughtful piece by Montoliu criticising Taylorism in 1915 is distorted to make Montoliu appear as the 'critical introducer' of Taylorism into Catalonia.

18   Eduard Masjuan has developed this idea in his article in the magazine *Archipiélago*, volume 7, 1991, and in *Urbanismo y Ecología en Catalunya* (Madrid: Editorial Madre Tierra, 1992).

19   Martínez Rizo, *La Urbanística del Porvenir* (The Town-planning of the Future), 1932, pp. 24–25, cited by Masjuan, *Urbanismo y Ecologia*. The emphases are mine.

20   Oriol Bohigas, *Reseña y Catálogo de la Arquitectura Modernista* (Catalogue and critique of modernist architecture) (Barcelona: Lumen, 1983).

NOTES TO CHAPTER 8

1   This chapter is based on the Twelfth Parisar Annual Lecture, delivered in Pune on 1 October 1993. I am grateful to the members of Parisar, especially Ravi and Vidyut Bhagwat, for inviting me to Pune, and to Professor Ram Bapat for his comments on an earlier draft.

2   Ramachandra Guha, *The Unquiet Woods: Ecological Change and Peasant Resistance in the Himalaya* (New Delhi: Oxford University Press, 1989).

3   Devendra Kumar, 'Kumarappa and the Contemporary Development Perspective', *Gandhi Marg*, volume 14, number 2, July–September 1992, p. 294.

4   *The Collected Works of Mahatma Gandhi*, which run to more than 90 volumes, are the basic source for all scholarly studies of Gandhi. For my own limited purposes, namely, the reassessment of Gandhi as an 'environmentalist', I have relied on three invaluable thematic anthologies of his writings: *Industrialize – And Perish!*, compiled by R. K. Prabhu (Ahmedabad: Navjivan Press, 1966); *Village Swaraj*, compiled by H. M. Vyas (Navjivan Press, 1962); and *My Picture of Free India*, compiled by Anand T. Hingorani (Bombay: Pearl Publications, 1965). However the citations in the text,which identify date and place of publication, can be followed by the interested reader to the *Collected Works*.

5   J. C. Kumarappa's important works include *Why the Village Movement?*, 2nd edn. (Rajahmundry: Hindusthan Publishing, 1938) and *The Economy of Permanence* 2nd edn. (Wardha: All India Village Industries Association, 1948). Kumarappa's ideas are examined in greater detail in my essay 'Prehitoy of Indian Environmentalism: Intellectual Traditions', *Economic and Political Weekly*, 4–11 January, 1992.

6   A fascinating selection of Mira Behn's writings compiled by her associate Krishna Murti Gupta, and on which I have drawn here, has been published in the journal *Khadi Gramodyog* (volume 39, number 2, November 1992).A fuller selection of articles, as well as tributes to her work, can be found in Krishna Murti Gupta, ed., *Mira Behn: Birth Centenary Volume* (New Delhi: Himalaya Seva Sangh, 1992).

7   Satish Kumar, quoted in Jonathan Porritt, *Save the Earth* (London: Dorling Kindersley, 1991), p. 132.

8   Bittu Sahgal, 'The Greening of India', *The Illustrated Weekly of India*, 22–28 June 1991.

9   'Social Aspects of Small and Big Projects' (speech of 17 November 1958), in Baldev Singh, ed., *Jawaharlal Nehru on Science and Society* (New Delhi: Nehru Memorial Museum and Library, 1988), pp. 172–75.

10 This story is narrated in Edward J. Thompson, *Report to the Rhodes Trust, 1938*, Thompson Papers, The Bodleian Library, Oxford. A copy of the relevant pages of the report was made available to me by Thompson's son, the historian E. P. Thompson.

NOTES TO CHAPTER 9

1   N. Georgescu-Roegen, 'Feasible recipes versus viable technologies', invited address at the 16th Atlantic Economic Conference, Philadelphia, 6–9 October 1983, footnote 3.

2   Grinevald, 'Vernadsky y Lotka como Fuentes de la Bioeconomia de Georgescu-Roegen', *Ecologica Politica*, number 1, 1991.

3   Cf J. Martinez-Alier, with Klaus Schluepmann, *Ecological Economics* (Oxford: Basil Blackwell, 1987, 1990).

4   Mirowski, *More Heat than Light: Economics as Social Physics, Physics as Nature's Economics* (New York: Cambridge University Press, 1987).

5 'Chrematistics' goes back to Aristotle, who distinguished it from *'oikonomia'*. Chrematistics is the art of researching prices in order to make money, *oikonomia* the provisioning of the household and all its members. This basic opposition is used by ecological economists to distinguish their work from orthodox economics, which restricts itself to the study of the economy as it is regulated by the price system.

6 Cf A-M Jansson et al. eds, *Investing in Natural Capital: the Ecological Economics Approach to Sustainability* (Covelo, CA: Island Press, 1994).

7 N. Georgescu-Roegen, 'The Entropy Law and the Economic Process in Retrospect', *Eastern Economic Journal*, volume 12, number 1, 1986.

8 *Quarterly Journal of Economics*, volume 50, number 3, pp.532-539.

9 As discussed in John Gowdy, 'Georgescu-Roegen's Utility Theory Applied to Environmental Economics', *Proceedings of the E. A. B. S. Conference on Entropy and Bioeconomics*, Nagard, Milan, 1993.

10 Georgecsu-Roegen, 'Comments on the papers by Daly and Stiglitz', in V. Kerry Smith, ed., *Scarcity and Growth Reconsidered* (Baltimore, MD: Johns Hopkins Press, 1979).

11 N. Georgescu-Roegen, 'Economic Theory and Agrarian Economics', *Oxford Economics Papers*, volume 12, number 1, February 1960, pp.1–40.

12 N. Georgescu-Roegen, 'The Institutional Aspects of Peasant Economies: a Historical and Analytical view', paper presented at the *ADC Seminar on Subsistence and Peasant Economics*, 28 February–6 March, 1965, East–West Center, Honolulu, Hawai.

13 Ester Boserup, *The Conditions of Agricultural Growth* (Chicago: University of Chicago Press, 1965).

14 Clifford Geertz, *Agricultural Involution* (Berkeley: University of California Press, 1963); Mark Elvin, *The Pattern of the Chinese Past: A Social and Economic Interpretation* (Stanford: Stanford University Press, 1973).

15 Utsa Patnaik, 'Neo-Populism and Marxism: The Chayanovian View of the Agrarian Question and its Fundamental Fallacy', *Journal of Peasant Studies*, volume 6, number 4, 1979; N. Georgescu-Roegen, 'On Neo-Populism and Marxism: A Comment on Utsa Patnaik', *Journal of Peasant Studies*, volume 8, number 2, 1981.

16 Cf. Robert M. Netting, *Smallholders, Householders: Farm Families and the Ecology of Intensive, Sustainable Development* (Stanford: Stanford University Press, 1993).

17 See R. B. Norgaard, 'Economic Indicators of Resource Scarcity: A Critical Essay', *Journal of Environmental Economics and Management*, volume 19, number 1, 1990.

18 As argued in Ramachandra Guha, *The Unquiet Woods: Ecological Change and Peasant Resistance in the Himalaya* (New Delhi: Oxford University Press, 1989).

19 Cited in footnote 9.

20 W. Lazonick, *Business organization and the myth of the market* (Cambridge: Cambridge University Press, 1994).

21 The most complete study of Georgescu-Roegen's work, with an extensive bibliography, is that published by his fellow countrymen J. C. Dragan and M. C. Demetrescu, *Entropy and Bioeconomics: the New Paradigm of Nicholas Georgescu-Roegen*, Nagard, Milan, 1986, 2nd ed. 1991. See also the last articles by and about Georgescu-Roegen and several good articles on his work in the papers of the conference on Entropy and Bioeconomics, Fondazione Dragan, Rome, November 1991 (published by E.A.B.S., Fondazione Dragan, Via Larga 11, Milan).

NOTES TO CHAPTER 10

1 In Ms. 10575, Geddes Papers, National Library of Scotland, Edinburgh.

2 Anne Chisholm, *Philosophers of the Earth: Conversations with Ecologists* (London: Sidgwick & Jackson, 1972). Mumford's invocation of the city as his university is in his *Sketches from a Life* (New York: The Dial Press, 1982), Chapter 11.

3 W. L. Thomas, ed., *Man's Role in Changing the Face of the Earth*(Chicago: University of Chicago Press, 1956); F. Fraser Darling and John P. Milton, eds., *Future Environments of North America* (Garden City, NY: The Natural History Press, 1966).

4 Roderick Nash, *Wilderness and the American Mind*, 3rd edn. (New Haven, CT: Yale University Press, 1982); Stephen Fox, *The American Conservation Movement: John Muir and his Legacy*, 2nd edn. (Madison: University of Wisconsin Press, 1985); Samuel P. Hays, *Beauty, Health and Permanence: Environmental Politics in the United States, 1955–85* (New York: Cambridge University Press, 1987).

5 Lewis Mumford (hereafter LM), *Sketches from a Life*, (New York: The Dial Press, 1982) p. 90.

6 Patrick Geddes, *Cities in Evolution* (first published 1915; revised edition, London: Williams & Norgate, 1949), p. 51f; Jacqueline Tyrwhitt, ed., *Patrick Geddes in India* (London : Lund Humphries, 1947), pp. 57–58, 78–83, etc. The latter work is an edited compilation of extracts from some of Geddes's reports on Indian towns. He wrote some 50 reports in all, as a guest of the colonial government and various Indian princely states.

7 R.P. McIntosh, *The Background of Ecology: Concept and Theory* (Cambridge: Cambridge University Press, 1985), pp. 293–94. Geddes was also one of the first to criticise conventional economics from the perspective of ecological energetics, as discussed in J. Martinez-Alier, *Ecological Economics: Energy, Economics, Society* (Oxford: Basil Blackwell, 1987), pp. 89–98.

8 Essay first published in *The Architectural Review* and excerpted in LM, *My Works and Days: A Personal Chronicle* (New York: Harcourt, Brace Jovanovich, 1979). See also LM, *Sketches from a Life*, p. 147, and LM, 'Patrick Geddes, Insurgent', *The New Republic*, 30 October 1929.

9 Patrick Geddes, *Report on Town Planning, Dacca* (Calcutta: Bengal Secretariat Book Depot, 1917), p. 17, emphasis in original.

10 LM, *The Brown Decades: A Study of the Arts in America* (1931: reprint; New York: Dover Publications, 1955), pp. 76–67. Years later, Mumford speculated that he was invited to co-chair the 1955 Wenner–Gren Conference on 'Man's Role in Changing the Face of the Earth' because of his memoir on George Perkins Marsh in *The Brown Decades* and as Geddes had introduced him to Marsh, in effect he owed that invitation to his master; LM, *Sketches from a Life*, p. 408. The proceedings of the Wenner–Gren symposium, edited by W.L. Thomas (see footnote 3), were dedicated to Marsh.

11 LM, 'Regionalism and Irregionalism', *The Sociological Review*, volume 19, number 4, 1927, p. 277.

12 LM, 'Regionalism and Irregionalism', op. cit.; LM, '*The Theory and Practice of Regionalism*', in two parts, *The Sociological Review*, volume 20, numbers 1 & 2, 1928.

13 Radhakamal Mukerjee, *Regional Sociology* (New York: Century Co., 1926). Mukerjee was also deeply influenced by Patrick Geddes, with whom he came in close contact during the latter's stay in Calcutta, c. 1915–16.

14 The following paragraphs are based on the essays cited in footnote 12.

15 Mumford rarely missed the opportunity to berate the pioneer for his crimes against nature. As late as 1962, he was still complaining that 'even when the pioneer didn't rape Nature, he divorced her a little too easily: he missed the great lesson that both ecology and medicine teach – that man's great mission is not to conquer nature by main force but to co-operate with her intelligently but lovingly for his own purposes'. LM, 'California and the Human Prospect', *Sierra Club Bulletin*, volume 47, number 9, 1962, pp. 45–46.

16 In the event, American economic development has continued to ignore regional realities. But ecological disaster has been forestalled only through the drawing in of natural resources from all over the globe. At the time of Mumford's *Sociological Review* series, America was still largely relying on its own resources. But, especially since World War II, the development of the consumer society has rested on a fundamentally exploitative relationship with the rest of the world. Consumers in the high centres of industrial civilisation can take for granted the continued supply of mink from the Arctic, teakwood from India and ivory from Africa, without being in the slightest degree responsible for the environmental consequences of their lifestyles.

17 LM, 'Science on the Loose' (review of Robert Millikan's *Science and the New Civilization*), *The New Republic*, 6 August 1930. See also the section entitled 'Pre-1970 Ecology', in L.M., *My Works and Days*, pp. 29–32.

18 LM, *Technics and Civilization* (New York: Harcourt, Brace & Co., 1934), p. 109.

19 Ibid., pp. 268, 110.

20 Ibid., pp. 111, 118, 147, etc.

21 Ibid., Chapter 4 (quotes from pp. 151, 168–69). Mumford is writing here of late 19th-century Europe and North America, but his description recognisably fits late 20th-century India and Brazil, those late and enthusiastic converts to carboniferous capitalism.

22 Ibid., p. 211.

23 Ibid., Chapter 5 (quote from p. 255).

24 Ibid., pp. 429–31.

25 LM, *The Culture of Cities* (New York: Harcourt Brace & Co., 1938), Chapter 1 (quotes from pp. 49, 51).

26 Ibid., Chapter 3 (quotes from pp. 162, 164, 191, 195).

27 Ibid., Especially. Chapters 5 and 6.

28 Hegel is mentioned only once in *Technics and Civilization* and not at all in *The Culture of Cities*. However, Mumford had read Karl Marx closely, and perhaps his stages approach unconsciously drew on Marx's interpretation of the Hegelian dialectic. Marx's theory of history is open to both an evolutionist and a cyclical reading: while Marxists have usually preferred the former, Mumford would have undoubtedly been more comfortable with the latter.

29 Martinez-Alier's chapter on Barcelona (Chapter 7) is a cameo ecological history that might be called 'Mumfordian' in its application of the master's framework to the life of a great European city.

30 *The Culture of Cities*, p. 331.

31 LM, *Technics and Civilization*, pp. 221–13, 247, 250, 267, etc; 'The Theory and Pracice of Regionalism', Part I, *The Sociological Review*, volume 20, number 1, 1928, p. 19.

32 LM, 'Preface' to his *The Condition of Man* (reprint, New York: Harcourt, Brace, Jovanovich, 1973), p. viii, emphasis in original.

33 LM, 'Technics and the Future of Western Civilization', in his *In the Name of Sanity* (New York: Harcourt, Brace, Jovanovich, 1954), p. 47.

34 LM, 'California and the Human Prospect', p. 43.

35 LM, 'Prospect', in Thomas, ed., *Man's Role in Changing the Face of the Earth*, volume 2, pp. 1147–48.

36 See for example Mumford's essays 'Gentlemen! You are Mad!', *Saturday Review of Literature*, 2 March 1946; 'The Morals of Extermination', *Atlantic Monthly*, October 1959; and the collection *In the Name of Sanity*. Cf. also Paul Boyer, *By the Bomb's Early Light: American Thought and Culture at the Dawn of the Atomic Age* (New York: Pantheon, 1985), especially pp.284–87.

37 LM, 'The Moral Challenge to Democracy', *Virginia Quarterly Review*, volume 35, number 4, 1959, p. 565.

38 ibid., pp. 562–67.

39 LM, *My Works and Days*, pp. 115-16.

40 LM, 'Looking Forward', *Proceedings of the American Philosophical Society*, volume 83, number 4, 1940, p. 541.

41 LM, 'California and the Human Prospect', pp. 45–47.

42 Benton Mckaye to Lewis Mumford, dated 3 December 1926, quoted in John L. Thomas, 'Lewis Mumford, Benton Mckaye and the Regional Vision', in Thomas P. Hughes and Agatha C. Hughes, ed., *Lewis Mumford: Public Intellectual* (New York: Oxford University Press, 1990), p. 89.

43 Donald Miller, *Lewis Mumford*, (New York: Weidenfeld and Nicolson, 1989) p. 166, emphasis in original.

44 LM, 'Prospect', p. 1146.

45 LM, 'Let Man Take Command', *The Saturday Review of Literature*, 2 October 1948, p. 35.

46 LM, 'California and the Human Prospect', pp. 58–59.

47 Cf. Alvin Gouldner, *Against Fragmentation: The Origins of Marxism and the Sociology of Intellectuals* (New York: Oxford University Press, 1985).

48 As suggested many years ago in James T. Farrell's essay 'The Faith of Lewis Mumford' (1944), reprinted in his *The League of Frightened Philistines and Other Papers* (London: Routledge, 1947).

49 It is, of course, not at all uncommon for writers to project their hopes, prejudices and aspirations in their tributes to other people. Thus, for Orwell's identification with Dickens, see John Rodden's suggestive study, *The Politics of Literary Reputation: The Making and Claiming of 'St. George' Orwell* (New York: Oxford University Press, 1989), pp. 181–182, 238–239.

50 LM, *Green Memories: The Story of Geddes Mumford* (New York: Harcourt, Brace & Co., 1947), pp. 114–115, 126–128, etc.

51 LM, 'Marsh's Naturalist–Moralist–Humanist Approach' (Review of David Lowenthal's *George Perkins Marsh: Versatile Vermonter*), *Living Wilderness*, number 71, winter 1959–60, pp. 11–13.

52 LM, 'A Universal Man', *New York Review of Books*, 23 May 1968, pp. 8, 10, 12, 15.

53 Donald Worster, 'Transformations of the Earth: Toward an Agroecological Perspective in History', *Journal of American History*, volume 76, number 4, 1990, p. 1087.

54 See Donald Miller, *Lewis Mumford*, p. 87.

55 Cf Alfred Runte, *National Parks: The American Experience* (Lincoln: University of Nebraska Press, 1979). Mumford had anticipated Runte's critique of monumentalism when he deplored the tendency of American planners in the past to 'single out the most striking forms of landscape'. He went on : 'If the culture of the environment had yet entered deeply into our consciousness, our esthetic appreciations would not stop short with stupendous geological formations like the Grand Canyon of Arizona: we should have equal regard for every nook and corner of the earth, and we should not be indifferent to the fate of less romantic areas.' *The Culture of Cities*, p. 322. This is yet another example of Mumford's prescience: for it is only in the last decade or so that the wilderness movement has begun to shift its priorities towards the protection of overall biological diversity and away from a narrow emphasis on the spectacular.

56 LM, 'The Corruption of Liberalism', *The New Republic*, 29 April 1940. For a critique by a conservative thinker of Mumford as anti-patriotic, see Edward Shils, 'Lewis Mumford : On the Way to the New Jerusalem', *The New Criterion*, volume 9, number 1, 1983.

57 LM, 'Let Man Take Command', p. 8; 'Looking Forward', p. 545.

58 One reason is, probably, the writers' own lack of interest in ecology; another is their methodological reliance on Mumford's books and private papers, ignoring the periodical essays that I have so heavily relied upon here. I may note too that my own reconstruction of Mumford's thought is itself based on a deliberately restricted focus; I have completely ignored his writings on American Studies and architecture, two fields in which his reputation is assured.

59 See LM, 'The Bolshevist Religion', *The New Republic*, 1 April 1928; LM, 'Alternatives to the H-Bomb', *The New Leader*, 28 June 1954.

60 Bahro, quoted in Kirkpatrick Sale, 'Lewis Mumford', obituary notice, *The Nation*, 19 February 1990 (emphases mine).

INDEX

*Numbers in **bold** refer to figures or tables*

A SELECTION OF TITLES ALSO AVAILABLE FROM EARTHSCAN

Winner of the 1996 Langhe Ceretto–Societa Editrice International Prize

The Food System: A Guide

Geoff Tansey and Tony Worsley

'Frank, devastatingly honest and expertly researched, this is the essential guide for anyone seeking to understand the global food jigsaw. If you want to understand why the world feeds itself in the way it does, you must read this book.' *Derek Cooper*, The Food Programme, *BBC Radio 4*

'The authors have done the growing area of food policy a great service. Anyone who teaches any aspect of food can now offer this to students.' *Times Higher Education Supplement*

As the headlines now demonstrate regularly, understanding the food system and managing it carefully are essential to ensure that all the world's people enjoy a secure, sufficient and sustainable food supply. This award-winning volume provides an essential overview of the key issues and players. Lively and accessible, it is appropriate both for students of any aspect of food, and for general readers.

£15.95 Paperback ISBN 1 85383 277 4

The Politics of the Real World

Michael Jacobs for the Real World Coalition

'An invigorating read' *New Scientist*

'The best shot at restoring grown-up politics in the UK for many years' *Town and Country Planning*

Many people feel that something is awry with British society and British politics. Quality of life is declining, crime soars, traffic and pollution spiral, mass unemployment is accepted as a consequence of low inflation, and growing poverty and inequality leave many British citizens effectively disenfranchised. Yet the culture of Westminster barely registers a blip. *The Politics of the Real World* represents the voice of over 40 of the UK's leading voluntary and campaigning organisations. It describes how conventional social and economic policies are creating the problems we face, not solving them; and it proposes new directions for the UK in an increasingly globalised system.

£6.99 Paperback ISBN 1 85383 350 9

Turning Point: The End of the Growth Paradigm
Robert U Ayres

This new book from one of the world's most eminent environmental economists challenges one of our society's most dearly-held beliefs; the need for 'growth'. He argues that the growth engine has run amok, and that its operation results both in the hopelessly inequitable distribution of wealth and resources, and in environmental contamination and unsustainable industrial practices. Ayres argues for a switch of emphasis, away from the production of goods and towards the production of services. By presenting feasible alternatives to conventional economics, Ayres presents the reader with a sense of the achievability of sustainable economies.

£13.95 Paperback ISBN 1 85383 439 4 £35.00 Hardback ISBN 1 85383 444 0

The World Who is Who and Does What in Environment and Conservation
Edited by Nicholas Polunin and Lynn M Curme

A unique guide to the world's most eminent and active environmental policy makers, campaigners, researchers, authors and academics. The volume gives details of some 1300 environmentalists and conservationists in a vast range of environmental disciplines from over 120 countries. The A–Z biographical listings include information on the chosen biographees' qualifications and affiliations, academic background and work experience, achievements and awards, and specialist interests and publications. Details are also given of the entrants' specialist capabilities and language skills, their willingness to be consulted for advice or by the media or to act as consultants, and their contact details. Fully cross-referenced indexes also list entrants by speciality and country or major state.

£50.00 Hardback ISBN 1 85383 377 0

For further information of these and other Earthscan publications, please contact us at:

Earthscan Publications Ltd
120 Pentonville Road
London N1 9JN
Tel: 0171 278 0433
Fax: 0171 278 1142
Email: earthinfo@earthscan.co.uk
WWW: http://www.earthscan.co.uk